Political Theory
Concepts and Debates

Political Theory
Concepts and Debates

Atlantic Research Division

ATLANTIC
PUBLISHERS & DISTRIBUTORS (P) LTD

Published by

ATLANTIC

PUBLISHERS & DISTRIBUTORS (P) LTD

7/22, Ansari Road, Darya Ganj, New Delhi-110002
Phones : +91-11-40775252, 40775214, 23273880, 23275880
Fax: +91-11-23285873
Web: www.atlanticbooks.com
E-mail: orders@atlanticbooks.com

Printed & bound in India by Atlantic Print Services

Preface

The purpose of the Political Science is to signify the political dynamics, political processes and leadership as well. Political theory is a core component in the discipline of Political Science. It is through political theory that the students in this discipline are introduced to the major concepts and critical debates on the subject. Political theory helps us to equip ourselves with the analytical tools necessary to differentiate between legitimate functions of government and the arbitrary use of power. Political theory helps the students to move beyond the 'apparent truths' regarding what is happening in politics. The job of the political theorist is to bring some precision to fundamental yet general political concepts like liberty, equality, democracy, development, human rights, justice, etc.

Equality is a multi-dimensional concept. It has many facets and so many implications. It means that each person, as a free legal agent in the scheme of the state, is equal to that of every other. The demand for equality has always been against the prevailing inequalities of the times. The existence of social inequalities is probably as old as human society and the debate about the nature and causes of inequalities is an old topic of political philosophy. Equality does not aim at a dead, mechanical level of uniformity in society. It does not stifle the free play of personality of any individual. The major rights are equality, liberty, security and property. By nature and before the law, all men are equal. Liberty is essential for the development of a man's personality. Liberty is not one but manifold, such as natural liberty, civil liberty, political liberty, personal liberty, economic liberty and national liberty. It is the most cherished ideal of a man's life. Liberty or freedom is the central problem of politics.

Political equality within the state is the essence of political dimension of justice. It is concerned with the actual policies through which the political process realises the norms of justice. Political justice lies in the relationship between the individual and the authority, i.e. the state. There should be political equality. Political justice stands for a free and fair participation of the people in the political processes. It involves the guarantee of universal adult franchise without any discrimination, and equality in matters of selection to public services. The notion of political justice requires that the state must protect and preserve certain valuable rights of the individual so that he may develop his personality as a citizen and thereby contribute his share to the welfare of the community.

Rights are the sum total of those opportunities which ensure enrichment of human personality. Rights are necessary conditions for the development of human personality. These are also necessary for the development of society and sustenance of social values. Rights are the social requirements of an individual for the development of his personality and society at large. Rights do not have an eternal character just by virtue of their force of long observance, otherwise the system of slavery would have been in practice even in modern times. Times change and with it changes the whole pattern of social life. The system of rights also undergoes a change. To emphasize the importance of rights, adjectives like 'natural', 'fundamental' and 'human' have been used in the long history of their development. Human rights constitute the very source of all rights of human beings. They provide for moral foundation of any system of rights. The idea of human rights descended from the philosophical idea of natural rights; some recognize no difference between the two and regard both as two labels for the same thing, while others choose to keep the terms separate to eliminate association with some features traditionally associated with natural rights.

There are multiple forms and institutions of power. The most powerful structure is state which is the aggregate and legitimate power structure of a country. Therefore, state is one of the core issues discussed and debated in political theory. State in fact is the central theme of Political Science. It is the most powerful and most universal of all social institutions. It is an association of society which serves its purpose during the various phases of its historical development. State is a political association that establishes sovereign jurisdiction within defined territorial borders, and exercises authority through a set of permanent institutions. The state includes such institutions as the armed forces, civil service or state bureaucracy, courts, and the police.

According to the liberal theory, civil rights constitute the foundation of citizenship, which is membership in a political community. The concept was developed by Aristotle in his book, *Poetics*. Aristotle regarded citizenship as a privilege of the ruling class. After the decline of the Greek city-states a new definition of citizenship was evolved in the Roman Empire. Citizenship most usually relates to membership of the nation state, but the term can also apply at subnational level. Subnational entities may impose requirements, of residency or otherwise, which permit citizens to participate in the political life of that entity, or to enjoy benefits provided by the government of that entity.

Sovereignty is the most important constituent element of a modern state. It is this element which distinguishes the state from all other associations. We cannot think of any state without sovereignty. It is the supreme power over citizens and associations. The concept of sovereignty has been called the very basis of modern Political Science. Sovereignty is the permanent quality of the state. The holder of sovereignty may die, but the power of the state survives. It is passed on to his successor. A state may lose its sovereignty only when it is conquered by some other state and converted into a colony or a dependency.

Political culture is the traditional orientation of the citizens of a nation towards politics, affecting their perceptions of political legitimacy and the traditions of political practice. It was brought into Political Science to promote the American political system. The political culture of a political community is characterized by the proportion of adherents of each way of life (its regime), and by the predominant alliance of two ways of life. Political culture is connected to notions of citizenship because it frequently includes an idea of what makes people good citizens. A citizen is a legal member of a political community, with certain rights and obligations.

The study of the concept of political culture constitutes an analysis of the sociological aspect of the theme of political development. The concept of property is crucial to modern political theory. It is the basis of modern state and society. Nothing else has played such a vital role in the development of state, civilization and culture. Ownership and control of material goods is property. It is the control of man over things or an appropriation of some material object recognised by society. Right to property requires social recognition. Property provides a means of harmony in the shape of security. Men get a sense of security. They develop their creative impulse. The institution of private property is not bad as such but it is possessed by a few capitalists who exploit others. It gives birth to the evils in capitalism.

Political theory has constantly been evolving with new sets of ideas and debates. These debates and concepts give new insights into the critical frame of understanding and interpreting politics. The book *Political Theory: Concepts and Debates* endeavours to introduce the students to these concepts and debates. It includes the discussion on all those topics which find a place in the syllabus of B.A. Political Science in Delhi University. But since the topics of Political Science at graduation level are the same everywhere, the book will also be useful for students of the subject in all the universities in India, including open universities.

Atlantic Research Division

Contents

1

Significance of Equality

Equality is a multi-dimensional concept. It has many facets and so many implications. It means that each person as a free legal agent in the scheme of the state is equal to that of every other. Laski first of all examines what equality is not. According to him, no idea is more difficult to be defined in the whole realm of political science than the concept of equality.[1] As Ernest Barker says, "Equality is a Protean notion; it changes its shape and assumes new forms with a ready facility".[2] It is so because equality has become like a multi-dimensional concept. It possesses more than one meaning. The controversies surrounding it arise partly because the same term is employed with different connotations. It may either purport to state a fact, or convey the expression of an ethical judgement. It may affirm that men are, on the whole, very similar in their natural endowments of character and intelligence. It may assert that while they differ profoundly as individuals in capacity and character, they are equally entitled to consideration and respect as human beings and that the well-being of society is likely to be increased if it so plans its organisation that, whether the powers are great or small, all its members may be equally enabled to make the best of such powers as they possess.[3]

He observes that "equality does not mean identity of treatment". There can be no identity of treatment so long men are different in want, capacity and need. The American and French revolutions have become the central plank of all modern forms of social change and the social movements for the reorganisation of societies. From the mid-seventeenth century, mankind advanced towards equality in a notable sense. The movements of Renaissance and reformation raised powerful voice against the legal privileges of the clergy and nobility based upon birth and demanded equality by birth. It were the seventeenth century exponents of natural law who postulated equality as a natural state for all men which finally created the theoretical basis for the political realization of the equalitarian concept. Henceforth, the affirmation that all men are born equal was to figure in the manifestoes all over the world. The revolutions in British in 1649 and 1688, in USA in 1776 and in France in 1789 made right to equality by birth as their central plank. "Men are born free and equal and they are free and equal in their rights". John Locke talked of a 'state of perfect equality'. Jefferson pronounced the self-evident truth that 'all men are created equal'. The demand for equality has always been against the prevailing inequalities of the times. The existence of social inequalities is probably as old as human society and the debate about the nature and causes of inequalities is an ancient topic of political philosophy. The declaration of 1793 proclaimed that 'governments are institutions to guarantee to men the enjoyment of their natural and imprescriptibly rights. The rights are equality, liberty, security and property. By nature and before the law, all men are equal. The movement to broaden the franchise was an offshoot of the industrial revolution which increased the social power of the urban middle class and converted a large section of the population into factory workers. The Reforms Acts of 1832, 1876 and 1884 in Britain were steps towards political equality. In the twentieth century, the demand for equality became more insistent. The declaration of Human Rights in 1948 extended the recognition of equality.

In classical Greece, Aristotle in his book 'Politics' distinguished three social classes and noted the significant difference between citizens and slaves, men and women in terms of rational and civic capacities. Participation in the police was restricted to the citizens only. Similarly, in our Hindu society, according to the classical text, the society was divided into four categories: Brahmin, Kshatriya, Vaishya and

Shudras. All rights and duties were based upon this classification. The medieval feudalism had legal privileges based on status and birth which were supported by Christianity. Such example can be extended but the point is simply this that various forms of inequalities have existed in all known societies. Different types of inequalities have been long enduring, giving rise to the notion that inequality is inevitable in social relations. In fact the pre-eighteenth century teachings argued that men were naturally unequal and that there was a natural human hierarchy. Different ideologies justified inequality on grounds of superior race, ancestry, age, sex, religion, military strength, culture, wealth and knowledge.

During the 19th century, the demand for political equality gained momentum. One basic element of this equality-universal adult franchise has become a reality in the 20th century in almost all parts of the globe. The struggle for economic equality has been partly in the socialist world. Nevertheless, the movement for equality has not yet run its course and peoples and classes are engaged in continuous fights to achieve various forms of equality in different parts of the globe. Equality is a multi-dimensional concept. It has many facets and so many implications. Equality broadly means that each person as a free legal agent in the scheme of the state is equal. However, absolute equality is an unattainable ideal. Nature has created so much difference among men that no power or objective condition can make them equal. "Equality implies fundamentally a certain leveling process".

The principle of equality warrants that "talent does not perish for want of encouragement". Equality does not aim at a dead, mechanical level of uniformity in society. It does not stifle the free play of personality of any individual. R.H. Tawney applies remark: "a large measure of equality, so far from being inimical to liberty, is essential to it". After the death of Aristotle in 22 BC, the most prominent star in the Greek philosophy was Zeno who founded the Stoic school and supported equality among men. The stoics concluded that all human beings possess reason and thereby all mankind is differentiated from other animals and is united. On this account, the concept of humanity does not admit of degree. As such, all men are equal as men. The stoic philosophers gave the idea of universal brotherhood and they were opposed to slavery. The promulgation of the 'law of the people' by the Roman empire was another way in which the Romans attempted to give effect to the principle that all men are equal and as an extension to that, they conferred citizenship both on the individuals and the entire communities. The climax reached in 212 A.D. when the notable edict of Emperor Caracalla conferred citizenship of Rome upon all free inhabitants of the empire. The trend initiated by Greeks and Romans was continued by the preachers of Christianity. St. Paul said to Gelatians, 'there is neither Jew nor Greek, there is all one in Jesus Christ. From fifth century to the end of fourteenth century, the demand for equality was a cry against serfdom, medieval gradations of rank and hereditary nobility, and the equality for career opportunities in the Church. From 15th to 17th century, the cry for equality was against the landowner's status and religious intolerance and was raised by puritans, levelers, doctrine of natural rights and John Locke. The struggle for equality did take place but equality in the modern sense of the term was missing.

It were the seventeenth century exponents of natural law who postulated equality as a natural state for all men which finally created the theoretical basis for the political realization of the equalitarian concept. Henceforth, the affirmation that all men are born equal was to figure in the manifestoes all over the world. The revolutions in British in 1649 and 1688, in USA in 1776 and in France in 1789 made right to equality by birth as their central plank. "Men are born free and equal and they are free and equal in their rights."

During this phase, the demand for equality coincided with the abolition of special privileges of the nobility and the achievements of political and legal equality with the nobility. It meant only juristic equality, i.e. all men are born equal and they are equal before law. Whether it was England, France or America, the issue at stake in the context of equality was not economic or social but only uniformity of legal rights. As stated earlier, since the demand for equality was primarily raised by the rising middle/bourgeois class which had acquired wealth but lacked legal status, and which was anxious to achieve political and legal equality with the nobility, the demand for legal equality served its purpose well.

In the strict sense it would imply provision of equal resources to all and ensuring equal economic condition to all. It means equality of economic power as the elimination of excessive inequalities of wealth and income. It does not require a flat equality of incomes. The laissez-faire policy of the state in the economic affairs created wide economic disparities in the society. As a result, along with legal equality, demand for economic and social equality was raised by liberal, socialist and Marxist writers alike such as J.S. Mill, T.H. Green, Babeuf, Karl Marx, etc. Simultaneously, the demand for political equality also grew stronger. The movement to broaden the franchise was an offshoot of the industrial revolution which increased the social power of the urban middle class and converted a large section of the population into factory workers. The reforms Acts of 1832, 1876 and 1884 in Britain were steps towards political equality.

The national liberation movements against imperialism and colonialism, movements against apartheid, socialist revolutions in Russia, China and East European countries brought the issue of equality, into the forefront. The declaration of Human Rights in 1948 extended the recognition of equality, which had hitherto been accepted as the aim of all industrialized countries, to the people of the third world countries who had been discriminated against, thus contributing to the eventual emergence of an international society based upon socio-economic equality. The concept of equality can be understood not in an abstract identity of treatment of reward. There can be no ultimate identity of treatment so long as men are different in wants, capacities and needs. As Laski wrote, "the purpose of society would be frustrated at the outset if the nature of a mathematician met an identical response with that to the nature of a bricklayer". Inequalities gifted by nature are an inescapable fact and it has to be accepted in the society.

Injustice arises as much from treating unequal equally as from treating equals unequally. Apart from natural inequalities, there are inequalities created by the society—based upon birth, wealth, knowledge, religion, etc. Claims for equality have always been negative, denying the property of certain existing socio-economic inequalities. When liberalism urged that all men are equal by birth, it meant to challenge the privileged position of nobility and aristocracy in the society. Similarly, when it was urged that all men are entitled to vote by reason of equality, it meant to challenge a property-owning franchise. The declaration of the rights of man explicitly recognized that superior talent and qualities of character are proper ground for distinction of wealth honour and power. During the twentieth century, we have been dismantling an educational and social system in which opportunities for advancement depended on the family means and replacing it with one that makes skill in passing examinations, one of the principal criteria. Thus, out of context, equality is an empty framework for a social ideal. It is concrete only when particularized.

Like liberty, equality can also be understood in its negative and positive aspects. Ever since the rise of the idea of equality, it has been engaged in dismantling certain privileges whether they were feudal, social, economic, etc. Hence negatively, equality was associated with 'the end of such privileges'. Positively, it meant 'the availability of opportunity' so that everybody could have equal chance to develop his personality. Explaining the meaning of equality in this context, Laski writes that equality means:

(i) It depends upon the training that is offered to the citizens. For the power that ultimately counts in society is the power to utilize knowledge; and disparities of education result, above all, in disparities is the ability to use that power. Opportunity should be given to everyone to realize the implications of his personality.

(ii) All must have access to social benefits and no one should be restricted on any ground. The inequalities by birth or because of parent and hereditary cause are unreasonable.

(iii) Absence of economic and social exploitation.

The most radical notion of equality is the equality of results. A programme of equality of results would seek to transform inequalities at the beginning into social equalities at conclusion. Social programmes of positive discrimination in favour of disadvantaged (i.e. scheduled caste, scheduled tribes, women, children, handicapped, etc.) are meant to compensate for significant inequality of condition in order to bring about a meaningful equality of opportunity to secure equality of results

DEFINITIONS OF EQUALITY

1. *Oxford English Dictionary.* Equality implies (i) the condition of having equal dignity, rank or privilege with others, (ii) the condition of being equal in power, ability achievement of excellence, (iii) fairness, impartiality, due proportion, proportionateness. Here equality is defined in the light of equal conditions guaranteed to each for making the best of himself.
2. *Barker.* Equality implies that "whatever conditions are guaranteed to me in the form of rights, shall also, and in the same measure, be guaranteed to others, and that whatever rights are given to others shall also be given to me".[4]
3. *Laski.* Undoubtedly, it implies fundamentally a levelling process. It means that no man shall be so placed in society that he can overreach his neighbour to the extent which constitutes a denial of the latter's citizenship.[5]
4. *Tawney.* In very simple terms, the idea of equality refers to the equality of rights and opportunities so that each member of the civilised community may have the best possible scope for the development of his personality. It obtains in so far as, and only in so far as, each member of a community whatever his birth or occupation, or social position, possesses in fact and not merely in form equal chances of using to the full his natural endowments of physique, of character, and of intelligence.[6] In other words, it

desires a state of life in which the strong and the weak share same privileges for the development of their personality irrespective of any artificial distinction like that of wealth, religion, colour of the skin, domicile, language, descent, sex and the like.

In defining Equality one may say with Laski, "It means that my realisation of my best self must involve as its logical result the realisation by others of their best selves. It means such an ordering of social forces as will balance a share in the toil of living with a share in its gain also. It means that my share in the gain must be adequate for the purpose of citizenship".[7]

POSITIVE AND NEGATIVE EQUALITY

1. *Positive equality*. In a positive sense, equality means the provision of adequate opportunities for all. It does not mean simply identical treatment for all. As men differ in their needs and capacities and also in their efforts, they require different opportunities for their self-development. The native endowments are by no means equal. As Benn and Peters say, "The goal of 'equality of opportunities' is achieved only when there is an appropriate opportunity for each; what is to be equalised is not the opportunity to enter professions or to be successful in business but the opportunity to lead a good life, or to fulfil one's personality".[8]
2. *Negative equality*. In a negative sense, equality means no discrimination on some artificial ground like that of religion, caste, wealth, creed, domicile, descent, sex and the like. However, discrimination can be made if the reason behind it is valid. For example, very hazardous jobs cannot be given to the females. But discrimination on the basis of caste cannot be justified by any rational standard. Thus, as Laski points out, there should be no arrangement whereby the authority of few is qualitatively more than that of the many.[9]

KINDS OF EQUALITY

Political Equality

Political Equality means the access of all to the venues of power. It means the equal right of all citizens, without any distinction, to participate in the affairs of the state. Every citizen has the right to direct or indirect share in the making of laws of formulation of public policy. It is ensured through universal adult franchise. All citizens enjoy political rights like the right to vote, the right to stand for election, the right to hold public office, the right to petition the government and criticize public policy, if necessary.

The principle is expressed in the right to vote, the right to stand for elections, to hold public office and no distinction on the basis of caste, colour, sex, religion, language, etc. According to Laski, political equality means that the authority which exerts that power must be subjected to the rules of democratic governance. However, in recent years, we have begun to realize that the principle of political equality is not as simple as the liberal meaning conveys. If the word political means the ability and skill to influence others which an individual exercises in controlling, managing and arranging things according to his will or to the will of the party to which he may belong, obviously, we cannot say that everyone is politically equal. In modern times, functioning of the government has become very complex and real political power vests in bureaucracy, police and army over whom people have virtually no control. The elite theory of democracy discourages the participation of the people in political affairs. Again, how much we may have political equality, the prime minister or the party boss of this or that party can never be said to be politically equal. Political equality and political power are distinct categories. There are many constraints put upon the common man to get his voice heard and the multiplicity of factors which include different ability, the ability to assert oneself and above all the differentiation imposed by the maladjusted property system. However, the merit of the political equality lies in recognizing the basic truth that if men are equal in law, then there should be equality amongst them regarding the right of governance.

Economic Equality

Economic equality prevails when all people have reasonable opportunities to develop themselves fully. Adequate scope for employment, reasonable wages, adequate leisure and share in the management of the economic concern make economic equality meaningful. Equality of opportunity does not only presuppose the equal allotment of certain rights but also requires application of another rule of distribution; equality of the satisfaction of certain basic needs. It means privileges for the economically underprivileged. As Tawney wrote, "Equality of opportunity is not simply a matter of legal equality. Its existence depends not merely on the absence of disabilities but also the presence of abilities. It obtains in so far as, and only in so far as each member of the community, whatever his birth or occupation, or social position, possesses in fact and not merely in form, equal chances of using to the full his natural endowments of physique of character and the intelligence".

It was also understood as freedom of contract or that everybody is equal in so far as the contractual obligation are concerned. Many a time it was also understood as equalization of wealth and income. However, all these meanings were considered insufficient. Examining the economic equality, Rousseau wrote, 'By equality' we should understand not that the degree of the poor and the rich be absolutely identical for everybody, but that no citizen be wealthy enough to buy another and none poor enough to be forced to sell himself. Economic equality is concerned with the apportionment of goods. To bring the poor to the general starting line, law must compensate them for those initial disadvantages by means of social legislation and social services such as minimum wages, tax exemption, unemployment benefits, free public schooling, scholarship, etc.

Economic equality is most largely a problem in proportion. It means that the things without which life is meaningless must be accessible to all without distinction in degree or kind. All men must eat and drink and obtain shelter. Equality involves, up to the margin of sufficiency, identity of response to primary needs. The equal satisfaction of basic needs as a precondition for equality of opportunity does require economic equality, i.e. reduction of extreme inequalities in the distribution of commodities.

In the social sphere, equality means absence of discrimination in the matter of social status on account of differences in caste, class, colour, race, creed or religion. The matter of status raises the issue whether the state should seek to turn the industrial production into something like a 'partnership of equals' and should introduce a system under which the directing and managing elements stand on an equal footing. With regard to property and income the issue is what methods the state should seek to correct inequality in their distribution. The liberal state through its policy of mixed economy, methods of differential taxation, regulation and raising the wages by methods of social expenditure, and other welfare services has been making corrections in the wide disparities of wealth. The state taxes the rich to provide welfare to the poor. While liberal sociologists like Dahrendorf, Raymond Aron, Lispet feel that through the extension of welfare services to all strata of society and redistribution of income and wealth though progressive taxation, the state has been able to lessen economic disparity and assure satisfaction of basic needs of all. Galbraith has gone to the extent of declaring that economic inequality has ceased to be an issue in men's mind in the Western democracies.

However, the liberal socialists feel that, in spite of the fact state action has resulted in greater diffusion of property, the permanent ownership of capital resources and the disparity between rich and poor continues and is 'still greater'. State action 'only touches the fringe of the problem of finding a general system of its more equitable distributions'. The state has yet to grapple with the problem of finding a general system of profit sharing.

Social Equality

The cardinal question which confronts us today is how the state and its law should go to promote equality of different castes, classes and race, emancipation of women so far as equality in property and voting rights is concerned, and equality of right of admission to educational institutions. Equality of race and colour denies that the class whose cause it champions is not inferior to any.

The case for equality of sexes can be understood as (i) that in spite of physical and psychological difference between men and women, there is no evidence that women are in general inferior to men in intelligence, business capacity, soundness of judgements, etc., and that discrimination resting on such assumed inferiorities is misplaced; (ii) the admitted differences will not support discrimination between the sexes in respect of voting rights, entry to profession, education opportunities, levels of remuneration, etc. Thus 'equal pay for equal work' means that men and women should be paid equally if they work equally well; (iii) there are admitted biological and psychological differences in the functions within the family. A mother is expected to occupy herself with house and children, a father with earning the family living. But this does not justify elevating the husband to the position of a lord and master, nor the complete sacrifice of women's personality to the demands of the family. The emancipation of women has to be expressed itself not only in law and economic but also in changes in conventional marital relations. For example, many husbands now recognize that the domestic burden carried by mothers of families in previous generations was out of all proportions to the difference in function implied by the difference in sex. Their readiness to share the household function and the baby minding is a sign of a practical extension of the principle of equal consideration.

Social equality also depends upon openness of educational institutions on an equal basis to facilitate social mobility. This is a field where extreme inequalities prevail. In almost all the liberal countries, education has been very much organized on the lines of social classes and educational opportunities are very much associated with wealth and position. There are different kinds of schools serving different social strata of society such as the elite, middle classes, lower middle class and the poor masses.

In the prestigious schools where children of the affluent section of the society receive their education, the boys are encouraged to regard themselves as one of the ruling classes whether in the field of politics, administration or business. On the other hand, an elementary school education, mostly run by the government, is always and still remains a cheap education. An elementary book is a cheap book adopted to the needs and powers of the children of certain section of society who are supposed not to require the same kind of education as the children of parents who have more money. Even if the elementary school boy, in today's changed circumstances, is not taught that the world is divided by God into rich who are to rule, and the poor who are to be ruled, the circumstances in which he is put provide ample proof of it. He is taught in unhealthy buildings, deficiency of playing fields, school libraries and laboratory facilities for practical work, shortage of books, non-availability of teachers, lack of funds, etc. The opportunities for the children of the poor masses are rationed like bread.

Moreover, public opinion is so much convinced by the influence of long-standing traditions of educational inequality that they have accepted it a social fact. Equality of educational opportunity is still largely only a paper realization. The inequality in educational opportunity could only be eliminated if the society becomes uncertified or the school system is totally undifferentiated. Neither outcome appears likely in the liberal countries and the present inequality in education nor will occupations persist.

Legal Equality

Rule of Law and Equality of Law. Rule of law means that the law is sovereign and no person, no matter how great he is or thinks he is, can declare himself above law because that would be tantamount to arbitrary rule. Equality before law means that law guarantees freedom and equality to each citizen. This is popularly explained as equality before law and equal protection of law.

Equality before law means that amongst equals the law should be equal and should be equally administered and that 'like should be treated alike'. In other words, the law is not to make any distinction between rich and poor, feudal lord or peasant, capitalist or worker. In the eyes of law, all are equal. Equality before law implies equality of rights and duties in law, i.e. equal protection of life and limb of everyone under the law and equal penalties on everyone violating them. However, since law creates classes with special rights and duties such as landlord, vs. tenant, police vs. people, Member of Parliament vs. judges, etc., in such circumstances, differences in rights are inevitable.

In spite of the fact that people may be equal before law, the judges may be corrupt or biased. Equality before law must ensure that the judges are free from political pressures, free from corruption, bias, etc. the inequality in the appreciation of law may also rise if poor men are kept from the cost of legal action; if a rich man can force a settlement on less favourable terms than a poor opponent would get in court by threatening to carry the cause to appeal.

J.R. Lucas writes that equality before law does not necessarily mean that the law will treat all alike, but rather determines that law will be within the reach of everybody. In other words, nobody will be small enough that he cannot take the shelter of law and nobody will be big enough that he will not be accountable to law. It means that anybody can ask for the help of court, everybody is bound to obey its orders, and the courts will also take decisions impartially. Equality before law means equal subjection to law and equal protection of law.

All may possess equal rights but all do not have an equal power to vindicate those rights, so long as the vindication demands expenditure and so long as some are more able than others to meet he expenditure demanded.

Natural Equality

Natural Equality implies that Nature has made all men equal. In ancient times, the Stoics of Greece and the Roman thinkers like Polybius and Cicero contradicted the principle of natural inequality of mankind as advocated by Plato and Aristotle. Cicero said: "For, no one thing is like as equal to another one as we human beings are like and equal to one another". The Stoics and the Romans took the argument of the 'law of Nature' that was equally applicable to all people irrespective of their country or race. Identifying the 'law of Nature' with the 'law of God' the Christian thinkers upheld the principle of natural equality of mankind as sanctioned by the Biblical injunction of the 'Fatherhood of God and brotherhood of man'. In modern times, Rousseau and Marx were the best exponents of the case of natural equality of mankind. However, though the natural equality of mankind is a very noble idea which constitutes one of the two foundations of democracy (the other being liberty), in practice things are not so. It is like an ideal to say that 'all earth is surface'. The social or civil equality is an actuality. It implies that the rights and opportunities of all are equal so that each may have the best possible development of his personality. In the world of law we come across the principle of equality before law and its equal protection for all. From the President or Prime Minister at the top to a constable or a watchman at the bottom the law of the land is applicable to all. The judicial system protects the rights of all irrespective of anybody's social and economic position. The noted English jurist Dicey defines it as one of the two essential principles of the 'rule of law'.[10]

International Equality

International equality means that all nations of the world must be treated equally without any consideration for any nation's demographic, geographical, economic, or military potential. Each member-state of the United Nations has one vote in the General Assembly. This is equality in the international sphere. But with the growth of internationalism, this term has acquired some more implications. It is also desired that nations must not resort to force. They must make use of pacific means of the settlement of their disputes. Evils like those of slavery and racial segregation must disappear from the face of the earth. There should be distribution of scientific and technological achievements among all nations of the world so as to usher in a new international social and economic order.

ASSUMPTIONS OF EQUALITY

Equality has been achieved in liberal countries. To a considerable extent, the problem of equality in the liberal societies boils down to the complex relationship between politics and economics. Although people are more equal socially than they were before the advent of the welfare state in the twentieth century, yet basic inequality in terms of power, prestige and wealth continues. While the liberal democratic state preaches public principles of impartiality and open government, it allows inequality in the economic sphere associated with capitalism. The liberal capitalist society generates massive inequalities in the distribution of wealth both through inheritance and personal achievements in the occupational field. At the industrial level, people experience a society which is economically unequal while the political stage suggests that democracy is open, free and equal especially at the level of opportunity. The government, being welfare state, cannot ignore the welfare and redistribution of resources, but at the same time, it has to pay attention to the requirements of free capitalist economy. The socialist states have tried to solve this dilemma but the results have not been encouraging.

Recently, American political sociologists like Talcott Parson, Kingley David, and E.M. Wilburt have declared that inequality is a necessary condition of all social organisations. Instead of worrying about the origin of inequality and social classes, they have attempted to demonstrate that social differentiation and stratification are indispensable to the very existence of the social structure. Each society has functional norms which promote the kind of inequality to be desirable. However, since the history of the idea of equality has been, to a considerable extent intermittent and sometimes violent, it is desirable that the debate over equality should be an unending one, with every new resolution a beginning for a new one.

LIBERAL VERSUS MARXIST INTERPRETATIONS

Liberal Doctrine

The central theme of Liberal view is that "equals should be treated equally, unequally, and the respects in which they are considered unequal must be relevant to the differences in treatment that we propose".[11] However, with the assimilation of the socialist content in the philosophy of liberalism, the real meaning of equality has been integrated with consideration of social good as a result of which the concept of social equality has become all-pervasive. John Rawls suggests two essential points inherent in the notion of equality:

1. Each person is to have an equal right to the extensive basic liberty compatible with similar liberty for others.
2. Social and economic inequalities are to be arranged in a way so that they are both (a) reasonably expected to be to every-one's advantage, and (b) attached to position and offices equally open to all.

The liberal doctrine of equality stands on the premise of the 'equality of adequate opportunities' available to every member of the society. All people have liberty to compete in the midst of equal opportunities with the result that those who can make best use of their chances may go ahead of others. Inequality in the midst of equal opportunities is thus a valid affair. It is egalitarianism. J.H. Schaar thus explains the meaning of egalitarianism: "The doctrine of equality of opportunity is the product of a competitive and fragmented society, a society in which individualism, in Tocqueville's sense of the word, is the reigning ethical principle. It is a precise symbolic expression of the liberal-bourgeois model society, for it extends the market-place mentality to all the spheres of life. It views the whole of human relations as a contest in which each man competes with his fellows for scarce goods; a contest resting upon the attractive conviction that all should be allowed to improve their conditions as far as their abilities permit. Thus, it is the perfect embodiment of the liberal conception of reform; the fundamental character of the social-economic system is altered in substance".[12]

Marxist Interpretation

The Marxist view of equality is different. It studies the whole case of liberty and equality through the prism of class war. Equality cannot exist in a society ridden with class contradictions. The class of the 'haves' enjoys all liberty. It is not available to the poor, weaker and backward sections who have to undergo the pangs of exploitation and oppression. The existence of a classless society is the sine qua non of the existence of the real conditions of liberty and equality. All kinds of artificial distinctions can be eliminated only when the dictatorship of the proletariat removes all kinds of contradictions in the society. Only then the real meaning of equality shall prevail that "lies in the existence of identical conditions and opportunities for the free development of the individual and the fulfillment of the requirements of all members of society, the equal position of people in society being understood differently in different historical epochs".[13]

View of Stalin

In a speech delivered in 1934 at the Seventeenth Congress of the Communist Party of the Soviet Union, Stalin declared that "equality in the sphere of requirements and personal life is a piece of reactionary petty-bourgeois stupidity worthy of a primitive sect of ascetics, but not of a Socialist society organised on Marxism lines, because we cannot demand that all people should have the same requirements and tastes, and that all people shall live their individual lives in the same way. By equality, Marxism means, not equality in personal requirements and personal life, but the abolition of classes, i.e., (a) the equal emancipation of all toilers from exploitation after the capitalists have been overthrown and expropriated; (b) the equal abolition for all private property in the means of production after they have been transformed into the property of the whole society; (c) the equal duty of all to work according to their ability and the equal right of all toilers to receive according to the amount of work they have done (socialist society); (d) the equal duty of all to work according to their ability and the equal right of all toilers to receive according to their requirements (communist society). And Marxism starts out with the assumption that people's tastes and requirements are not, and cannot be, equal in quality or in quantity, either in the period of socialism, or in the period of communism. It is time it was understood that Marxism is opposed to levelling".[14]

Distinction in Liberal and Marxist Views

In the view of the liberals, a classless society under the dictatorship of the proletariat is the model of a single-interest society that guarantees no liberty and hence no equality of any kind to its members. It is a totalitarian set up. Real equality prevails in an open society having different interests living in competition with each other. Thus, equality means equal rights and opportunities to all to play their part in the competitive pattern of life. The distinction between the rich and the poor subsists due to the fact that they have different capacities and different levels of merit to play their part in the competition of life. The Marxist view condemns the model of a liberal society. It desires a thoroughly new social and economic system free from exploitation and oppression of man by man in any form. A liberal or bourgeois society cannot ensure the boons of equality of the individuals in general; bourgeois democracy proclaims the formal or the legal equality of the property-owner and the proletarian, the exploiter and the exploited, thereby grossly receiving the oppressed classes".[15]

AFFIRMATIVE ACTION

"Affirmative action" means positive steps taken to increase the representation of women and minorities in areas of employment, education, and business from which they have been historically excluded. Affirmative action is intended to promote equal opportunity. It is a policy or a program that seeks to redress past discrimination through active measures to ensure equal opportunity, as in education and employment. It is the practice of giving preference to racial minorities or women when hiring employees, giving awards or deciding whom to admit. The term "affirmative action" was first used in the United States. It first appeared in Executive Order 10925, which was signed by President John F. Kennedy on March 6, 1961, and it was used to refer to measures to achieve non-discrimination. President Kennedy explored the concept of affirmative action but it was President Lyndon Johnson who first applied this concept by taking steps to equalize the presence of individuals in government positions. Affirmative action arose out of a desire to bring minority groups into institutions and professions that had traditionally been dominated by white males. It first appeared after the Civil Rights movement of the 1960s as an attempt to accompany the new legal equality gained for minorities with social and economic equality.

The legal status of affirmative action was densified by the Civil Rights Act of 1964. This landmark legislation prohibited discrimination in voting, public education and accommodations, and employment in firms with more than fifteen employees. Title VII of the Civil Rights Act offered a similar understanding of affirmative action as Executive Order 10925. It stated that the act was not designed "to grant preferential treatment to any group because of race, colour, religion, sex, or national origin". Two important issues were controverted with the awakening of the Civil Rights Act of 1964. It was, whether unintentional or structural discrimination constituted violation of the principle of equal opportunity; and the extent to which preferential treatment should be given to affected groups. These issues came out during the Johnson administration. President Johnson argued that instead of simply ending discrimination was not enough; there was strong requirement for equality of opportunity. He also argued for a more active interpretation of affirmative action that would assure "equality as a result".

Reservation in India

Reservation in India is a form of affirmative action designed to improve the well-being of perceived backward and under-represented communities. The main aim of the reservation policy is to uplift the submerged sections of society. Its objective is to increase the opportunities for enhanced social and educational status of the underprivileged communities and, thus, enable them to take their rightful place in the mainstream of Indian society. Many citizens from the upper classes opposed the reservation policy of the government as it takes away their rights to equality.

Reservation or Affirmative Action Program is one such policy, which has the following three goals:

(i) To remove social and religious disabilities of the deprived people, on account of their social segregation and cultural isolation.

(ii) To facilitate and promote equal participation of all in the nation building activities.

(iii) To protect underclass from all forms of social injustice and exploitation.

Reservation system has been a matter of contention ever since it was first introduced in the British occupied India and remains a point of conflict. In 1891, there was a demand for reservation of government jobs with an agitation against the recruitment of non-natives into public service overlooking qualified native people.[16] In 1901, reservations were introduced in Maharashtra by Shahu Maharaj. Chatrapati Sahuji Maharaj, Maharaja of Kolhapur in Maharashtra introduced reservation in favour of non-Brahmin and backward classes as early as 1902. The notification of 1902 created 50% reservation in services for backward classes/communities in the State of Kolhapur. This is the first official instance providing for reservation for depressed classes in India.[17] In 1905, Vice-Roy Curzon banned the employment of Hindu Bengalis in the government services. In 1909 and in 1919 similar reservation system was introduced for the Muslims in British India. In 1935, for pure political reason, the British government had provided job reservation for the backward castes. After Independence in 1947, the Indian Parliament passed resolutions and made amendments to the Constitution passing Acts to facilitate reservations for backward people in education and in jobs. The Constitution of India states in Article 15(4), "All citizens shall have equal opportunities of receiving education. Nothing herein contained shall preclude the State from providing special facilities for educationally backward sections of the population". It also states that "The State shall promote with special care the educational and economic interests of the weaker sections of society, and shall protect them from social "injustice" and all forms of "exploitation". The Article further states that nothing will prevent the nation from helping SCs and STs for their betterment.

Although Reservation provides facilities to a small group of people, on the basis of caste and religion, yet it also creates dis-satisfaction in a comparatively larger group of the discriminated people. The demand for reserving seats in jobs, both in government as well as private sector, on the basis of caste, religion, and minority is increasing day by day. The recent Gurjar (Gujjar) outbreak in Rajasthan is one of the burnished example of it. Reservation in India is always controversial topic in India.

NOTES

1. Laski, *The Danger of Being Gentlemen and other Essays*, Ch. 3.
2. Barker, *Principles of Social and Political Theory*, p. 151.
3. R.H. Tawney, *Equality*, p. 22.
4. Barker, *op. cit.*, p. 151.
5. Laski, *op. cit.*, p. 153
6. Tawney, *op. cit.*, p. 103-104
7. Laski, *op. cit.*, p. 153
8. Benn and Peters, *op. cit.*, p. 119.
9. Laski, *op. cit.*, p. 153-154.
10. A. Appadorai, *The Substance of Politics*, p. 81.
11. Rawls, *op. cit.*, p. 61.
12. Schaar, *Equality of Opportunity and Beyond* in Nomos. IX, p. 237.
13. *A Dictionary of Scientific Communism*, p. 85.
14. Emile Burns (ed.), *A Handbook of Marxism*, pp. 937-938.
15. Lenin, *Collected Works*, Vol. 31, p. 145.
16. Laskar, Mehbubul Hassan. "Rethinking Reservation in Higher Education in India". ILI Law Review
17. Chhatrapati Shahu Maharaj. "Shri Chhatrapati Shahu Maharaj". History. Bahujan Samaj Party. Retrieved 20 October 2011.

2

Importance of Liberty

Freedom means the absence of the initiation of physical force or absence of any form of coercion. When one has freedom, it means that he is free of or free from the initiation of physical force by other people in any form including the form of majority rule or government. Freedom is a natural right. According to Mccallum, freedom is a triadic relationship: "X is/is not free from Y to do/not to do or become/not become Z".

"Freedom," "independence," and "liberty" refer to an absence of undue restrictions and an opportunity to exercise one's rights and powers. "Freedom" emphasizes the opportunity given for the exercise of one's rights, powers, desires, or the like (e.g., an organization promoting freedom of speech). "Liberty," though most often interchanged with "freedom," is also used to imply an undue exercise of freedom (e.g., taking liberties with the text of the manuscript). Liberty is a concept of political philosophy and identifies the condition in which an individual has the right to act according to his or her own will. Freedom on the other hand, is the state of not being imprisoned, enslaved, or otherwise constrained, or more specifically.

The word liberty owes its origin to Latin word "liber" which means "freedom". Thus, liberty means freedom from restraints. It implies complete freedom to do anything one desire. There must not be any limitation on the individual actions. Liberty is a fundamental concept without which a man is hardly a man. A man clothed with liberty is a man, otherwise he is dehumanized, aimless and a mere slave. Like the state and sovereignty, it is a product of specific historical circumstances. It is often identified with the absence of restraint. It can be termed as the availability of certain socio-economic conditions in which a man may develop his personality. Liberty is generally considered a concept of political philosophy and identifies the condition in which an individual has the ability to act according to his or her own will. Political philosophies rooted in individualism and socialism often conceive of liberty differently; individualist and liberal conceptions of liberty relate to the freedom of the individual from outside compulsion; a socialist perspective, on the other hand, regards liberty as the equal distribution of power, arguing that liberty without equality amounts to the domination of the most powerful. Seeley said that Liberty is the opposite of over government. G.D.H. Cole defined that Liberty is freedom of individuals to express without external hindrances, his personality. Rousseau said that Liberty consists in obedience to general will. Laski said that the eager maintenance of that atmosphere in which men have the opportunity to be their best selves. Gettell defined that Liberty is the positive power of doing and enjoying those things which are worthy of enjoyment and work.

Liberty is essential for a man's personality. Liberty is not one but manifold. Such as natural liberty, civil liberty, political liberty, personal liberty, economic liberty and national liberty. Liberty is the most cherished ideal of life of a man. Liberty or freedom is the central problem of politics. History shows that freedom is the basic thing that goes to make up the ethos of man and civilization. Without it no one can attain happiness which is the true end of man's life. Men want to be free to live their own lives in their own way. Rights are means to an end and that end is liberty. Freedom means absence of restraints. Liberals pleaded for the freedom of an individual from the authority of the state. The Marxists fought for the freedom of proletariat from bourgeoisie. The right to liberty is one of the most important rights because it contributes to the evolution of a man's individuality. History has amply shown that liberty is the basic thing that goes to make up the ethics of man civilisation. Without it no one can attain happiness which is the true end of all human beings. Men want to be free to live their own lives, in their own way and the attainment of that ambition constitutes liberty. The purpose of rights is enabling men to live, to enjoy life and to develop to the full potentialities of their individual personalities. Rights are only means to an end and the end is liberty. Men want to be free to live their own lives in their own way and the attainment of that ambition constitutes liberty or freedom.

DEFINITIONS OF LIBERTY

In order to understand the essence of the word liberty it is necessary to examine some definitions:

1. **Seeley.** "Liberty is the opposite of over Government".
2. **Laski.** "I mean by liberty the absence of restraints upon the existence of these social conditions which a modern civilization are the necessary guarantees of the individual happiness".
3. **Liber.** "It is the faculty of willing to the power of doing what has been willed without influence from any other source".
4. **D.D. Raphael.** "Freedom means absence of restraints. A man is free so far as he is not restrained from doing what he wants to do or what he would choose to do if he knew that he could".
5. **Ramsay Muir.** "By liberty I mean to secure enjoyment by individuals and by the natural and spontaneous groups of individuals. Such as a nation, church, trade, union, of the power to think their own thoughts and to express and act upon them using their own gifts in their own way under the shelter of the law, provided they do not impair the corresponding right of others".

In brief, liberty is the affirmation by an individual or a group of his or its own essence. The ideal of liberty has made its powerful appeal to man in all ages. John Locke was a great exponent of liberty.

Thus, liberty means man's right to do what is worth doing. Social life is regulated by a set of principles or norms that make man's life civilised. These restraints distinguish between good and bad, right and wrong, moral and immoral, legal and illegal. Thus liberty means man's right to do what he wants for the sake of making the best possible development of his personality by following a course that is good, or right, or moral, or lawful. In fine, the real meaning of liberty should be understood with this point in view that the liberty of an individual is relative to that of others.[1] Sidgwick holds that freedom, when employed without qualification, signifies primarily the absence of physical coercion or confinement. A is clearly not a free agent if B moves his limbs, and he is not free if he cannot get out of a building because B has locked the door. But in another part of its meaning—which from our present point of view is more important—freedom is opposed not to physical constraint but to the moral restraint placed on inclination by the fear of painful consequences resulting from the action of other human beings".[2]

POSITIVE ASPECT OF LIBERTY

Positive liberty is an idea that was first expressed and analyzed as a separate conception of liberty by John Stuart Mill but most notably described by Isaiah Berlin. It refers to the opportunity and ability to act and fulfill one's own potential, as opposed to negative liberty, which refers to freedom from coercion. Positive liberty is described as freedom to achieve certain ends, while negative liberty is described as from external coercion. The concept of positive liberty is emphasized by those on the left-wing of the political spectrum, whereas negative liberty is most important for those who lean towards libertarianism. The right-wing also embraces some forms of positive liberty. Many anarchists and others considered to be on the left-wing, see the two concepts of positive and negative liberty as interdependent and thus inseparable. While he described the concept of positive liberty, Isaiah Berlin was deeply suspicious of it. Berlin argued that the pursuit of positive liberty could lead to a situation where the state forced upon people a certain way of life. The state judged that it was the most rational course of action, and therefore, was what a person should desire, whether or not people actually did desire it.

Defenders of "positive liberty" say that there is no need for it to have such totalitarian undertones, and that there is a great difference between a government providing positive liberty to its citizens and a government presuming to make their decisions for them. Many on the left see positive liberty as guaranteeing equal rights to certain things like education and employment.

In the present times individual liberty is sought to be reconciled with the growing authority of the state. If the state desires to achieve the goal of public welfare restraints are essential. Human actions cannot be divided into water-tight forms as was done by Mill more than a hundred years back. Man lives in society, his actions have an effect on the liberty of others. There can be nothing like a strictly private or self-regarding sphere. Man cannot be allowed to commit suicide or read obscene literature. As L.T. Hobhouse points out, "There is no side of a man's life which is unimportant to society, for whatever he is, does, or thinks may affect his own well-being, which is and ought to be a matter of common concern, and may also directly or indirectly affect the thought, action and character of those with whom he comes into contact".[3]

NEGATIVE ASPECT OF LIBERTY

The concept of negative liberty reflects the phase of liberalism in the 17th and 18th centuries. The main exponents are: J.S. Mill, Hobbes, Locke, Tocqueville, Jefferson, Burke, Adam Smith, Thomas Paine, Isaiah Berlin, Friedman, Nozick, and Hayek. The philosophical concept of negative liberty refers to an individual's liberty from being subjected to the authority of others. In this negative sense, one is considered free to the extent to which no person interferes with his or her activity. According to Thomas Hobbes, for example, "a free man is he that...is not hindered to do what he hath the will to do". The distinction between negative liberty and positive liberty was drawn by Isaiah Berlin in his lecture entitled *Two Concepts of Liberty*. According to Berlin, this distinction is deeply embedded in the political tradition: the notion of negative liberty being associated most strongly with the classical British political philosophers (e.g. Locke, Hobbes and Smith) and positive liberty with continental European thinkers such as Hegel, Rousseau, Herder and Marx. The concept of negative liberty has several noteworthy aspects. First, negative liberty defines a realm or "zone" of freedom (in the "silence of law"). In Berlin's words, "liberty in the negative sense involves an answer to the question 'What is the area within which the subject—a person or group of persons—is or should be left to do or be what he is able to do or be, without interference by other persons'. Some philosophers have disagreed on the extent of this realm while accepting the main point that liberty defines that realm in which one may act unobstructed by others. Second, the restriction (on the freedom to act) implicit in negative liberty is imposed by a person or persons and not due to causes such as nature, lack, or incapacity. The dichotomy of positive and negative liberty is considered specious by political philosophers in traditions such as socialism, social democracy, libertarian socialism, and Marxism. Some of them argue that positive and negative liberty are indistinguishable in practice, while others claim that one kind of liberty cannot exist independently of the other. A common argument is that the preservation of negative liberty requires positive action on the part of the government or society to prevent some individuals from taking away the liberty of others.

The meaning of liberty has two dimensions—negative and positive. In a negative sense, liberty implies the absence of restraints as far as possible. All restraint is bad, because it effects curtailment or diminution of individual freedom. These should be as little as possible as liberty lives within restraints. Here the burden of argument is to accept the fact of restraints with a sense of compulsion. John Stuart Mill says that "all restraints qua restraints is an evil...leaving people to themselves is always better than controlling them".[4] In order to make his meaning more clear, Mill divides man's action into two parts —self-regarding and others-regarding. The state has no right to interfere with the liberty of man if his action affects himself alone. Professing any religion, worshipping the Deity, and reading a book are examples of man's strictly self-regarding actions. However, the state may intervene in the liberty of a man if he harms liberty of his fellow-beings. If a man does something that has its effect on others, it pertains to the realm of others-regarding. As Mill puts it, "The sole end for which mankind is warranted, individually or collectively, in interfering with the liberty of action of any of their number, is self-protection. That the only purpose for which power can be rightfully exercised over any member of a civilised community against his will is to prevent harm to others. His own good, either physical or moral, is not a sufficient warrant.... Over himself, his own body and mind, the individual is sovereign".[5]

F.A. Hayek says that every individual has some assured area of personal freedom with which others cannot interfere. The element of 'choice' should be taken as decisive.[6] A man is really free when he is not subjected to coercion of any kind. Coercion means subjection to the arbitrary will of others. It occurs when an agent's actions are made to serve the will of another, not for his own but for other's purposes. It implies action in the sense that a person, who is coerced, chooses to be what he does. It occurs only when one person threatens with the intention of thereby getting the other to act in conformity with his will".[7]

KINDS OF LIBERTY

Liberty implies "a condition of freedom especially opposed to political subjection, imprisonment, or slavery".[8] However, it is a multiple concept having following varieties:

1. **Natural Liberty.** Natural liberty implies complete freedom for a man to do what he wills. Hobbes called it 'license' by the liberty of the woods. It means no restraint of any kind whatsoever on the doing of a man. In the world of nature all creatures live according to their will. So should be the pattern of a man's life. Let a man do what he wills.

Criticism

Liberty lives within restraints. Therefore, the idea of natural liberty is an errant nonsense; it cannot prevail in a society of human beings. As a social creature, man should lead a life regulated by social restraints. Rousseau begins with the assumption that 'man is born free, he is everywhere in chains' but he ultimately stresses the point that "what man loses by the social contract is his natural liberty and an unlimited right to everything he tries to get and succeeds in getting; what he gains is civil liberty and the proprietorship of all he possesses".[9]

2. **Social Liberty.** Liberty lies in its civil or social variety in personal, political, religious, economic, national and international spheres. It relates to man's freedom in his life as a member of the social organisation. It refers to a man's right to do what he wills in compliance with the restraints imposed on him in the general interest. This kind of liberty consists in the rights and privileges that the society recognises and the state protects in the spheres of private and public life of an individual. Following are its sub-varieties:

(i) ***Personal Liberty.*** According to Laski, Private liberty "is that aspect of which the substance is mainly personal to a man's self. It is the opportunity to be fully himself in the private relations of life".[10] According to Blackstone, this kind of liberty consists in three directions—(i) personal security not only of health and life but also of reputation, (ii) personal freedom especially of movement, and (iii) personal property or the free use and enjoyment and disposal of all acquisitions.

(ii) ***Political Liberty.*** Political liberty refers to the power of the people to be active in the affairs of the state. It is integrally connected with the life of man as a citizen. It consists in the provisions for universal adult franchise, free and fair elections, and freedom for the avenues that make a healthy public opinion. Its existence shows that the people may curb, control and change their government.

(iii) ***Economic Liberty.*** Economic liberty pertains to the individual in his capacity as a manual or mental producer or worker engaged in some gainful occupation or service. It means security and opportunity to find reasonable significance in the earning of one's daily bread. The individual should be free from the fear of unemployment and insufficiency which saps the whole strength of personality. It includes freedom from want and right to produce and distribute goods. It stands for the establishment of industrial democracy enabling the workers to participate in the management of industry. Economic freedom is, however, a matter of controversy. The liberals desire a free and competitive economic system. The socialists advocate the system of state controls, even nationalization of private property in the public interest. The communists seek to abolish private economy. They define economic freedom as man's emancipation from evils like unemployment and exploitation. Absence of unemployment and provisions for social security are the marks of economic freedom in the country.

(iv) ***Domestic Liberty***. L.T. Hobhouse talks of domestic liberty which means a responsible and respectable position of the wife and children in the family, freedom for the members of the family to have marriage of their choice, and responsibility of the parents to seek moral and mental development of the members of their family.

(v) ***National Liberty.*** National liberty is another name for national independence. It rejects the colonial or imperial subjection of one nation by another. Freedom struggles are national movements. The Americans gained national liberty in 1776 and the Indians in 1947. Love for one's country is so deep-seated in human hearts that millions of people lay down their lives for the sake of protecting the honour and security of their motherland.

(vi) ***International Liberty.*** The ideal of liberty covers the world as a whole. In the international sphere, it implies renunciation of war, limitation on the production of armaments, abandonment of the use of force and pacific settlement of international disputes. This ideal is based on the assumption that as the world becomes free, the use of force becomes irrelevant. There is no sense in aggression if it is not to issue in national subjection in one form or another.

3. **Moral Liberty.** Moral freedom is contained in the idealistic interpretations of thinkers from the ancient Plato and Aristotle to the modern Rousseau, Kant, Hegel and Green. Though a person may have all kinds of freedom, he lacks the essential quality of a human being if he does not have moral freedom. Moral freedom lies in man's capacity to act as per his rational self. Every individual has a personality of his own. Unless he seeks best possible development of his personality and desires the same thing for others and pays sincere respect for the real worth and dignity of his fellow beings, he is not free in the moral sense. Kant calls it the 'fulfillment of the will to categorical self-imposed imperative of duty' and the 'autonomy of the rational will.' To Hegel such freedom has its objective realisation in the state. It has its place in the observance of complete loyalty to the state. It is necessarily connected with man's self-realisation that has a meaning only in the context of the common good.

CONTRIBUTION OF T.H. GREEN

The meaning of liberty in its positive aspect is a contribution of T.H. Green. He defines liberty as a positive power of doing or enjoying something that is worth doing or worth enjoying in common with others. As man is a social creature, his life should be regulated by certain social bonds. Liberty of the individual should be considered in relation to the norms of goodwill. Paraphrasing the meaning of Green, Barker says: "Liberty can only be liberty for this goodwill; it can only be liberty for the pursuit of objects which such a will presents to itself. It is, therefore, no negative absence of restraints any more than beauty is the absence of ugliness. Inhering as it does in the goodwill and in that will only; it is not a power of pursuing any and every object, but a power of pursuing these objects which the goodwill presents to itself. In a word, it has two qualities. It is positive—a freedom to do something, not a freedom from having something done to one. It is determinate —a freedom to do something of a definite character, something which possesses the quality of being worth doing, and not any and everything".[11] Today the meaning of liberty has come to involve within itself both the individual and social sides of man's existence. As the social life requires a network of regulations, the idea of liberty has been bound with the necessity of due restraints. Liberty has come to have a derivative value arising from the supreme value of the moral personality acting and developing its capacities as such. The liberty which the state upholds and makes a principle of its action must be a liberty relative to and, regulated by the nature of moral personality. As like Prof. Leo Strauss says: "There is no relation of man to man in which man is absolutely free to act as he pleases or as it suits him.... By virtue of his rationality man has latitude of alternatives such as no other earthly being has.... The sense of the latitude of this freedom is accompanied by a sense that the full and unrestrained exercise of that freedom is not right. Man's freedom is accompanied by a sacred awe, by a kind of divination that not everything is permitted. Restraint is, therefore, as natural or as primeval as freedom".[12] To quote Sir John Seeley "We may say then that liberty is primarily the absence of restraint or the opposite of government, but in a secondary sense, which is also convenient, it is the absence of excessive restraint or the opposite of over-government".[13]

Thus liberty has both its negative and positive dimensions. The negative view disfavours the case of restraints on the liberty of man as far as possible. Mill and Hayek subscribe to this view. The positive view appreciates the system of reasonable restraints in the name of public good. Green and Strauss subscribe to positive view. As Prof. Isaiah Berlin of the Oxford University has pointed out, the real meaning of liberty involves both sides, and the two cannot be separated from each other. In some area of a man's life he must be free from the restraints of any kind so that he may wish to determine the course of his action without any direction from others. As Berlin affirms: "The extent of my social or political freedom consists in the absence of obstacles not merely to my actual, but to my potential, choices to my acting in this or that way if I choose to do so".[14] The state may impose some fetters on the freedom of man, but no fetter should be like one killing his area of choice. "Liberty is increased when sovereignty is put into right hands".[15] N.P. Barry says: "The old lag may deliberately commit a crime in order to recapture the security of prison life, but it would be absurd to describe his resulting condition as one of liberty".[16]

J.S. MILL'S VIEWS ON LIBERTY

Liberty or freedom is the central problem of politics. The purpose of rights is to enable men to live, to enjoy life and to develop to the full potentialities of their individual personalities. Rights are only a means to an end and the end is liberty. Men want to be free to live their own lives in their own way and the attainment of that constitutes liberty or freedom. The rights and duties arise only if the citizens are provided with the environment in which they are truly free to be themselves. Liberty is free choice of creation of an individual. It is freedom from restraints. J.S. Mill has been the great champion of liberty. In his famous *Essay on Liberty*, he strongly pleaded for the liberty of the individual against legislative interference as well as against the public opinion. An individual needed protection not only against the tyranny of magistracy but also against the tyranny of society. The growth of democracy and the increasing legislative power of the state tend to reduce individuals to a common type and to, "swamp them in the tyranny of the collectivism". Social progress depended upon giving to each individual the fullest opportunity for the fullest development of his personality. Hence, Mill forcefully pleaded for the freedom of the individual. According to Mill an individual is sovereign over his body and mind. He should be left free in all that concerns himself alone. Society has no right to impose any restraint over the individual because restraint as such is an evil thing. Mill divided the actions of individuals into two parts; self-regarding and others-regarding actions. The self-regarding actions include those matters which affect the doer only, having no concern with others. The individual was to be free in doing those things which affected him alone. But his independence was to be restricted in those cases in which his action had a direct or indirect bearing on others. As it is difficult to divide actions into watertight compartments, the principle was to be followed in a general way.

Regarding the relation of the state to liberty, Mill's analysis implied three propositions:

(1) An increase in the power of the state is prejudicial to liberty,

(2) A distinction can be drawn between the part of human life in which it is chiefly the individual that is interested, and the part which chiefly interests society and that liberty is infringed if the state interferes with the first part, and

(3) The most valuable element in human life is spontaneous choice, anything which is done by a compulsory power, diminishes the scope of that choice and thus infringes liberty.

Criticism of Mill's Concept of Liberty

(1) ***Individual freedom.*** Mill assumed that the individual is sovereign over his body and mind and therefore, he should be left free in all that concerns himself alone. This is not a sound proposition. Neither it is a self-evident truth nor is it in harmony with the facts of total life. Mill, himself admits that, "there can be circumstances under which it may become legitimate for others to intervene in a purely personal matter i.e., where one is about to commit suicide. No one will call it an attack upon one's safety".

(2) ***Division of human action.*** Mill's division of human action into two self-regarding and other-regarding is

a misnomer. Individuals are not isolated beings in a society. The action of each individual directly or indirectly definitely affects others. Therefore, it is not possible to set apart a sphere of conduct which may concern the individual alone.

(3) *Nature of energy*. Critics have also pointed out that, "in his argument he is adamant to identify the individual's energy with genius or originality and to forget that energy may be mere electricity—not strength of character; but weakness consequently need to be repressed rather than encouraged".

Contribution of Mill

Mill not only propounded the negative conception but forcefully pleaded for positive freedom also. He favoured freedom of speech, thought and action. He believed in the toleration of opinions and unhampered freedom of discussion. He was convinced that in the struggle of ideals, ultimately the truth will triumph.

HAROLD LASKI'S VIEWS ON LIBERTY

Laski was a consistent believer in the dignity of human personality. In thought and action, he was an uncompromising individualist. He contended that the individual must consult his conscience before deciding to obey or disobey the particular command of the sovereign. The state which insists upon an unquestioning obedience to its orders by the citizens reduces the states of moral slaves. Laski criticised the modern society because it prevents a large majority of people from securing the material foundations of a spiritually enriched life. Laski revised some of the well-known dogmas which Mill stated in his *Essay on Liberty*. He discussed them in the context of an international situation when the success of Fascism was posing a serious danger to the ideal of freedom in all countries. He always remained a consistent champion of human freedom in all its variegated aspects.

Meaning of Liberty According to Laski, 'Liberty' means the eager maintenance of that atmosphere in which men have an opportunity to be their best selves. He regarded rights as an essential condition of liberty. Without right, there can be no liberty because in that case men are the subjects of law unrelated to the needs of personality. Freedoms are opportunities which history has shown to be essential for the development of personality. Freedoms are inseparable from rights. If the rights are not guaranteed liberty becomes uncertain and illusory. Giving a very comprehensive definition of liberty, Prof. Laski says, "Liberty is the eager maintenance of the atmosphere in which men have the opportunity to be their best selves. It is a product of rights. Without rights, there can be no liberty because in that case men are the subjects of law unrelated to the needs of personality. Liberty, therefore, is a positive thing. It does not merely mean absence of restraints".

No Classification of Human Actions. Laski did not approve of Mill's classification of human actions into two parts i.e., self-regarding actions and other-regarding actions. According to him all conduct was social in the sense that whatever a man did, affected the other members of society. Laski therefore, lays emphasis upon the relationship of the individual's liberty with the society. He is convinced that personal liberty cannot be enjoyed in isolation from society. He maintains that liberty also, "involves restraints, because the separate freedom I use not freedom to destroy the freedoms of those with whom I live".

Three different aspects of liberty:

1. Private or individual liberty
2. Political liberty
3. Economic liberty.

Three conditions for the realisation of liberty:

1. There should be no special privileges in society. Freedom cannot exist in the presence of special privileges.
2. Another condition for the realisation of liberty is the presence of rights. There cannot be liberty where the rights of some depended upon the pleasure of others.

3. The third condition for the realisation of liberty is the existence of a responsible Government whose incidence of action should be unbiased.

Thus, Laski was a great champion of a positive liberty. He attached great significance to human rights. But there was shift in his attitude later on.

MARXIST VIEWS ON LIBERTY

The Marxist interpretations regarding the meaning and nature of liberty hinge on the nature and scope of economic liberty available in the pattern of social life. The liberals define liberty as a bundle of rights that enable a man to seek the best possible development of his personality. They do not bother for the kind of social life of man. The Marxist view of liberty covers the case of man's life in the society he lives and the conditions he is subjected to. There is no liberty for a man of the 'dominated' class in a bourgeois society. In it, all privileges are available to the members of the 'dominant class' by virtue of having the ownership of the means of production and distribution. After the occurrence of a socialist revolution, conditions change with the change of society.

Abolition of Capitalism

In the Marxist view, there can be no real freedom unless the capitalist system is replaced with the socialist system. The bourgeois order with its system of private property and wage slavery throws man at the mercy of the blind forces of the market producers at all levels in society. The freedom of man "is crucified upon a cross of gold".[17] According to James Maritain, "Marx had a profound intuition which is to my eyes the great lightning flash of truth which traverses all his work of the condition of heteronomy and loss of freedom produced in the capitalist world by wage slavery, and of dehumanisation with which the possessing class and proletariat alike are thereby simultaneously stricken".[18]

Meaning of Freedom

While Marx takes liberty as synonymous with the end of exploitation of man by man in a class-contending society, he also integrates it with the 'glorious human values' possible only in the stateless era of social development. For him, the abolition of capitalism or the establishment of socialism only makes the truly human society, possible. As he says: "Every emancipation is a restoration of the human world and of human relationship to man himself".[19] The aim or purpose of human life is not to bear the pangs of exploitation and subjection and injustice but to have a life of real freedom. This is possible only in a classless society. An alienated man has no freedom. Freedom can only be achieved by means of changing society so that the 'have-nots' of today are converted into the 'haves' of tomorrow. Huberman and Sweezy put it, "Freedom means living life to the fullest—the economic ability to satisfy the needs of the body in regard to adequate food, clothing and shelter, plus effective opportunity to cultivate the mind, develops one's personality, and asserts one's individuality".[20]

The Marxist concept of liberty rejects 'free will' as the ingredient of liberty. Man is not only a social creature; he is also a conscious creature. He can understand the pattern of his social existence and then change it by means of his conscious revolutionary social activity (praxis). A man can know the implications of his free or unfree life only when he is conscious of the objective laws of nature and social existence. Knowledge makes possible the mastery of man over nature and society, but this knowledge is useless without man's revolutionary social activity. Thus, freedom as the laws of nature and society comes as a result of practical revolutionary activity based on such knowledge of the laws of historical development.[21]

Universal Principle

Marxist interpretation of freedom is universal. It has implications to all. It has its different implications to the people of different classes in a bourgeois or class-ridden society. There it means right to exploit and oppress the working class at the hands of the feudal or capitalist lords. It means bearing the condition of exploitation and subjection by the people of the working class. According to Marx, it signifies the freedom of the wolves in a society of sheep with shepherdship in the hands of the wolf. This is no freedom. Freedom means freedom for all in an equal measure. All people should be free from the pangs of exploitation, coercion, subjection, injustice, alienation etc. According to Marx, this is possible only in a socialist society that is committed to convert itself into a communist way of life. Freedom implies activity aimed at creating real conditions for the all-round development and flowering of man's individuality. The full significance of this fact lies in the all-round development of all members of the society.

1. ***Criticism of Marxist view.*** The Marxist view of liberty was not appreciated by the liberal thinkers who identify liberty with constitutional government, political democracy and orderly administration based on common law system. By the argument of their free-market liberalism Joseph Schumpeter and Milton Friedman reject the Marxian contention.
2. ***Louis Fischer, Arthur Koestler and J.K. Galbraith*** describe the socialist system as a condition of perfect regimentation of life under the iron rule of a small section of the communist leadership. Their whole argument boils down to two important propositions. First, that competitive capitalism is a necessary condition of political freedom. Second, a socialist society is so constructed that it guarantees no political freedom.[22]

FREEDOM OF BELIEF AND EXPRESSION

Freedom of Religion or Belief

Freedom of religion is a principle that supports the freedom of an individual or community, in public or private, to manifest religion or belief in teaching, practice, worship, and observance; the concept is generally recognized also to include the freedom to change religion or not to follow any religion.[23] Freedom of religion and belief is a fundamental human right protected by a number of international treaties and declarations, including article 18(1) of the International Covenant on Civil and Political Rights (ICCPR). This right provides freedom of thought on all matters and the freedom to manifest religion and belief individually or with others, in public or in private.

Article 18 of ICCPR

1. Everyone shall have the right to freedom of thought, conscience and religion. This right shall include freedom to have or to adopt a religion or belief of his choice, and freedom, either individually or in community with others and in public or private, to manifest his religion or belief in worship, observance, practice and teaching.
2. No one shall be subject to coercion which would impair his freedom to have or to adopt a religion or belief of his choice.
3. Freedom to manifest one's religion or beliefs may be subject only to such limitations as are prescribed by law and are necessary to protect public safety, order, health, or morals or the fundamental rights and freedoms of others.
4. The States Parties to the present Covenant undertake to have respect for the liberty of parents and, when applicable, legal guardians to ensure the religious and moral education of their children in conformity with their own convictions.

IARF

The International Association for Religious Freedom (IARF) founded in Boston in 1900, is a charitable organization that works for religious freedom around the world. IARF has over ninety affiliated groups, spread over twenty countries. IARF was granted consultative status with the United Nations Economic and Social Fund (ECOSOC) in 1972. It was the catalyst for the formation of the "Committee on Freedom of Religion or Belief" in 1989 which was granted formal status with ECOSOC in 1992.

Freedom of Expression

Freedom of expression is enshrined in the Constitution of India as a fundamental right under Part III of the Constitution. Article 19 guarantees the Freedom of speech and expression, as one of six freedoms. The freedom of expression is the basic right of every human being, irrespective of colour, race, gender or status, to live with dignity which means the right to food, clothing, shelter, primary health and education. The right to freedom of expression is recognized as a human right under Article 19 of the Universal Declaration of Human Rights and recognized in international human rights law in the International Covenant on Civil and Political Rights (ICCPR).

Article 19

(a) Everyone shall have the right to hold opinions without interference.

(b) Everyone shall have the right to freedom of expression; this right shall include freedom to seek, receive and impart information and ideas of all kinds, regardless of frontiers, either orally, in writing or in print, in the form of art, or through any other media of his choice.

(c) The exercise of the rights provided for in paragraph 2 of this article carries with it special duties and responsibilities. It may, therefore, be subject to certain restrictions, but these shall only be such as are provided by law and are necessary:

(i) For respect of the rights or reputations of others;

(ii) For the protection of national security or of public order (order public), or of public health or morals.

Article 19 of the Universal Declaration of Human Rights, adopted in 1948, states that: "Everyone has the right to freedom of opinion and expression; this right includes freedom to hold opinions without interference and to seek, receive and impart information and ideas through any media and regardless of frontiers".[24]

Today, the freedom of expression is recognized in international and regional human rights law. The right is enshrined in Article 19 of the International Covenant on Civil and Political Rights, Article 10 of the European Convention on Human Rights, Article 13 of the American Convention on Human Rights and Article 9 of the African Charter on Human and Peoples' Rights.[25]

NOTES

1. Barker, *Principles of Social and Political Theory*, p. 145.
2. Sidgwick, *Elements of Politics*, p. 45.
3. L.T. Hobhouse, *Liberalism*, p. 65.
4. Mill, *Essay on Liberty*, pp. 150-51.
5. *Ibid.*, pp. 72-73.
6. Hayek, *The Constitution of Liberty*, p. 13.
7. *Ibid.*, pp. 12-13.
8. Encyclopaedia Britannica, Vol. 13, 1967 Ptg., p. 1029.
9. Rousseau, Social Contract, Book I, Ch. VIII
10. Barker, *Political Thought in England*, p. 24.
11. Strauss, *Natural Right and History*, pp. 129-30.
12. Seeley, J., *Introduction to Political Science*, p. 120.
13. Berlin, *Four Essays on Liberty*, pp. xxxix-xl.
14. *Ibid.* p. 166. The element of 'choice' is very important in the meaning of liberty.
15. Barry, *op. cit.*, p. 160.
16. Laski, *op. cit.*, p. 146.
17. Caudwell, *The Concept of Freedom*, p. 75.
18. Cited in Harry Slochower, *No Voice is Wholly Lost*, pp. 220-21.
19. De Caute (ed.), *The Essential Writings of Marx*, pp. 187-88.
20. Huberman and Paul Sweezy, *Introduction to Socialism*, p. 76.
21. M. Petrosyan, *Humanism*, p. 179
22. C.B. Macpherson, *Democratic Theory*, p. 143
23. Universal Declaration of Human Rights, Article 18.
24. Universal Declaration of Human Rights, Article 19.
25. Andrew Puddephatt, *Freedom of Expression, The essentials of Human Rights*, Hodder Arnold, 2005, pp.128.

3

Indispensability of Justice

Justice is a flexible term which is stretched to fit any idea of good. The Greek philosopher Plato tried to define justice as virtue. For him justice is not to give every man his due but is based upon 'just proportion' among various parts of society. As an egalitarian of concept, justice is there where highest place is accorded to the value of equality. In the liberal scheme of things, justice lies in liberty. Some identify justice with duty, others with the maintenance of law and order, still others with social ordering of individual rights. Some relate it with legal system and punishment. Socialists base justice upon 'need and fundamental equality'. In political arguments, justice is regarded as the property of distribution of something. According to Kolb, justice is used in two senses: (i) to give man his due, and (ii) setting right of wrong either by compensation or by punishment. In the first place, justice is concerned with deciding the principles of allocation of rights and duties, material goods, security, dignity and opportunities in the society. Since the distribution of goods and services is determined by historical circumstances of a particular society, the principles of justice are never absolute and keep on changing with the change in circumstances. Secondly, justice is related with the legal system and punishment. If what is due to man is because he is man, then it is natural justice. If what is due is according to certain customary rules which happen to be accepted by the community, then the justice is conventional. If the due is in virtue of a rule the breaking of which makes the breaker answerable for his action or actions to the public power, then the justice is legal.

MEANING OF JUSTICE

The term justice is derived from the Latin word which implies the idea of joining or fitting the idea of bond or tie. According to Barker "Primarily, the Joining or fitting implied in this root ideas is that better men and man in an organised system of human relations". Prof. Barker extends the meaning of justice by including in it the idea of joining or fitting between value and value in a general synthesis of values—the supreme values for a just system of human relations being liberty, equality and fraternity. Thus according to Barker, justice is the reconciler and synthesis of political values. C.E. Herriam has defined justice as consisting in a system of understandings and procedures through which each is accorded what is agreed upon as fair. Actually the concept of justice is a relative concept. It is related to the social system of the society. When the social system changes, the concept of justice also changes. That is why Rawls writes, "The nature and aims of a perfectly just society is the fundamental part of the theory of justice". Regarding the place and value of justice, Plato, Augustine, Acquinas, etc. suggest that the concept of justice is absolute, eternal, and permanent. It does not change with time or changing circumstances. Like truth, justice is infallible and unchangeable though it is governed by certain specific rules. On the other hand, Aristotle, Bentham and Mill opine that 'justice' is a relative concept and is susceptible to change with changing times, conditions, values and circumstances.

SOURCES OF JUSTICE

1. **Religion.** Medieval Christian writers believed the idea of justice is planted by God in the human mind. It is sacred and preserved through the authority of law. Saint Thomas said that there were four kinds of law corresponding to four forms of reason—External law, natural law, divine law and the human law. Religion, as a source of justice, has lost much of its significance since the separation of church from the state. The norms of justice enunciated by religion ought to be applied without any legal coercion. If legal coercion is applied, it may not succeed at all. Religion as a source of ethical principles is

an ultimate source of notice of justice. It cannot be considered as the immediate validating principle.

2. Nature. Stoics supported the idea of nature being of a source of justice. The stoic conception of Nature combined their moral philosophy and religious beliefs. The word Nature related to a spiritual world. For them nature, God and Reason was one thing. They believed that men who lived in conformity with nature also shared something of Reason and God. It implied three things—men must be free, men should be treated as equal, and men should be associated with their fellow men by the common factor of reason. Thus, the three coordinal sources provided by Nature for justice were Liberty, Equality and Fraternity. The stoics identified justice with the rule of reason or God.

3. Economics. Some thinkers considered economics as the most important source of justice. The Marxists believe that economics is the source of justice. Positive law or the law of the state is enacted by the dominant ruling class. It represents their economic interests. It is imposed on society by the authority of the ruling class which also controls all the means of production. Marxists believe that the bourgeoisie is the repository and dispensary of justice. When the revolution of the proletariat has succeeded in establishing a proletariat state, class based justice will come to an end. The laws of the state will now reflect the wishes of the common people. The idea of justice and its content varies with the interests of the ruling class. It is only when the state has withered away and a stateless society is established without classes, that the interests of society as a whole will be served.

4. Ethics. The Idealist thinkers Plato, Aristotle, Kant, Green, and Barker believe that the true source of justice is to be found in ethics. Law is made by a properly constituted state authority. It should also fulfil the requirements of moral conscience. Law and ethics are not the same thing. Law is concerned with the external actions of human beings whereas ethics is concerned both with the external acts as well as internal motives of man. In spite of these differences ethics and law are related to each other in the sense that law seeks to secure the external conditions necessary for the moral action or the general framework of external order in which the moral conscience can act and determine itself most easily and most freely. Sanctioned and enforced by the general moral conscience, the moral standard of community constitutes the real basis of the idea of justice. The system of values accepted by a community should be the impersonal source of positive law enforced by the state.

DIMENSIONS OF JUSTICE

1. Legal Dimension. Legal justice consists in codes enacted by the state and supplemented by customary rules observed by the community. In every country there is a general body of rules recognised and enforced by courts. The Constitution and Acts of legislature determine the legal dimension of justice. The Constitution of India prohibits discrimination among the citizens on grounds of religion, race, caste, sex, and place of birth or any of them. The laws of legislature prohibit Sati or child marriage. This is a legal way of promoting justice. A legal dimension of justice requires laws of the state and faithful adherence to them. Those who do not obey them are punished by the courts. The laws are framed by the legislative bodies which should be truly representative bodies. If the representative bodies make unjust or unreasonable law, the people should have right to oppose such law. The independent judiciary is a check on the legislative body. It does not allow legislature to make unjust laws. But the ultimate check should be the people. Strong public opinion will never allow legislature to behave irresponsibly.

The judicial system of the state should be simple and cheap. It should not be difficult to understand. A poor man cannot get justice if it is costly. The judiciary should be independent. The judges should be qualified and well paid. They should have secured service. The judiciary should be separated from the executive and legislature. The judges should not be allowed to accept legal profession after retirement. Infliction of punishment is based on various theories of punishment such as Retribution Theory, the Deterrent Theory and the Reformative Theory. The Retribution Theory believes in immediate punishment and therefore the theory is rejected. The Deterrent Theory brings fear complex in the criminals. The most acceptable theory is the Reformative Theory as the aim of punishment is to reform the criminals and turn them into good citizens.

2. Political Dimension. 'Political equality' within the state is the essence of political dimension of justice. It is concerned with the actual policies through which the political process realises the norms of justice. Political justice lies in the relationship between the individual and the authority i.e. the state. There should be political equality. All citizens should have the same political rights and equal voice in government and an equal access to all offices of authority provided the necessary qualifications are fulfilled. This means democracy and adult suffrage. It is through the exercise of this right that democracy actually comes into existence. Only a democratic constitution ensures political justice to the people. The Constitution, the Parliament and the courts give shape to the legal dimension of justice. The political parties the interest groups in the country give shape to the political dimension of justice. They try to translate the legal norms of justice into political programmes. The political dimension has a great force in democratic countries. It is a guide to the legal authority. The preamble and directive principles enshrined in the Constitution of India are the best examples of political dimension of justice. They envisage the creation of a just social order in the country. The public opinion should always be respected. The views of the minority should not be ignored. The healthy criticism by the opposition should be welcome by the ruling party. A democratic form of government assures political justice to the people.

3. Social Dimension. The socio-economic dimensions of justice are an extension of the legal and political dimensions of justice. In the ancient and medieval times, the societies were hierarchical. The division of the community into ranks, castes or orders was regarded as an expression of justice. In these societies there were the masters and the slaves, the lords and the serfs. While the masters and the lords were destined to rule from birth, the slaves and serfs were destined to serve and obey from their birth. It was considered as a natural phenomenon of society. It was justified in terms of god's will, reason and morality. In India, the division of society into a caste hierarchy was sanctioned by the law of Karma and ordained by Dharma. The aim of social justice is to protect the interests of minorities to eradicate poverty, unemployment and illiteracy from the society. It helps in removing social evils. It removes all those hindrances which hamper common good. Social justice gives protection to downtrodden and weaker sections of society. Equality before law and independent judiciary are necessary for achieving social justice. Social justice demands elimination of all discrimination between citizens on any ground. There should be freedom of conscience and free profession.

4. Economic Dimension. With the advent of socialism we are laying more emphasis on the economic dimension of justice. Without economic justice, we cannot achieve the objectives of social and political justice. For economic justice there should be sufficient production of essential goods. Basic necessities of life must be available to all. Everyone should get adequate food, clothing and shelter. There should be equitable distribution of wealth and income. Cooperation should replace cut throat competition in society. There should be no exploitation of man by man. A just socio-economic order is possible only in a classless communist society of the future. "Everyone should do according to his capacity and will get according his needs". Economic justice means, socialism or economic democracy. As M.C. Chagla, former education minister said, "Freedom is meaningless if it prevents the achievements of economic justice. To a hungry man or to a man who is denied human dignity, political freedom is an empty word. The problem of today is how to bring economic and social justice without sacrificing the individual to the ever increasing power of state".

NATURE OF JUSTICE

The term 'justice' is given different meanings by different people at different times. Its implications vary from man to man and from situation to situation. The idea of justice is a dynamic affair. Its implications change with the passage of time. What was justice in the past may be injustice today or vice versa. One may talk of moral justice or divine justice, but it will hardly be conformable to any set of empirical standards and, for this reason, not capable of practical application. Due to this, Potter said that "most men think that they understand the meaning of justice, but, in fact, their notions prove to be vague".[1]

Implications of Justice

The concept of justice has these important implications:

1. *A just state of affairs*. It is impossible to assess the justice of actions without a prior identification of the just state of affairs.[2]
2. *Aligned with the conditions of morality*. For instance, a fair race is one in which a person who wins morality deserves to win but one in which there is no cheating, nobody jumps the gun, or has an unfair advantage through the use of bad things like drugs.[3]
3. *Proper distribution of favours and losses*. It means that justice is primarily concerned with the way rewards and punishments are distributed among the individuals in a rule-governed practice and its intimate connection with fairness indicates that if a ruler were to boil his subjects in oil, jumping in afterwards himself, it would amount to an act of injustice though there would be no inequality of treatment.[4]
4. It prevails in a congenial atmosphere that is provided by a democratic set-up. As N.P. Barry says, "Fair rules may be impartially enforced in regimes which allow little political participation and majority rule democracies may generate arbitrary treatment of individuals and minorities".[5]

Traditional and Trans-traditional Justice

According to Brecht, "not only do different individuals hold various ideas about the ideal state of affairs they would consider really just; every individual is capable of several such ideas. Our ideas and feelings of justice may be two-fold, or three-fold, or manifold in accordance with different systems of values to which we respond positively at different times, or even simultaneously. Justice, in the light of personal ideas, is or at least may be a barrel with several bottoms".[6] Brecht divides justice into two broad categories.[7]

1. ***Traditional Justice.*** It accepts the fundamental institutions which constitute the basis of our daily life. It takes them for granted. It does not question them. In so far as these institutions have been established by the positive law, written constitutions, legislation, judicial precedents and the like, the traditional idea of justice is positivistic.
2. ***Trans-traditional Justice.*** It detaches itself from the existing institutions, either in whole or in part. It criticises them according to principles which are taken from a trans-traditional Scheme of evaluation. These two levels are the subjective and objective aspects of the same theme of justice. In a normative sense, justice implies the idea of joining or fitting, the idea of a bond or a tie.[8] In an empirical context it has its relation with the concept of positive law with the result that law and justice become sister-concepts. The fundamental purpose of law is the quest for justice which is to be administered without passion as when it (passion) "comes at the door, justice flies out of window".[9] Viewed in this sense, justice implies the fulfillment of.the legitimate expectations of individual under the existing laws and ensuring him the benefits promised there and to afford him protection against any violation of his rights or against any encroachment on his rights.[10]

THEORIES OF JUSTICE

1. The Philosophical Theory of Justice. It is found in the religious injunctions, or in the highly abstract ideas of philosophers. Hindu scriptures identify justice with Dharma or righteousness that involves duties in the category of actions. Plato in his *The Republic* treats justice as the principle of right ordering of human personality so as to have a right ordering of social classes. In the case of individual, the principle of justice means that he should discover his place according to the best element of his personality (reason, courage, appetite). In the case of society it means that it should have three classes (ruling class, military class, economic class) and in each class individuals should be accommodated according to the best element of their personality. There should be no interference of one element or of one class into the domain of another. This shall open the way for proper division of labour and specialisation of functions. Here is the profile of a just man and a just society. Justice means proper ordering of the three elements of human personality and reorganisation of society in three classes in correspondence to these three elements of human personality.

Criticism

Critics of philosophical theory say that (i) it is too abstract to be understood by a man of average comprehension, (ii) it is too difficult to be put into practical terms.

2. Natural Theory of Justice. Men should follow the principles of a moral life as sanctioned by the law of nature. The observance of the principle of natural equality of mankind is a precept of natural justice. Slavery is not a natural but a conventional institution. With the advent of Christianity the word 'Nature' came to have its substitute in God. Therefore, natural justice came to be identified with divine justice. The law of Nature became the law of God. Not law of Nature but law of God (as contained in the holy books) became the determinant of justice. Even in modern times, the canons of natural (or divine) justice are invoked to say that the strong should not oppress the weak, the victor should not kill the vanquished when the latter surrenders, even criminals should be treated in a human way inside the jails.

Criticism

(i) Like philosophical justice, the idea of natural or divine justice is a matter of myth, (ii) it is abstract and metaphysical in nature.

3. The Legal Theory of Justice. It identifies the idea of justice with the working of the courts. The magistrate is the administrator of justice. He should interpret the meaning of law and then pronounce a verdict whether the accused is guilty of a certain crime or not and, if guilty, what punishment should be given to him. The advocates of imperative theory of jurisprudence like Hobbes, Bentham, Austin and Dicey fully endorse this view. The legislature has the authority to make a law. The courts have authority to administer justice according to the law of the land. Where law is silent, the courts may act according to the norms of natural justice from which arises a new kind of law based on the principles of equity. A dispute must be settled by a court of competent jurisdiction. The accused must be given opportunity to defend himself. The procedure of trial must be fair and open. The judges should act freely and honestly. The accused should be given punishment according to the nature and magnitude of the wrong.

Evaluation

Legal theory is the best of all theories on this subject. It constitutes the basis of western jurisprudence. Proper implementation of this theory leads to the creation of an ideal situation what Dicey calls the 'rule of law'.

4. The Marxian Theory of Justice. In Marxian theory, law and justice are identified with the fact of class domination. State is an instrument of exploitation and oppression by one class over another. Law and justice are nothing else than a part of the entire state structure. The legislature makes a law that is in the interest of the ruling class. The courts act in a way that strengthens and defends the position of the class in power. If the instruments of law and justice protect and promote the interests of the bourgeois class, they will serve the purpose of the proletariat after the successful socialist revolution. The judiciary should have a 'committed' character. It should not defend the system of exploitation in a bourgeois society. It should finish the class of exploiters in a socialist society.

Thus, while the liberal interpretation of justice is quite flexible that places judiciary in an impartial and independent position; the Marxist notion desires its committed form. The liberal theory is too flexible and amenable to diverse, even conflicting, interpretations in various important directions. The Marxist view is inherent with very rigid postures. Highlighting this essential point of distinction between liberal and totalitarian (including Fascist and Communist) varieties, W. Friedman says: "In modern democratic society the judge must steer his way between the Scylla of subservience to government and the Charybdis of remoteness from constantly changing social pressures and economic needs...the administration of law under these systems becomes a predominantly political function and an instrument of government policy".[11]

KINDS OF JUSTICE

1. Social Justice. It relates to the balance between an individual's rights and social control. It ensures the fulfillment of the legitimate expectations of the individual under the existing laws. It assures him benefits thereunder and protection in case of any violation or encroachment on his rights. It is consistent with the unity of the nation and needs of the society.[12] Social justice requires the sacrifice of certain rights of an individual at the altar of general interest. However, viewed in a wider perspective the idea of social justice aims at the proper reconciliation of the interest of an individual with the overall interest of the community or prevalence of the latter over the former in the event of any conflict. It constitutes "an essential part of the great complex of social change, for which something may have to be sacrificed for a greater good".[13]

The concept of social justice is a very wide term covering within its fold everything pertaining to the norm of general interest ranging from the protection of the interests of the minorities to the eradication of poverty and illiteracy. It relates to the observance of the principle of equality before law and independence of judiciary. It also relates to the eradication of gigantic social evils like those of pauperism, disease, unemployment and starvation. All this also relates to the liquidation of vested interests that obstruct the achievement of common good. In the backward countries of the world, the idea of social justice enjoins upon the state to make concerted efforts for the improvement of the lot of the down-trodden and weaker sections of the community. Its area widens itself to cover the economic domain of a people's life because it demands non-exploitation of the working class.

Criticism

1. The ideal of social justice lacks a precise connotation on account of varying social and economic theories and in view of the conflicting interpretations of thinkers and jurists belonging to the liberal and the Marxist schools.
2. Allen observes: "We hear much today of 'social justice'. I am not sure that those men who use the term most glibly know very clearly what they mean by it. Some mean distribution or redistribution of wealth; some interpret it as 'equality of opportunity' —a misleading term, since opportunity can never be equal among human beings who have unequal capacities to grasp it. Many, I suspect, mean simply that it is unjust that anybody should be fortunate than themselves and the more intelligent mean that it is just—I would rather say benevolent—that every effort should be made at least to mitigate the asperities of natural human inequality and that no obstacle should be offered, but rather help offered, to practicable opportunities of self-improvement".[14]

2. Economic Justice. Social and Economic justice are closely related. Social justice demands eradication of gigantic social evils. Most of these, such as exploitation of the workers by the capitalists or concentration of national wealth into fewer hands etc. find their place in the economic sphere. As M.C. Chagla said, "Freedom is meaningless if it prevents the achievement of economic justice. To a hungry man or to a man who is denied human dignity, political freedom is an empty word. The problem of today is how to bring about economic and social justice without sacrificing the individual to the ever-increasing power of the state".[15]

The idea of economic justice means non-discrimination between man and man on the basis of economic values. In positive terms, it implies adequate payments for work without any discrimination on some artificial ground. It enjoins freedom for all in the sphere of production and distribution of goods subject to the conditions of social welfare. It demands that the state of national economy be reshaped in a way that the benefits are made more and more available to the common man. Thus, the idea of economic justice comes to imply a socialist pattern of society. Like social justice, the economic justice is also a matter of acute controversy between the liberal and Marxist thinkers. It is a matter of acute controversy among the proponents of liberalism. The Communists desire to abolish the institution of private property for the sake of bringing about an era of economic justice. The liberals invoke varying standards ranging from the maintenance of private property system to the imposition of reasonable restrictions on its use and enjoyment by the people. Both notions suffer from inherent fallacies. For instance, while one may say that the Marxist formula of 'to each according to his work' in the era of socialism and 'from each according, to his ability, to each according to his need.' In the final stage of socialism (communism) it would be contrary to the just principle of distribution as well as to the humanistic norm of helping the weak and the disabled even when they do not work. The norm of regulatory legislation or reasonable restriction as laid down by the courts of free and democratic countries would make the whole idea of economic justice fluid, perhaps touching the verge of meaninglessness. Justice and ideas about it are, therefore, to seek a new balance and a new harmony in the present conflicts between large national economic and social interests, on the one hand, and the individual or group rights and interests on the other.[16]

3. Political Justice. Political justice stands for a free and fair participation of the people in the political sphere. It involves the guarantee of universal adult franchise without distinction on some artificial grounds in matters of recruitment to public services. What the policy of the state should be, and how the society should be organised in political and economic directions are matters which should be decided by the people themselves according to prevailing needs and circumstances. The idea of the preservation of political rights of the individual dominates the scene. The very notion of justice assumes an individualistic tenor in view of the fact that despite being a social creature, some of his deeper pursuits in the field of knowledge, mind and spirit are individual affairs. As a matter of fact, they "are the springs from which civilisation grows".[17]

The notion of political justice requires that the state must protect and preserve certain valuable rights of the individual so that he may develop his personality as a citizen and thereby contribute his share to the welfare of the political community. It desires a liberal-democratic order in which rights of the individuals, including those of the minorities, are well protected. It covers much of what falls under the category of social and economic justice. It makes itself coterminous with the case of a full-fledged democratic order. It involves recognition and protection of rights relating to the maintenance of a political creed. It also enjoins the prevalence of right to dissent and duty to tolerate.

4. Distributive Justice. The earliest notion of distributive justice was given by Aristotle who said that equals should be treated equally and unequally. Injustice arises when the reverse comes to take place. It establishes an organic relationship between the norms of justice and the principle of equality. The modern interpretation of this term, however, establishes an organic relationship of a juristic norm with a particular system of economy. In this sense, distributive justice desires equal distribution of income among the equals only. It is traceable in the writings of J.W. Chapman and John Rawls.

(i) *View of Chapman.* Chapman seeks to integrate the idea of justice with his principles of 'economic rationality of man' and 'consumer's sovereignty' coupled with individual's claim of 'moral freedom.' To him; the first principle of justice is the distribution of benefits which maximise benefits in accordance with the principle of consumer's sovereignty. The second principle is that a system is unjust if the material well-being of the few is purchased at the expense of the many. In simple terms, it implies that no one shall gain at the expense of another.[18]

(ii) ***View of Rawls.*** Rawls sets out two basic moral principles of justice which constitutional democracy should satisfy. Firstly, each person engaged in institution affected by it has an equal right to the most extensive liberty compatible with a like liberty for all. Secondly, inequalities as defined by the institutional structure or fostered by it are arbitrary, unless it is reasonable to expect that they will work out to everyone's advantage and provided that the positions and offices to which they attach or from which they may be gained are open to all.[19] Such a view of distributive justice has been offered by the thinkers of the liberal school. They have made serious efforts to reconcile their notion of an affluent society with a challenge posed by the socialist order. In their affirmations, democracy "is reduced from a humanistic aspiration to a market equilibrium system".[20]

5. Corrective Justice. It is contained in the verdict of the judicial bodies that is delivered after hearing the statement of parties in a dispute. It aims to correct the erratic behaviour of the party in dispute. It emanates from the decisions of the courts in which we find an interpretation of the law of the land, a wise distinction between 'just' and 'unjust' situations, award of punishment to the wrongdoers, strictures passed against the delinquent authority and the like. In certain cases the courts may significantly reduce the scope of inequality created by the statutory provisions of the land. In brief, corrective or 'positive' justice is what is done by the courts to correct the erratic behaviour of a person by following the law of the land.

Thus justice is essentially a normative concept having its place in various spheres like religion, philosophy, ethics and jurisprudence, though its ramifications also cover social, political and economic spheres. Justice is necessarily related with the function of judicial organisations. It is the bond that connects important political values like those of rights, liberty, equality and fraternity. There can be no liberty if there is no equality. There can be no equality if there is no justice. Again, there can be no liberty if there are no rights. There can be no protection of rights if there is no well-organised system of law so as to ensure proper administration of justice. Thus, justice is the synthesiser and reconciler of great political values. In the words of Daniel Webster "justice is the chiefest interest of man".

CONTEMPORARY DEBATE ON JUSTICE

Herbert Spencer (1820-1903), F.A. Hayek (1899-1992), Milton Friedman (1912) and Robert Nozick (1938) and John Rawls (1921) are the main exponents of justice. The notion of procedural justice is closely related to the tradition of liberalism. The champions of procedural justice hold that it is necessary to determine a just procedure for the allocation of social advantages, viz. goods, and services, opportunities and benefits, power and honours; then its outcome with automatically be accepted as just. The contemporary debate as the nature of justice focuses on the distinction between procedural justice and substantive justice. The allocation or distribution of social advantages among various sections of society itself should be just- that is the primary issue, the procedure for making such allocation is a secondary issue, which can be adjusted suitably to meet the requirements of just distribution. The function of justice is to regulate the mutual relations between individuals and groups. The quest for justice should aim at evolving reasonable rules which should be applied impartially to all categories. Freedom of contract is the mainstay of procedural justice.

It requires the state to ensure that no individual or group would oppress another by force or fraud. As Norman Barry (*An Introduction to Modern Political Theory*, 1989) has aptly illustrated, procedural justice is exemplified in competition, such as races. A fair race is not one in which the person who wins morally deserves to win but one in which there is not cheating, nobody jumps the gun or has an unfair advantage through the use of drugs. Procedural justice treats the rules of market economy as the model rules of human behaviour. It holds that the market mechanism creates necessary conditions for the most efficient use of resources; any artificial social policy designed to restrict this process will lead to wastage of the rare material and human resources.

Procedural justice repudiates all discrimination between human beings on the basis of caste, creed, sex, race, region, language and culture, etc. and accepts equal dignity and moral worth of all human beings. In this respect, it is a progressive idea. But it stretches the principle of open competition too far; Spencer went to the extent of suggesting that the state should not extend only help to the handicapped and let the weaker go to the wall. C.B. Macpherson (1911-87) has rightly pointed out beings who are constrained to employ their talents, skills and punishing their self-appointed goals. The idea of substantive justice corresponds to the philosophy of socialism. It holds that rest of justice in society consists in ascertaining whether the poor and the underprivileged have adequate opportunity to improve their lot. It demands that the opportunities of self-development should be progressively extended to the underprivileged and disadvantaged sections of society.

What is Free Market

The notion of a free market is closely associated with *laissez-faire* economic philosophy. It is a market where the price of each item or service is arranged by the mutual consent of sellers and buyers; the opposite is a controlled market, where supply and price are set by a government, with government force limited to a defensive role, government itself does not initiate force in the market place beyond levying taxes in order to fund the maintenance of the free market place. Some free market advocates oppose taxation as well.

Between a just punishment and the just judge who impose it, which of these senses is more fundamental? Justice has been thought, primarily, the morally right assignment of good and bad things; alternatively, it has been thought the virtue of a person who expresses or acts for that right assignment. Either actions are just because a just person does them, or a person is just because they do just things. The twentieth-century moral philosophers Elizabeth Anscombe influentially argued that modern philosophy had gone wrong in focusing on actions and their results over the character of actors, and so inspired modern virtue ethics, which follows Aristotle in considering justice as one of the virtues of a good person, and only indirectly as a property of a state of affairs.

NOTES

1. Harold Potter, *The Quest of Justice*, p. 3.
2. David Miller, *Social Justice*, pp. 17-18.
3. Brian Barry, *Political Argument*, p. 103.
4. W.K. Frankena, "The Concept of Social Justice" in R. Brandt (ed.), *Social Justice*, p. 17.
5. N.P. Barry, *An Introduction to Modern Political Theory*, p. 116.
6. Brecht, *Political Theory Foundations of Twentieth Century: Political Thought*, pp. 147-48.
7. *Ibid.*, p. 148.
8. Ernest Barker, *Principles of Social and Political Theory*, p. 102.
9. C.K. Allen, *Aspects of Justice*, p. 34.
10. Bakhshish Singh, *The Supreme Court as an Instrument of Social Justice*, p. 33.
11. W. Friedman, *Law in Changing Society*, pp. 65-66.
12. Bakhshish Singh, *op. cit.*, p. 73.
13. Boalding, "Social Justice in Social Dynamics" in R. Brandt (ed.), *Social Justice*, p. 92.
14. Allen, *op. cit.*, p. 3.
15. M.C. Chagla, *The Individual and the Slate*, p. 8.
16. P.B. Mukharji, *The Elemental Principles of Indian Constitution*, pp. 12-13.
17. *Ibid.*, p. 20.
18. J.W. Chapman, "Justice and Fairness" in Friedrich and Chapman (ed.), *Justice in Nomos*, VI, pp. 30-34.
19. Rawls, "Distributive Justice" in Peter Laslett and W.G. Runciman (eds.), *Philosophy, Politics and Society*, III Series, p. 61.
20. C.B. Macpherson, *Democratic Theory*, pp. 78-79.

4

Punishment

Wikipedia states that punishment is the "authoritative imposition of something negative or unpleasant on a person or animal in response to behavior deemed wrong by an individual or group". The word 'punishment' literally means torture that a person should undergo on account of doing a wrong. It may be seen from a religious or an ethical point of view. The religious injunction is that God being the ruler of this world punishes those who break His laws. 'The mills of God grind surely though slowly'. A man should always act according to his best rational judgement. If he makes a wrong by default, he should correct it by undergoing a self-imposed penance or remorse. But a jurist desires the positive role of the state in a matter relating to the determination of the guilt. He awards suitable punishment according to the law of the land. Thus there are different views about the meaning of punishment.

Criteria of Punishment

Prof. Flew has suggested five criteria for the use of the word punishment in its primary sense:[1]

1. It must involve an evil or an unpleasantness to the victim.
2. It must be for an actual or supposed offence.
3. It must be for an actual or supposed offender.
4. It must be the work of personal agencies (i.e., not merely the natural consequences of an action).

5. It must be imposed by authority (real or supposed), conferred by the system of rules against which the offence has been committed.

Benn and Peters add one more item to the above list: that the unpleasantness should be an essential part of what is intended and not merely incidental to some other aim.[2]

Punishments are applied for various purposes, most generally, to encourage and enforce proper behaviour as defined by society or family. Criminals are punished judicially, by fines, corporal punishment or custodial sentences such as prison; detainees risk further punishments for breaches of internal rules. Children, pupils and other trainees may be punished by their educators or instructors. Punishment may also be applied on moral, especially religious, grounds, as in penance or imposed in a theocracy with a religious police by Inquisition.

Justification of Punishment

1. **The utilitarian argument.** It has been advanced by Jeremy Bentham. According to it, by violating a law of state the wrong-doer adds to the unhappiness of the society and for, that reason, he must be punished. However, the nature of punishment should be such that the wrong-doer is reformed so that the stock of social happiness is increased by excluding the possibilities of a greater evil. Bentham suggests the scheme of having a semi-circular jail (Panopticon) with the seat of the jailor in the centre and the rooms of the prisoners on the periphery so that the jail staff may keep a close watch on the activities of the jail inmates. The aim of the jail staff should be to convert the criminals into better citizens. As Bentham says: "All punishment is mischief, all punishment in itself is an evil. Upon the principle of utility, if it ought at all to be admitted, it ought only to be admitted in so far as it promises to exclude some greater evil".[3]
2. **The argument of the idealists.** It is peculiarly harsh. Rousseau says that a state has every right to punish

the wrong-doer in the interest of protecting a system based on the 'general will of the community'. A wrong-doer may be forced to be a good man, or 'he must be forced to be free.' Kant says that a 'penal law is a categorical imperative'. Hegel says that a state can do no wrong and if a criminal is punished, he should be happy to feel that he is being made a free or an intelligent citizen of the civil society. Green and Bosanquet contend that the aim of punishment should be 'removal of obstacles' in the way of the 'good life' of the people by very harsh means. Thus, in the view of the idealists, "Punishment, like all State action, has a moral purpose and a positive quality".[4]

TYPES OF PUNISHMENTS

In this day and age there are four types of punishment:

1. **Capital punishment:** This means the death penalty. It is a legal process whereby a person is put to death by the state as a punishment for a crime. Capital punishment has in the past been practised by most societies; currently only 58 nations actively practise it, and 97 countries have abolished it.
2. **Prison sentences:** Life Imprisonment is any sentence of imprisonment for a serious crime. This requires the criminal to spend a term in prison. This can be anywhere from a week to life. This sentence doesn't exist in all countries. Portugal was the first country in the world to abolish life imprisonment by the Prison reforms of Sampaio e Melo, in 1884.
3. **Fines:** This is when the guilty criminal has to pay the government a fine as compensation for the crime. This is the most common punishment for small or petty crimes. The most usual use of the term, fine, relates to a financial punishment for the commission of minor crimes or as the settlement of a claim. A synonym, typically used in civil law actions, is mulct. One common example of a fine is money paid for violations of traffic laws.

4. **Community service:** Community service is where the person convicted of crime has to serve the local community in ways such as removing graffiti, cleaning streets, and helping the young and elderly.

THEORIES OF PUNISHMENT

1. Retributive Theory

From a justification of punishment, we may trace three important theories on this subject. According to it, a wrong-doer must be punished because he has done a wrong. It is based on old saying—an eye for an eye and a tooth for a tooth'. It imbibes element of revenge or retaliation with this difference that while the action of an individual can be taken as revengeful, it cannot be so in the case of the state. The guilty should suffer pain for an act that gives pain to the society. The guilty should get punishment as a matter of his right in such a situation "of which he must not be defrauded".[5]

According to the German philosopher Kant, the offender should not be punished for the reason that it is the means to his or another's benefit but for the simple reason that he has committed a crime. A court of law repays to one only that which he has acquired. He has done crime and it is logical the reward of his crime, the equivalent of his destructive value, be given to him. The punishment which the society confers upon him does not deprive him of his right but gives to him that which he has earned and deserves. According to Hegel and Aristotle, punishment is the negative reward of the criminal, who acquires it by infringing the moral law. It is his award which he must receive. For this reason, when some offenders escape with lighter punishment than the merit of their crimes, they try to reap the reward of their misdeeds by penance. According to Bradley, "We pay the penalty because we owe it and for no other reason, and if punishment is inflicted for any other reason whatsoever, than because it is merited by wrong, it is a gross immorality, a crying injustice; punishment is inflicted for the sake of punishment". In this view punishment is the rewards of the violation of moral law. In the words of Sir James Stephen, "Criminal procedure is to resentment what marriage is to affection". Thus the purpose of punishment is to vindicate the superiority of moral law. By punishing the person who has perpetrated the crime the authority of moral law is vindicated. Bosanquet has enumerated two features of this theory—(1) In it personal revenge and punishment coalesce, and (2) It has been recognised in this theory that the punishment is quantitatively equal to the crime. Both of these features are defective. Mill and Leaslie Stephen have laid great emphasis upon the element of revenge in punishment. The retributive theory has two forms—rigorist and liberal. According to the rigorist retributive theory the criminal should be punished severely for a serious crime. The liberal retributive theory also includes the consideration of the circumstances of the crime.

Criticism. But even the liberal form of the retributive theory is not satisfactory. It is not essential that the criminal will, after having been punished, realise his mistake in violating the moral law and feel remorse for his misdemeanour. Mackenzie has said, "If the aim of punishment is to vindicate the authority of the law, this will be partly done in so far as the offender is reformed and in so far as similar acts are prevented. And indeed neither reformation nor prevention is likely to be effected by punishment unless it is recognized that the punishment is a vindication of the law".[6] But this can be possible only when the criminal himself decides the punishment and is prepared to repent for his wrong violation. It cannot be expected, when the punishment has been administered by the state or any foreign agency that the criminal will repent. In practice it has been seen that a criminal becomes even worse after punishment. Actually, too, the retributive theory is not practical; it does not remove the cause of crime. Prevention of crimes or transformation of the criminal can be achieved only by preventing crimes or transforming the criminal and not by punishment. Johan Dewey has said quite correctly, "We are not relieved of the responsibility for the consequences of our procedure by the fact that the offender is guilty". It is more important to remove those economic, social, mental and physical causes which spur on the ordinary and the more numerous type of offender. Though it is not herein implied that punishment is unnecessary in every circumstance because it sometimes does become unavoidably necessary to mete out punishment.

2. Preventive Theory

According to the Preventive theory the aim behind punishment is to set an example to others and to prevent them from criminal tendencies. In this way, the object of punishment is prevention. This theory is expressed by the judge's formula, "You are not punished for stealing sheep, but in order that sheep may not be stolen". This theory does not invalidate even capital punishment because though there is no question of improvement in the criminal, the other people derive a lesson not to indulge in homicide.

Criticism. The major defect of this theory is that it uses the offender as means and not as an end. This does not affect any improvement in the culprit. He is made the means of the improvement of others. This theory is incorrect from the practical viewpoint. Actually everyone cannot become a criminal. People who know how to respect laws are in no need of any such exemplary exhibitions. On the other hand, those who have criminal tendencies can be prevented from crime by necessary preventions and the removal of conditions constituting the breeding ground of crime. To punish a man in order to convey a lesson to others is improper and inhuman. This theory is more defective than even the Retributive theory.

3. Reformative Theory

According to the reformative theory, the aim of punishment is the improvement of the offender himself. The modern age seems generally to favour and apply this theory. In this theory, the behaviour directed at the criminal shows him the consideration due to an individual and not conduct analogous to treatment of objects and means. An offender is punished for his own benefit. This theory concurs with the modern humanitarian trend in thought. This theory has been supported from many viewpoints. Some of the major ones are the following:

(i) *Criminal Anthropology.* The modern criminal anthropology propounds that crime is a disease, a pathological state or the state of inherited or acquired degeneration. Thus, it is necessary to treat a criminal instead of punishing him. Hospitals, lunatic asylums, and welfare homes are better adapted to the execution of projects to decrease crime than prisons. Crime is not the result of a willful violation of moral law. The most usual causes of crime are mental or physical defects. For example, kleptomania forces the patient to steal.

Criticism. The major short-coming of this theory of criminal anthropology is that it assumes the causes of limited number of crimes to be the causes of all crimes. If some person steals due to kleptomania he should undoubtedly be interned in a hospital rather than jail but the number of kleptomaniacs is negligible among the number of thieves. All crimes cannot be attributed to diseased conditions. Criminals who resort to illegal means due to mental or physical deformities form only a very small minority in the realm of criminals. Thus people who commit crimes due to reasons other than these should be curbed by other methods.

(ii) *Criminal Sociology.* Criminal sociology emphasises the responsibility of social circumstances for crime. Thus, it is more efficacious to induce improvements in social and economic conditions, to remove inequalities and immoralities, than to punish the criminal. Crime can be stopped not by punishment, but by the organisation of human society on the basis of justice and equality.

Criticism. The opinion of criminal sociology is as partial as is the opinion of criminal anthropology. Social inequality is, of course the cause of some crimes and can be credited as such. But the causes of all crimes cannot be analysed in this way. Many people commit crimes while fully conscious of the fact. And, especially the crimes of white collar criminals cannot be included in the explanation offered by criminal sociology.

(iii) *Psychoanalysis.* Psychoanalysis joins hands with criminal anthropology and sociology in supporting the reformative theory. According to Freud and his followers, crimes are caused by repressed complexes, and tendencies of sex and jealousy caused by desires and frustrated sexual passions. Thus, education and psychoanalytic treatment is needed for preventing crimes instead of punishment. Crime is a mental or neural disease which can be eliminated by searching out repressed unconscious complexes and transporting them to the conscious level, finding their causes and effecting their sublimation through means acceptable to society.

Criticism. The psychoanalytic suggestions hold true only in relation to particular criminals. Actually, this opinion is not universally true as was the case with criminal anthropology and criminal sociology.

Reformative Theory is Superior to Others

The reformative theory is effective in all such conditions in which the criminal commits the crime in ignorance and compelled by circumstances for, where this criminal tendency is attributable to a mental or physical defect. But the reform of a criminal who willfully violates moral laws is not so easy a proposition. Thus, for some criminals it becomes unavoidable to arrange for punishment. It can be said that the reformative theory is the most superior among the theories of punishment because it is compatible with the modem humanitarian ideals and seeks to eliminate the causes of and prevent crime but it cannot be applied to all crimes. Some crimes are more conducive to the preventive theory.

All the three theories on the subject of punishment have their own merits and demerits. The retributive and preventive theories are appreciated for discouraging persons from committing a crime and thereby protecting the system of rights in an effective way. The reformatory theory is criticised for being too idealistic and thereby encouraging the tendency of committing crimes. Let the punishment be as harsh as possible so that its repetition may not take place. But the retributive and deterrent theories hurt the norm of a civilised way of thinking. The reformatory theory treats crime as a conventional affair that may be checked by reforming the character of the individual with the force of love and fellow-feeling. Though reformative treatment "might cure criminal inclinations by relaxing the rigours of punishment, it might still defeat the ends of punishment, if it reduced the deterrent effects for others".[7]

The best way of punishment should imbibe the essential elements of all the theories discussed above. Sidgwick says: "I conclude, then, that from a political point of view, it is evidently necessary to take as the primary end of punishment and prevention of mischiefs and not the retribution of wickedness; and to decide on this principle any doubtful question as to the allotment of punishments".[8] For this sake, Sidgwick offers a set of following important principles:[9]

1. To realise the principle of justice that similar cases should be treated similarly, it is important that the punishment should be equal, e.g., if imprisonment then same kind of imprisonment to all the delinquents.
2. Avoidance of excess in punishment is impossible not only in order to inflict no more pain than is needed but even more in order that different degrees of punishment may all be adequately deterrent, where the criminal has choice of alternatives differing in degrees of mischievousness. Punishment should be so chosen that clearly greater punishments may be allotted to more mischievousness.
3. Punishment should be of an exemplary kind — more in appearance less in reality as appearance is more deterrent. But it should be offensive to public feeling and so likely to arouse aversion to the administration of law and dangerous sympathy with the criminal punished.
4. Punishment should be as little burdensome to the community as possible.

5. Punishment should be remissible if possible in the name of humanity.

Thus, the best form of punishment will be a union of the elements of retribution, deterrence and reformation. Using the word 'discipline' for punishment, James Seth says, "The goal of punishment should be to bring home to a man such a sense of guilt as shall work in him a deep repentence for the evil past, a new obedience for the time to come".[10]

NOTES

1. A. Flew. "The Justification of Punishment" in *Philosophy*, Vol. xxix (1954), pp. 291-307
2. Benn and Peters, *Social Principles and the Democratic State*, p. 174.
3. Bentham, *An Introduction to the Principle of Morals and Legislation*, edited by W. Harrison, p. 281
4. See Barker, *Political Thought in England*, p. 38
5. Bosanquet, *The Philosophical Theory of State*, p. 211.
6. Mackenzie, J.S., *A. Manual of Ethics*, p. 376
7. Benn and Peters, *op. cit.*, p. 180.
8. Henry Sidgwick, *Elements of Politics*, p. 114.
9. *Ibid.*, pp. 123-125
10. Seth, J., *Study of Ethical Principle*, p.323.

5

The Universality of Rights

Rights are the sum total of those opportunities which ensure enrichment of human personality. Rights are necessary conditions for development of human personality. These are also necessary for the development of society and social values. Rights are the social requirements of an individual for the development of his personality and society at large. According to Laski, "Any system of right, therefore, has three essential aspects from which it must be regarded. There is the interest of the individual always, at least ultimately isolated from his fellow men. There is the interest of various groups in and through which his personality finds channels of expression. There is the interest of the community which is the total result of the whole pressure of social forces". The concepts of right find its broad manifestation in the liberties of the individual on the one hand and in the sphere of state activities on the other. As a subject, necessarily it involves within its fold a discussion of individual as well as to the development of his personality, rights occupy a prominent place. Laski correctly observes that "Without rights there cannot be liberty" and that "every State is known by the rights it maintains. Most modern conceptions of rights are universalist and egalitarian—in other words, equal rights are granted to all people".

The study of rights occupies a very important place in the discussion of political theory. Rights are regarded as bedrock of a democratic system. Their ideological development, their political, social and economic contents and implications and their legal status in the present day world is of paramount importance to political theorists. Rights define the position of the individual in a State. They offer a positive purpose to the state. Through them alone, the state promotes the general welfare of the society as a whole. The presence of rights is a proof that the state exists for the individual not the individual for the state. Rights virtually determine the status of a political civilisation achieved by the state. A right is the claim by an individual or by a group or association which is allowed and confirmed by other individuals and other groups. Rights enrich an individual's life. If there is an all-round development of individual life, the social life will automatically be enriched.

According to Harold J. Laski, "Any system of rights, therefore, has three essential aspects from which it must be regarded. There is the interest of the individual, always, at least, ultimately, finally isolated from his fellow men. There is the interest of various groups in and through which his personality finds channels of expression. There is the interest of the community which is the total result of the whole pressure of social forces".[1]

Rights, liberty and equality are the three inter-related themes. Possession and enjoyment of certain rights requires liberty. Possession and enjoyment of such rights by all without any distinction on some artificial ground require equality. To talk of liberty means to talk of rights; to talk of liberty for all means to talk of equality. As Laski said "without rights there can be no liberty"[2] and "every state is known by the rights it maintains".[3]

DEFINITIONS OF RIGHT

1. *Laski.* Rights are "those conditions of social life without which no man can seek in general, to be himself at his best". They are the sum total of opportunities which ensure an adequate development and expression of an individual's personality.
2. *Bosanquet.* "A right is a claim recognised by society and enforced by the state".
3. *Barker.* "Any particular right which I have in a capacity of enjoying some particular status or

employing some particular power of action which has been secured and guaranteed to me by law".

Thus, a right is a claim of an individual recognised by the community and the state. Thus, a proper definition of the term 'right' has three ingredients.

(i) **A claim of the individuals.** Though every claim cannot be a right. In order to be a right a claim should be like a disinterested desire, or something which is capable of universal application. What an individual wills should be of common interest. In asserting a claim one should feel like rendering a public service. The motivating force should be a rational consideration and not a personal caprice of the individual. As Barker says, the will that issues in the form of a claim to something not only wills the good of itself, it wills the goodness of itself in relations to others. To quote his words, "It wills the goodness of society which is constituted by such relations. The goodness of the relations which constitute society means a system of rights".[4]

(ii) **Social recognition.** As individual's claim is backed by a disinterested desire, it receives social recognition. For example, an individual's claim that none should take his life, receives social recognition as every individual wills in the same direction. The right to life is created by recognition of the claim of this type. An individual's desire that none should take away his property creates in him a sense that he should not take away the property of others. It becomes right to property when it gets social recognition. In the words of Barker, "Claims thus recognised are translated into rights, and it is such recognition that constitutes them rights. Thus, if we care to make the distinction, we may say that rights have a double aspect. On the one hand, a right is a claim of an individual arising from the nature of self-consciousness for permission to will his own ideal objects; on the other hand, it is the recognition of that claim by society and, therein and thereby, the addition of new power to pursue these objects".[5]

(iii) **Political recognition.** Until they are protected by the state, rights are like moral declarations. When they think in terms of patterning their conduct according to the rules of 'common behaviour', individuals are guided by their real wills. However, in most of the cases, they are motivated by their selfish wills. This violates the system of rights. Therefore, there must be some coercive force to ensure the exercise of these rights. The state translates socially recognised claims of moral rights into terms of law. It accords them legal recognition. It acts like a coercive agency to prevent the operation of selfish wills of the individuals. A proper definition of the term 'right' should involve all the three ingredients. However, in the realm of political theory, the most important ingredient is the fact of political recognition that connects the element of disinterested claims of the individuals with the sovereign authority of the state. Gilchrist says: "Rights arise, therefore, from individuals as members of society and from the recognition that for society there is ultimate good which may be reached by the development of the powers inherent in every individual".[6] However, the view of Laski is better when he says, "Rights, in fact, are those conditions of social life without which no man can seek, in general, to be himself at his best. Since the state exists to make possible that achievement, it is only by maintaining rights that its end may be secured".[7]

Rights, therefore, have a three-fold nature:

(i) **Ethical.** When we deal with claims of the individuals based on their real wills, they are recognised by the community.

(ii) **Legal.** When translated into law by the state, rights are legal.

(iii) **Political.** In politics we are concerned with 'moral rights' which would be legally enforceable if law were what it ought to be.

BASES OF RIGHTS

The concept of rights emerged with the rise of modern state and out of the criticism of the old social and political order. Its tone was radical and in its ultimate employment, was revolutionary. Historically, the demand for individual rights was made by the rising commercial/middle class which was the product of industrial revolution. It became the accepted ideology of American and French revolutionaries and was expressed in the Declaration of Independence and the constitutional Bill of Rights in America and the Declaration of the Rights of Man in France. Prominent liberal writers such as Locke, Rousseau, Bentham, J.S. Mill, T.H. Green, Harold Laski, Ernest Barker and a host of others have advocated the rights of the individual on one ground or the other. In the post-war period, the concept of rights has been further expanded by John Rawls, Robert Nozick, Ronald Dworkin and others.

THEORIES OF RIGHTS

On what basis the rights should be given to the individual? No universal answer has been provided to this question. In their long history of development, different rights have been justified on different basis. These bases are commonly known as theories of rights. The main theories are:

1. Theory of Natural Rights
2. Theory of Legal Rights
3. Historical Theory of Rights
4. Idealist/Moral Theory of Rights
5. Social welfare Theory of Rights
6. Recent Liberal-Individualistic Theory of Rights
7. Marxist Theory of Rights

The Theory of Natural Rights

It holds that rights are rationally deducible from man's nature. They have their universal application irrespective of the difference of place, time and environment. Nature is the author of certain rights that have a universal, rational, eternal and immutable character. The Stoics of ancient Greece upheld the right to equality as given to us by Nature. The Roman thinkers like Polybius and Cicero emphasised that the laws of the state must conform to the Law of Nature. Though the principles of the law of nature may be understood by rational power, they are of a universal and eternal character. Thomas Hobbes defined right to life as a natural right which even the sovereign of the state could not jeopardize. John Locke treated three rights relating to life, liberty and property as natural rights. Effective protection of the natural rights is the responsibility of the state. If the sovereign authority is incapable of fulfilling the trust of the people, the contract may be dissolved and a new sovereign may be chosen to secure effective protection of natural rights.

The doctrine of natural rights was incorporated into important declarations as those of American independence of 1776 and of French Revolution of 1789. The Universal Declaration of Rights adopted by the General Assembly of the United Nations in 1948 is based on theory of Natural Rights when it says: "All human beings are born free and equal in dignity and rights". Thus, the whole idea of natural rights is based on the assumption that irrespective of his merit as an individual in his personal or moral capacity, man is at least equal to all others in human worth. Even convicted criminals have the right not to be treated in cruel or in-human ways by the jail staff".[8]

Implications of 'natural rights':[9]

1. *Historical affirmation.* There is a historical affirmation that man pre-existed society.
2. *Moral and metaphysical assumption.* There is a moral and metaphysical assumption that man is a creature who possesses certain rights by virtue of the general nature and plan of the universe and of the part which he has to play in carrying out the plan of the universe.
3. *Formation of society.* In order that these rights may be preserved, he forms society.

4. *Rights brought by men.* Rights, then, are not created by society, but are brought by men into society.
5. *Purpose of society.* The purpose of society is to secure man's rights.
6. *Right to rebel.* If it does not do so, the individual has a right to rebel.
7. Man has no right to rebel because society is formed to secure his rights, as a whole. Even if on a particular occasion society appears to violate one of the rights, it does so only that it may better secure them as a whole; or it may better secure the rights of the most of its members even if it does not secure the rights of a particular member at a particular moment, or of a particular member at any moment.

Criticism of the Theory of Natural Rights

1. It is incorrect to say that rights may be available in the pre-political stage. To say that some rights are created by Nature is to say that some rights are available to man just after his birth. But, there are no rights unless there is some machinery to give them effective recognition or protection.
2. Rights are created in a well-organised social system. A man living in a forest or in some unknown island has no rights of his own. Robinson Crusoe had no rights until he met Man Friday.[10]
3. It is impossible to prepare a list of natural rights. Cicero, Hobbes and Locke, did not offer a precise definition of the term 'natural right', nor did they prepare a catalogue of such rights. There "is no official, or complete, or generally agreed upon list of natural rights".[11]
4. To treat rights as pre-political is to make them absolute or beyond the control of the state. It becomes like a dogma at the hands of anti-statists. The new notion is that the state may impose reasonable restrictions on the exercise or enjoyment of any right that a man possesses. The rights must be

associated with the usefulness or utility to the community. Therefore, Jeremy Bentham scoffed at the doctrine of natural rights by calling them as 'rhetorical nonsense upon stilts'. Laski also rejected the case of natural rights though he realised the significance of this theory in a different way when he says that rights "are not natural in the sense that a permanent and unchanging catalogue of them can be compiled, rather they are natural in the sense that under the limitations of a civilised life, facts demand their recognition".[12]

Legal Theory of Rights

It holds that a right is a creation of law. If there is no law, there is no right. Custom may sanction some right, but as there is no law to enforce it, it is no right. Hobbes advocated this theory. In his view people made a social contract and thereby established a Leviathan to protect their rights by the force of law. Bentham holds that rights are the creatures of law and of organised society. John Austin says that every right, whether divine, legal or moral, "rests on a relative duty; that is to say, a duty lying on a party or parties other than the party or parties in whom the right resides. And manifestly that relative duty would not be a duty substantially if the law which affects to impose it were not sustained by might".[13]

Limitation of Legal Theory

1. To say that law alone creates right is to dismiss the importance of custom in the life of a community. People have so many rights because of the force of custom behind them. The law of the state protects the system of rights. But to dismiss the value of custom altogether is not justified.
2. To say that law is the creator of rights and that the state is the possessor of legal sovereignty is to make the state omnipotent and the people helpless in fighting for their rights in the event of any encroachment upon them by the action of the state. It deprives the people of their right to resist state absolutism.

3. Legal theory discards the role of ethical considerations. "It does not help us to make the state what it should be".[14]

Historical Theory of Rights

In the creation of rights it takes the factor of time. Every right is based on the force of long observance. On account of its long observance the essential sanction behind a right is a tradition or custom. As R.M. Maclver says a law is nothing else than an action of the state in the form of the crystallisation of the age-old custom into a legal sanction. A better affirmation of this view may be found in the ideas of Edmund Burke in his theory of prescriptive institutions. According to him, the people have a right over anything that they exercise or enjoy uninterruptedly over a fairly long passage of time. Maclver condemned the philosophy behind the action of French revolutionaries who desired to uproot the established system of institutions and suddenly erect a new one in its place.

Limitations of Historical Theory

Rights do not have an eternal character just by virtue of their force of long observance; otherwise the system of slavery would have been in practice even in modern times. Times change and with it change the whole pattern of social life. The system of rights also undergoes a change. The rulers may abolish a particular system of rights and instead impose a new one in the light of new conditions without bothering for the factor of prescription or long observance. For example, the British rulers finished the rights of the Indian people to burn alive a widow, to settle disputes in a panchayat, to excommunicate a person by the caste or community panchayat. They introduced a new system of rights that had to be accepted by the people of India. However, no one can deny that rights are created by the passage of time. History "cannot be ignored, but history cannot be relied on alone".[15]

Idealist/Moral Theory of Rights

According to Idealism, man's rational will issues in the form of claims and leads to the creation of a system of rights when moral recognition of such claims is converted into legal sanction.

T.H. Green begins with the assumption that human consciousness thinks of the goodness of the self as well as of other human beings. Thus, he recognised that a claim conducive to common interest brings about a system of rights. In the words of Barker: "Human consciousness postulates liberty: liberty involves rights; rights demand the state".[16] As Bernard Bosanquet said, "It is a claim which can be enforced at law, which no moral imperative can be; but it is also recognised to be a claim which ought to be capable of enforcement at law; and thus it has a moral aspect.... A typical right unites the two sides".[17]

Idealistic theory looks at rights from a highly moral point of view. Rights are rooted in the mind of man. They are powers granted to him by the community so that he may realise a common good of which his good is an intrinsic part. A right must establish two things (i) the individual claiming it must be able to convince society that in doing so he is not interfering with like claims of his fellow beings, and (ii) he must be able to convince society that his claim is absolutely necessary for the sake of his self-development. Thus, a right "is a freedom of action possessed by a man of virtue of his occupying a certain place and fulfilling a certain function in a social order".[18]

Limitations of Moral Theory

1. The idealistic interpretation of the origin and nature of rights is too abstract to be understood by a man of average comprehension.
2. The whole idea of the 'best possible development of a man's personality' is so vague that the state cannot prescribe a particular pattern that may be equally relevant for all.
3. This theory seems to sacrifice social good for the sake of individual good.

However, the merit of idealistic theory lies on the theoretical plane. It furnishes a safe test to rights which can be applied at all times. Herein, it is superior to the legal, historical, and social welfare theories. The one absolute right of all human beings is the right of personality.[19]

Social Welfare Theory of Rights

It implies that the rights are the creation of the society. They are based on the consideration of common welfare. They make what is conducive to the greatest good of the greatest number. They are the conditions of social good. Claims not in conformity with the general welfare fail from being rights as they would not be recognised by the community. Jeremy Bentham developed the principle of utility to show that the system of rights is beneficial both to the individual and to the society. Laski reinterprets the premises of Benthamite utilitarianism in his positive liberalism. As he says: "We are making the test of rights utility; and that, it is clear, involves the question of those to whom the rights are to be useful. There is only one possible answer. In any state the demands of each citizen for the fulfillment of his best self must be taken as of equal worth; and the utility of a right is, therefore, its value to all the members of the state".[20]

Limitation of Social Welfare Theory

1. It dwells on the factor of social welfare which is a term too vague to be put into a precise form. The Benthamite formula of 'greatest good of the greatest number' may mean different things to the liberals, the socialists and the Marxists.
2. If carried to extremes, the point of individual welfare may be lost, as it seeks to sacrifice individual good at the altar of social welfare. N. Wilde believes that if rights are created by the consideration of social expediency, the individual is without an appeal and helplessly dependent upon its arbitrary will.[21]

However, the essential merit of social welfare theory lies in its linking up the idealistic version of rights with its utilitarian counterpart and thereby making it a commendable affair so far as liberal political theory is concerned

Recent-Liberal-Individualistic Theory of Rights

For the last thirty years, the liberal-individualistic theory of rights has come to be dominated by the views of John Rawls and Robert Nozick. Both of them have achieved much prominence in the liberal tradition and have been instrumental in influencing other writers like Dworkin, Gallstone, Ackerman, Barry to propound alternative theories of rights. They represent two dominant socio-economic views of our times. While Nozick represents the classical-liberal view of free market, free trade capitalism and minimal state, Rawls represents the Keynesian tradition of liberal egalitarianism. He appeals to those who believe in the desirability, efficiency and future of capitalist market but that the later may not function well and generate serious inequalities. He wants to find efficient ways to address to those inadequacies, without altering the essential nature of the system.

According to Nozick, the theory of rights is derived the principle of natural right of 'self-ownership' which means treating people as they are an end in themselves. The opening sentence of his book reads: 'The individuals have rights and there are no things people or groups may do to them (without violating their rights).' Society must respect these rights because individuals are ends and not means. Rights affirm the separate existence of man, and taken seriously, they mean that the individuals are not the resources of some other persons. Respect for rights is respecting people's claim to be equal. A libertarian society by respecting the individual respects his rights, it allows individually or with whom we choose, to choose our life and to realize our ends, aided by the voluntary cooperation of other individuals possessing the same dignity. As far as the substance of rights is concerned, Nozick holds an extremely strong doctrine of individualistic rights, particularly right to acquire and hold property and freedom of contract. His concept of property right excludes welfare rights of the individual and their protection by the state. According to Nozick, an individual is an owner of himself and his talent, and free to use his powers as he wished. Every individual has an exclusive domain which must not be breached without his consent. All political institutions are coercive by definition and must command the unanimous assent of the governed. That is they must be brought into existence purely by voluntary transaction. The state has no legitimate powers beyond the function of protection, justice and defence. Rights are prior to the civil law from which the latter is derived.

John Rawls uses the words 'rights' and 'justice' interchangeably. According to him, an account of rights must be embedded in justice. Rights belong to all disinterested political individuals beyond the veil of ignorance. But they had no natural rights except those which they chose unanimously in their original position. They were accepted because of the considered judgement of the people. The rights which people accepted in their original position included an equal right to the most extensive liberty compatible with a similar liberty for others; and arrangement of social and economic inequalities in such a way that they (i) benefit the greatest to the least advantaged, and (ii) attached to positions and offices open to all under conditions of fair equality of opportunity. By basic liberties, he means the standard civil and political rights recognized by the liberal democracies such as right to vote, to run for offices, due process of law, free speech, etc. But what is important for Rawls is that the rights should guarantee a fair share of economic resources. Hence, the second category gives certain egalitarian rights to citizens. The social and economic inequalities should be so regulated that those with least material goods such as income, wealth, education, etc. will get a larger share. Hence Rawls assumes a market economy in which material inequalities serve as incentives, increasing the overall stock of goods available for distribution. In practical terms, it means that the tax system should be proportionately used to redistribute goods to the worst off. He believes that the people's rights to social goods should not be dependent upon their natural endowments. The talented do not deserve any greater income and they should only receive more income if it benefits the less well off.

Both Rawls and Nozick reject the utilitarian theory of rights and believe that individual is an end in himself. However, whereas for Nozick, the most important right is the right over oneself, i.e. the right to self-ownership, for Rawls, it is the right to a certain share of society's resources. According to Nozick, the goods produced by the talented should not be used to improve the well-being of the disadvantaged since 'If I own myself, then I own my talent as well as what is produced of that talent'. Hence, any redistributive taxation is wrong. Rawls' position is that the right over the talent does not necessarily include the right to unequal rewards from those talents. Since talent is unequally distributed by nature, it is the duty of the state to guarantee that the untalented have a right over the naturally advantaged.

Yet another theory of rights has been advanced by Ronald Dworkin in his book *Taking Rights Seriously* (1978). He has tried to build a new theory of politics based on the primacy of moral rights. Dworkin identifies only two moral rights of the citizens to be treated as natural or inalienable: (i) the right of the citizen to be treated equally, and (ii) right to have respect for human dignity. The theory is not based upon history or philosophy or tradition but on a speculative claim based upon reason. Dworkin's theory is different from other liberal writers because of his emphasis that there can be no general right to liberty. 'The idea of a right to liberty is a misconceived concept that does disservice to political thought'. Though some specific liberties are important but only because they are based upon right to equality. He writes that citizens 'have distinct rights to certain liberties like the liberty of free expression and of free choice in personal and sexual relations, but do not have a right to free use of property. Another aspect of Dworkin's theory is his extreme individualism. In the context of the right to freedom of speech and expression, he writes that it is wrong for a law to ban speakers in a demonstration on the grounds of public safety because such rights restrict the individual right of the demonstrators to speak. In the name of equality and human dignity, he justifies right of the blacks to get admission in the colleges with lower qualifications than a white (just as we have reservation policy in India).

Thus a new type of liberal radicalism from 1960s onwards has given rise to a number of theories of individual rights. But the question is: can we formulate a coherent theory of fundamental rights? According to Birch, it seems unlikely because these new theories lack a view of human nature, a view of society and a view of functions of the state. Moreover, as Peter Jones writes, there are still fundamental disagreements among philosophers over the conceptual question of what it is to have a right. If there has been a progress in recent years, it has been the progress of an unfolding diversity rather than progress towards a single truth.

Marxist Theory of Rights

It links up the case of rights with the prevailing economic system of the society. It holds that rights cannot be understood in isolation from the pattern of social classes and struggle going on between them as a necessary consequence of the laws of dialectical materialism. The dominant class owns the means of production and distribution. It creates a system of rights to keep itself in power. The dominant class claims the right to exploit and oppress the dominated class who has no control over the means of production and distribution. Until the capitalist system is replaced by the system of socialism, the working class cannot have rights. After the successful revolution the proletariat has a new kind of social life in which its rights shall be associated with the set of duties so as to consolidate the new socialist order. The people would have rights like those relating to work and social security. They would also be tacked with duties like obedience to law and protection of the socialist system. With the advent of the socialist system the society would be able to dispense with the idea of rights prevailing in the bourgeois society.[22] Thus, Marxian theory of rights is unique in telling us about the meaning and nature of rights.

Criticism of Marxism

1. As every system whether pre-feudal, feudal, bourgeois or socialist, has its own system of rights, it cannot be accepted that the whole system of existing rights would disappear with the establishment of a socialist society.
2. To say that rights must be tacked with duties is a good thing, but to destroy the whole system of rights

in the name of the fulfillment of duties by the role of an omnipotent state is equally bad.

3. Milovan Djilas and Stojanovic of Yugoslavia have rabidly denounced the Russian political system for allowing no meaningful rights to the people.

KINDS OF RIGHTS

1. **Moral Rights.** Moral rights are the claims of the individuals based on the conscience of the community. These are the claims recognised by the good sense of the people. For example, a teacher has the moral right to be respected by his students. But such rights cannot be enforced by the courts. Their enforcement depends upon the good sense of the community. It is only when moral rights are converted into legal rights, that they become enforceable by the action of the state.

2. **Civil Rights.** Civil rights relate to the person and property of the individuals. As they relate to the essential conditions of a civilised life, they are civil or social rights. They include a number of rights like those relating to life, personal liberty, thought and expression, property, religion and the like.

   (i) *Right to life.* Right to life is most important of all the civil rights. The enjoyment of all other rights depends upon it. It implies that no person can take the life of another, and a person has the right to save his life even by killing another if his opponent makes an attempt to kill him. It is called 'right to self-defence'. Suicide is a crime.

   (ii) *Right to personal liberty.* The right to personal liberty includes right to live as a free citizen. A person cannot be detained without a proper cause. He cannot be punished physically or economically unless he is held guilty by a court of competent jurisdiction. The trial of the accused must be free and open.

(iii) *Right to think and express.* It also comes in this category.

(iv) *Right to keep arms and property.* In legal parlance, it means equality before law and its equal protection for all.

(v) *Right to religion.* It is also a civil right.

3. **Political Rights.** Political rights relate to a man's participation in the affairs of the state. They include right of giving vote, fighting elections, taking public employment, supporting or opposing the government and changing it by constitutional means. Political rights enable a person to send petitions to the government for the redressal of certain wrongs, following or abandoning a particular policy, making or unmaking a particular law, and expressing views for the creation of a healthy public opinion. Democracy is regarded as the best form of government because it ensures all such rights.

4. **Economic Rights.** Economic rights relate to a man's vocation, his engagement in a gainful employment so as to solve the problem of food, clothing and shelter. It includes right to earn livelihood by proper means and the right to work. The right to rest and leisure makes a person take relief for the sake of maintaining and increasing his efficiency. The workers must have a right to form unions and associations for protecting and promoting their interests. They should have right to bargain freely for remunerative work. They should have some share in the management of industry. The socialists include right to social insurance and self-government in industry in economic rights.

5. **Human Rights.** 'Natural rights' and civil rights have assumed more significance since the formulation of the Universal Declaration of Human Rights by the Human Rights Commission and their adoption by the General Assembly of the United Nations in December, 1948. The Declaration incorporates a host

of rights that have a necessary connection with moral and civil rights pointed out above. It says that all human beings are born free and equal in dignity and rights; they are endowed with reason and conscience and should act towards one another in a spirit of brotherhood. It speaks of the right to security in the event of unemployment, sickness, disability, old age, or other conditions of destitute hood beyond one's control.

RIGHTS OF A CITIZEN IN A MODERN STATE

A. Civil Rights

(i) ***Right to life.*** The right to life is a basic civil right given to each and every citizen. Without life and security of a person other rights are of no use. Green regarded it as the most fundamental of all rights. The state must provide protection to the individual against the foes, internal and external even against himself because he must be prevented from committing suicide.

(ii) ***Right to family.*** The family is the hope and cradle of civilisation. Its right implies the right to marriage, right to the custody and control of the children and the right of inheritance. The right to family is great importance for the continuation of the human race. The right includes the liberty to rear and bring up children in the way the parents like.

(iii) ***Right to property.*** Right to property is based on the assumption that owning property is a natural instinct in man and it provides incentive to hard work. Since early days of human society the idea of property has been a supreme factor in the evolution of modern civilization. The right to property means the freedom to the individual to enjoy his property. It implies that the individual has the right to acquire, hold and dispose of property without any restriction or hindrance. It also means that he is free to alienate property by way of gift, exchange or will.

(iv) ***Right to worship.*** The right to worship is right to freedom of religion and conscience. It guarantees to every citizen the right to liberty, belief and worship. It means that everyone is free to progress and follow any religion and perform the necessary rites connected with his religious practices. The modern secular states remain neutral between different religious faiths and permit the citizens to enjoy the right to profess, to propagate and practise any religion. The Constitution of India also guarantees this right to all the Indian citizens.

(v) ***Right to work.*** The individual is born in the world in which if it were organised rationally he would live only on his labour. It is the duty of the state to provide him with a job. If state fails to provide him with a job, his development will stop. The socialist states strongly advocate right to work. They plead that society should provide him with work or it should feed him. Right to work does not mean the right to particular work. Laski says, "A Prime Minister who has been over thrown has not the right to be provided labour of an identical character. Society cannot afford each man the choice of the effort he will like. It cannot in any ultimate way afford under emphasis occupation which carry with them special dignity. It means supply of goods and sources to maintain life". If a man is deprived of right to work he is entitled for an equal reward or compensation. Right to work carries with it the right to an adequate wage for one's labour. The wage earner needs the food which can keep him physically fit. He needs clothing and shelter which can enable him to start life. A worker needs those small comforts which make life a thing of some interests. Proper service conditions are necessary for good life of the workers.

(vi) ***Right to contract.*** Right to contract enables the individual to enter into contracts freely with others. An individual can enter into agreements with others

regarding subjects of mutual interest. But the state can regulate or ban contracts those which are against the interests of society.

(vii) ***Right to speech.*** The right to freedom of thought and expression along with the freedom of speech and press has been highly valued by all the democratic states. It is considered as fundamental for the development of human personality. Therefore, poets, philosophers, and political scientists have passionately pleaded for freedom of thought and expression. J.S. Mill strongly advocated for the liberty of thought and speech. According to Bury, "It is one supreme condition of mental and moral progress". Laski opines, "To allow a man to say what he thinks is to give his personality the only ultimate channel of free expression and citizenship the only means of moral adequacy". Freedom of speech and expression is also the cornerstone of democracy. A government can always learn more from the criticism of its opponents than from the eulogy of its supporters.

(viii) ***Right to free movement.*** While governments in democratic states pass various laws to regulate the life of the individuals and society, they see to it that there is no arbitrary restriction on the free movement of the individual.

(ix) ***Right to equality.*** Right to equality is given great importance in the modern welfare states. The right means the absence of legal discrimination against anyone, individual group, class or race. Democracy can only exist and flourish in a society of equals.

(x) ***Right to education.*** This right is considered very necessary to the citizens. Every developing state spend sufficient amount for the education of its citizens. Schools, colleges, universities, research centres are established by the state. The state provides proper educational atmosphere in these institutions. The education makes people perfect citizens. Without education there will be a mockery of people's government. Education alone can provide conditions for developing all faculties of mind and body.

B. Political Rights

The political rights are those legal rights which enable the citizens to take part in the work of the government. The following are the important political rights given in all modern welfare states:

(i) ***Right to vote.*** Right to vote enables a citizen to choose his representatives in the elected bodies as parliament or legislative assembly. This right to vote, also called 'franchise', is both a condition and product of democracy. Modern democracies because of their large areas and populations are not direct but indirect representative democracies. Every adult citizen has the right to express his opinion by casting a vote at the time of election what person he desires should undertake the task of government. The right to vote should be as wide as possible irrespective of sex, property, race, creed, religion and education. One man one vote ought to be the maxim of a democratic government. Aliens, bankrupts, paupers, criminals and minors are denied the right to vote.

(ii) ***Right to be elected.*** The right to be elected is a corollary to the right to vote and most of the democratic states grant to their citizens the privilege of contesting elections to the different legislative bodies. It has been argued by some that it would be desirable to prescribe a qualification demanding experience of work on a representative body. Laski suggests a representative must possess adequate knowledge of the working of a local body.

(iii) ***Right to public work.*** In a democracy, every citizen has the right of equal eligibility for any office executive, administrative or judicial and to be protected against discrimination on grounds of religion, race, caste, sex, and descent, place of birth or residence. The Indian Constitution ensures to all citizens in India equality of opportunity in matters of appointment to any office under the state. It does not mean that academic, professional and other qualifications cannot be laid down for filling the various posts.

(iv) ***Right to petition.*** The right to send petition for the redress of grievances is an old and valued right of the people. The right entitles every citizen to send petition either individually or collectively to the competent authority for the redress of grievances. In a democracy, the government cannot ignore the legitimate desires and grievances of the people because they are the ultimate sovereign. The government must always be above to the grievances of the people and promptly respond to their needs.

(v) ***Right to criticise the government.*** This right is available only in free and democratic states. This right is beneficial not only for the people but also for the government. Public criticism of the government policies keeps the government alert and efficient. A responsible opposition party in the legislature is therefore considered essential. The role and importance of healthy public opinion in a democracy cannot be over emphasised. Democracy is really a government by criticism, for truth only comes by the clash of opinions.

(vi) ***Right to resist.*** The citizen has the right to resist the authority of the state if he honestly feels that a particular law or action of the government is inimical to his moral sense of justice. But the resistance of this type is only a moral right and not a legal right. Obviously, no state can permit an action which defies the authority and may jeopardise even its very existence.

MEASURES FOR PROTECTION OF RIGHTS

(i) **Constitutional safeguard.** The rights of the people must be enshrined in the Constitution of the state so that they may have the character of fundamental rights. By doing so the state accords them constitutional protection and empowers the courts to issue prerogative writs for their enforcement.

(ii) **Rule of law.** Another safeguard is the rule of law as available in Britain. There is no written Constitution in Britain and yet the people enjoy their rights because in the words of Dicey, this country is known for having the 'rule of law.' It has two essential features: (i) every citizen is under the same law of the land irrespective of his social, economic or political status, and (ii) a person cannot be arrested without sufficient cause and he cannot be made to suffer in body or in goods unless declared guilty by a court of competent jurisdiction after a fair trial.

(iii) **Free and honest press.** There should be a free and honest press in every country so that the people may have a straightforward dissemination of news and views. The press would highlight if there is any encroachment upon the rights of the people. Thus, a healthy public opinion may be created for the protection of their rights against encroachment of any kind.

(iv) **Decentralisation of powers.** Concentration of powers creates conditions under which the rights of the people are in jeopardy. But decentralisation of powers creates conditions that minimise the possibility of the abuse of power.

(v) **Independent and impartial judiciary.** The existence of an independent and impartial judiciary is also necessary so that if the people feel aggravated by any action of the state or some other institution, they may move the courts for the protection of their rights. In democratic countries the courts are given special power of issuing prerogative writs for the enforcement of constitutional provisions.

(vi) **Extension of state's activities.** It is suggested that the state should not extend its area of activity into the legitimate domain of voluntary groups and associations.

(vii) **Eternal vigilance of the people.** If the people are apathetic or indolent, their rights can never be secure. It is well said: "It is the proud spirit of the citizens, less than the letter of the law that is their most real safeguard".[23]

NOTES

1. Laski, *A Grammar of Politics*, p. 141.
2. *Ibid.* p. 142.
3. *Ibid.*, p.89
4. E. Barker, *Political Thought in England* (1848-1914), p. 25.
5. *Ibid.*
6. R. N. Gilchrist, *Principles of Political Science*, p. 135.
7. Laski, *op. cit.*, p. 91.
8. Barry, *An Introduction to Modern Political Theory,* p. 192.
9. C.E.M. Joad, *Guide to the Philosophy of Morals and Politics*, p. 545.
10. Benn and Peters, *Social Principles and the Democratic State*, p.97
11. E. Asirvatham, *Political Theory*, VIII, ed., p. 163.
12. Laski, *op.cit.*, p. 91
13. Austin, *The Province of Jurisprudence Determined*, edited by H.A.I., Hart, p. 285
14. Asirvatham, *op. cit.*, p. 167.
15. Hocking, *Law and Rights*, p. 7.
16. Barker, *op. cit.*, p. 23.
17. Bosanquet, *The Philosophical Theory of State*, p. 188.
18. N. Wilde, *The Ethical Basis of the State*, p. 12.
19. Asirvatham, *op. cit.*, pp. 175-76
20. Laski, *op. cit.*, p. 92.
21. Wilde, *op. cit.*, p. 124.
22. J. Plamentaz, *Karl Marx's Philosophy of Man*, p. 312
23. Laski, *op. cit.* , p. 104

6
Human Rights

To emphasize the importance of rights, adjectives like 'natural', 'fundamental', 'human' have been used in the long history of their development. Twentieth century has been described as the century of human rights because the concept of 'Human Rights' became increasingly important in liberal-democratic as well as in the socialist countries and the underdeveloped world. Virtually, all states now subscribe officially to some doctrine of human rights and in every case, there is a general political theory justifying the kind of society and the political institutions. Human rights refer to inherent, universal rights of human beings regardless of jurisdiction or other factors, such as ethnicity, nationality, or sex. Human rights constitute the very source of all rights of human beings. They provide for moral foundation of any system of rights. The idea of human rights descended from the philosophical idea of natural rights; some recognize no difference between the two and regard both as labels for the same thing while others choose to keep the terms separate to eliminate association with some features traditionally associated with natural rights. The horizons of human rights are very wide. They set the standards for the provision and expansion of civil, political, and socio-economic rights.

The history of human rights would reveal that it was a struggle for freedom of men against tyranny, oppression, injustice and exploitation down the ages. Rights are the facts of life. The Greek city-states recognized a number of rights of the individual including that of freedom of speech (Insogoria), equality before the law (Isonomia), and equal respect for all (Isotimia). In modern times almost all the states provide their citizens with rights through their respective Constitutions and Statutes.

Human Rights in the Ancient Philosophies

Although the expression 'Human Rights' came into every day parlance in the post-second World War era, it owes its origin to the classical writings of Indian thinkers like Manu, Kautilya, etc. These thinkers prescribed many duties to the rulers to protect the dignity of the citizens. Among the western thinkers, Plato made a systematic attempt to protect the citizens in his grand scheme of Justice. Cicero provided the philosophical foundations for later theories of Natural Law. Religious Universalists like Thomas Aquinas, based his religious arguments on the fundamental values of human dignity and universality of Natural Law. The most systematic thinking about human rights could be found in the writings of the Social Contract Tradition of Hobbes, Locke and Rousseau, who made a determined effort to protect individuals from the state abuse. Hobbes wanted to make the 'Leviathan' all-powerful to protect individuals from the anarchical state of nature through a contract. The individuals in the Civil Society acquired certain rights which are inalienable and inviolable. Locke recognised right to life, right to liberty and right to property as three Natural Rights of men enjoyed by them even in the State of Nature. Locke's individualism reaches its climax in the recognition of individual's right to Revolution against despotic and autocratic government. Unlike Hobbes, sovereignty belongs to the whole people in the philosophy of Rousseau. Reviving the organic theory of the state, he stressed on the fact that real freedom for an individual is not what he thinks it is, but what he ought to think it is, and that a man can be forced to be free. The works of Rousseau were the Text books of the French Revolution, which is a milestone of the human rights movement. He prescribed a socialistic model where economic exploitation could be avoided and common man could be glorified. His contemporaries like Montesquieu and Voltaire contributed to the philosophy of human rights in their own ways. Montesquieu's 'Theory of Separation of Powers' and Voltaire's 'Attack on Censorship and the Call for Freedom of Expression' were important facts in the evolution of human rights. Even hedonist like Helvetius had contributed to human rights by laying fingers on universal education.

Human Rights at the Hand of Idealists and Utilitarians

The real groundwork for the modern human rights was done by the German Idealist Immanuel Kant. In his words, "The only original right, belonging to each man, in virtue of his humanity, is freedom. Every action is in accordance with Right which enables the freedom of each man's will to subsist side by side with the freedom of every other man, according to a universal law". He realised that a person who is really free is one who is morally free. He believed in the oneness of human race. Thomas Paine who followed the liberal tradition of the Rights of man believed in the sovereignty of individual and advocated for minimum state interference. Following Paine's line of thinking Mary Wollstonecraft wrote "A Vindication of the Rights of Women" which later became one of the important works in the Women's Rights Movement. Utilitarian thinkers like Bentham recognized Right to Education as essential both for happiness and efficiency. He regarded Democracy as the best form of government to promote the greatest happiness of the greatest number.

J.S. Mill's essay "On Liberty" is not merely concerned with the advocacy of freedom of thought and discussion but it is also concerned with the development of individuality of men and women in the community. To him, there can be no self-development without liberty. He has pointed out that the best government is not that which is the most efficient, but that which serves as a training ground in the art of citizenship and imparts political education. He was the first advocate of Women's Suffrage.

T.H. Green has pointed out that, "through seeking self-perfection or self-improvement that true freedom is to be found". He realized that there can be no individual well-being apart from social well-being. State as a natural and necessary ethical institution is to enforce rights for the moral development of man. As a believer of International Law, Green believes that the right of every man as man to free life involves the conception of a common humanity and of a common social organism. Herbert Spencer was an ardent advocate of 'Natural Rights', which he described as pre-social. According to him, there are two fundamental laws of human nature: (i) Law of Free Energy of Faculty, and (ii) Law of Equal Freedom and if these laws are not allowed to operate, the personality of the individuals will not be perfectly developed.

Human Rights from Marxian Angle

The individuals in the liberal western democracies are 'free', but in Communist countries they are 'unfree'. Marx has pointed out that in Capitalist countries neither the rich nor the poor are free. While the rich are slaves of property, the Poor are the slaves of their material needs. To him, in Capitalism, the man is "dehumanized", he is alienated from his labour, from the society, etc. He is just a commodity in the market. To Marx, all those who live in bourgeois society are unfree, for bourgeois society is not giving them what they desire.

Rawls' Concept of Human Rights

The contemporary thinking on Human Rights is associated with John Rawls' work *A Theory of Justice*. By making extensive use of the traditional social contract tradition, Rawls has tried to construct his theory of Justice. To him, Justice is the first virtue of social institutions and therefore is important for understanding human rights. He has clarified his stand by saying that "in a just society the liberties of equal citizenship are settled; the rights secured by justice are not subject to bargaining or to the calculus of social interests". His idea of Justice consists of two principles. The first principle is that "each person is to have an equal right to the most extensive total of equal basic liberties compatible with similar system of liberty for all". This implies equality of political rights to all citizens in a democratic country. These rights are necessary for the development of individual liberty. The second principle deals with distributive justice. According to him, "social and economic inequalities are to be arranged so that they are both (a) to the greatest benefit of the least advantaged and

(b) attached to the position and offices open to all under condition of fair equality of opportunity". Rawls has identified 'primary goods' which include Rights, Liberties, Power, Wealth, Opportunity and Self-respect. In a Just Society these goods are distributed equitably among its citizens. This theory of Justice is criticized for being highly abstract and complex philosophy.

INDIAN PERCEPTIONS AND PERSPECTIVES

The term "human right" is a dynamic concept and it endeavours to adapt itself to the needs of the countries and their people. These rights are sometimes known as basic rights, fundamental rights, natural rights or inherent rights. The protection of human personality and of its fundamental rights is the ultimate purpose of all the national and international laws. Although human rights are necessary for sustaining human life and promoting development of man, yet the internal political structure, levels of social, technological and economic development, the resource bases and the religio-cultural background of the countries, do have a profound bearing on the policies and priorities of various countries towards human rights. Human rights like fundamental rights are paramount, sacrosanct, eternal and transcendental in nature and ought to be treated as inalienable and inviolable for preserving the dignity of the people. These rights, however, cannot be imagined without the security and existence of a well regulated society. The society and the state cannot only guarantee the human rights to the individual but also demand observance of social norms from the citizens. The imperfections and frailty of human nature is the justification for the law of social control. They do not reject liberty but only regulate it to keep it on the trail of social justice. Human rights are those minimal rights which every individual must have against the state or other public authority by virtue of being a "member of the human family" irrespective of any other consideration. These are rights, which are inherent in all citizens, because of their being human. These are the rights, which are inalienable because the enlightened conscience of the community would not permit the surrender of those rights by any citizen. These are rights, which are inviolable because they are not only vital for the development of human personality and for ensuring its dignity, but also because without them men would be reduced to the level of animals.

Little effort has been made to create a comprehensive map of the totality of human rights, and there has been little discussion on the detailed content of particular rights. Often even the very concept of human rights is left obscure. The United Nations Charter refers to human rights in its preamble and six other articles. Learning about one's own rights builds respect for the right of other and points the way to more tolerant, peaceful societies.

The Universal Declaration of Human Rights adopted and proclaimed by the General Assembly resolution of 10th December 1948, forms one of the main milestones in the history of human rights. Indian Constitution contains a variety of human rights termed as fundamental rights, the India human rights have been defined under "the protection of Human Rights Act, 1993 (No 10 of 1994)" as under: 2(l)(d) "Human rights" means the rights relating to life, liberty, equality and dignity of the individual guaranteed by the Constitution or embodied in the International Covenants and enforceable by Courts in India.

It is a matter of great national pride for all Indians that human rights concept prevailed in its highest form in our Indian scriptures and religious books. Human rights were known in ancient India. For example, in 1367 B.C. Bahmani and Vijayanagar kings entered into an agreement for the humane treatment of prisoners of war and the sparing of lives of the enemy's unarmed subjects. Human rights as a concept is very ancient and some references pertaining to human rights can be found even in ancient Indian Scriptures:

Man is not an individual. He is a social organism. God loves him only who serves other being: men, cattle and other creatures. His glory lies in being a member of a big family. On the one hand, man is bound by blood kinship his parents, his wife, his children and on the other, he is linked with every individual of society whether near or far. It is given to man to link himself with those who constitute his ancestry, and also think of those who could be his posterity. Man thus lives, works and dies for society possessed of certain inalienable rights. Man is expected to develop his craft, sciences and technology and society from poverty to prosperity, with a happy today and a happier tomorrow.

This work contains a systematic body of political ideas and embodies a comprehensive theory of kinship, government and preservation of war. In ancient age there was a rule that from evening to morning there will be no firing by the troops and there used to be cease-fire with setting of the sun. The Yajnavalkya Smriti and Narada Smriti, both are still authoritative source books of Hindu law, specifying inter alia rules of drafting, pleading, procedure and judicial conduct. Both are authoritative sources of human law, specifically various rules pertaining to protection of human rights. The concept of Dharma has been internal spring of Hindus' ethic and has been all-pervading, governing and regulating conduct of human beings. The five Yarmas-ahimsa (non-violence), truth, non-theft, total abstinence and non-possession and five Niyamas—purity, contentment, penance, study of scriptures and surrender to God were enunciated by great saint Patanjali to attain self-discipline and to establish equilibrium in the society. The creation of perfect man, son of eternity, was aimed at establishing an egalitarian, non-exploitive and humane social order. Chapters 39 to 108 of the celebrated Tamil book on philosophy, *Tirukkural*, speak almost all the civil, political, economic, social and cultural rights. Ideas of freedom of criticism, curriculum of education, freedom from corruption, seeking advice from foreign experts, duty of a country to sustain the burden of the influx of refugees and socialist pattern of society could be found in the text of Tiruvaltuvar who authored it almost two thousand years ago. In Valmiki's *Ramayana*, Lord Rama advised Lakshman not to use a weapon of war which could destroy the entire humanity including those who did not bear arms because such destruction in mass was forbidden in ancient laws of war. In the *Mahabharata*, Arjun observing the laws of war refrained from using "Pasupataastra", the hyper-destruction weapon because human rights of civilians have to be kept in mind.

In the post independent era India has enacted the protection of Human Rights Act, 1993 (No. 10 of 1994) with a view to providing for the constitution of a National Human Rights Commission, State Human Rights Commissions in states and Human Rights Courts for better protection of human rights and for matters connected therein or incidental thereto. The Act received the assent of the President of India on January 8, 1994 and was published in the Gazette of India Extraordinary part II, Section 1 dated 10 January, 1994. The Protection of Human Rights Act, 1993 (Act No. 10 of 1994) contains 43 sections and is divided into the following eight chapters. Chapter I: Preliminary—Sections 1 and 2 National Human Rights Commission. Chapter II: National Human Rights Commission, Sections 1 and 2. Chapter III: Functions and Powers of the Commission, Sections 12 to 16. Chapter IV: Procedure Sections 17 to 20. Chapter V: State Human Rights Commissions, Sections 21 to 29. Chapter VI: Human Rights Courts, Sections 30 to 31. Chapter VII: Finance, Account and Audit, Sections 32 to 35. Chapter VIII: Miscellaneous, Sections 36 to 43. This Protection of Human Rights Act 1993 is a very important landmark in the history of human rights jurisprudence.

The Constitution of India in Part XVIII (Articles 352-360), provides a separate set of provisions to deal with situations such as a war or external aggression or even internal rebellion, civil war, etc. which render it impossible for the normal constitutional machinery to cope with the abnormal situation. During emergency certain human rights can be derogated in the international covenant of civil and political rights, 1966. During public emergencies which threaten the organized life of the nation (communities), certain human rights can be derogated as a temporary measure till continuance of an exceptional situation of crisis or emergency crisis or threat to the nation may be either actual or imminent and such provisions exist in Article 352(1) of the Indian Constitution which has been as under: "Explanation—A Proclamation of Emergency declaring that the security of India or any part of the territory thereof is threatened by war or by external aggression or by armed rebellion may be made before the actual occurrence of war or of any such aggression or rebellion, if the President is satisfied that there is an imminent danger thereof (Article 4.1). In time of public emergency which threatens the life of the nation and the existence of which is officially proclaimed, the State parties to the present covenant may take measures derogating from their obligations under the present covenant to the extent strictly required by the exigencies of the situation, provided that such measures are not inconsistent with their own obligations under international law and do not involve discrimination solely on the ground of race, colour, sex, language, religion or social origin".

Human rights are thus of two categories. One category is called "non-derogable rights" and the other category is called "derogable rights" under the Indian Constitution. Articles 358 and 359 make provisions derogating from the fundamental rights during the operation of a proclamation of Emergency by the President. Under Indian Constitution, "armed rebellion" implies "something like the offence of waging war against the Government in power or a conspiracy or combination to overthrow lawful government by force" (Section 121 of Indian Penal Code is relevant). The 44th Constitutional Amendment Act, 1978 got 352(1) by substituting "armed rebellion" for "internal disturbance". The 42nd Amendment Act, 1976 empowers the President to proclaim emergency confined to a particular area only without affecting the rest of India.

Limitations

Under the exercise of the right of "Derogation", for preserving the life and existence of the nation-State itself, the State is free from the obligations imposed by the human rights in time of "war" and other emergency. When the violation of human rights are sought to be justified under a limitation clause, the law would be saved only if the terms of the relevant clause such as reasonableness, public interest and the like are satisfied. Article 29(s) of the Universal Declaration of Human Rights, Articles 12(3), 14(1), 18(3), 19(3), 21, 22(2) of International Covenants on civil and political rights, and

Articles 8(2), 9(2), 10(2), 11(2) of European Convention on Human Rights append specific limitations to each of human rights, apart from some generic provisions. No human right is absolute and some limitations are needed for the protection of the society and the nation. Indian Supreme Court in words of Das J. had held that "putting restraint on the freedom of wrong-doing of one person is really securing the liberty of the intended victims. Therefore, restraint on liberty should be judged not only subjectively as applied to a few individuals who come within their operations but also objectively as securing the liberty of a greater number of individuals. Constituting the state [Gopalan vs. State of Madras 1950) S.C.R. 88 (292)]. In the Indian Constitution, for human rights the limitation clauses are to be found in Article 19. It provided the conditions of reasonableness of the restrictions imposed and the grounds specified in the relevant clause are satisfied. (Ram vs. Union of India) A-1965 SC 1178 (Para 10. 13). In Indian Constitution, Article 31 offers complete exceptions to the fundamental rights guaranteed by Part-Ill of the Constitution and if any law comes within the ambit of above referred articles (Article 31A or 31B or 31C) the law enacted to upheld even though its provisions are unreasonable or arbitrary [State of Tamil Nadu vs. Abu A. 1984 SC 326; Niyarni vs. Union of India, Air 1990 S.C., 2128 (para 3)]. It has been held that there cannot be anything as absolute or uncontrolled liberty for that would lead to anarchy and disorder [Vide Gopalan vs. State of Madras (1950), SCR 88, Santosh Singh vs. Delhi Administration AIR 1973 SC 10911].

HUMAN RIGHTS IN THE INDIAN CONSTITUTION

The struggle for the recognition of human rights and the struggle against political, economic, social and cultural oppression, against injustice and inequalities, have been an integral part of the history of all human societies. The conception of the rights, which every human being is entitled to enjoy by virtue of being a member of the human species, has evolved through history in the course of these struggles.

India has played the most significant role in the promotion of the cause of human rights. With the attainment of

Independence, a declaration of rights, the most elaborate in the world, was incorporated in the new constitution. India has made the most sincere efforts for the protection and promotion of human rights the world over and is the greatest champion of the human rights in the Third World. India has not only incorporated an elaborate Bill of Rights in her Constitution but efforts have been made to translate these into reality. Thus, we find that India has incorporated the most elaborate Declaration of Human Rights, 1948 in its Constitution. The spirit of providing for human rights pervaded the minds of the Founding Fathers of the Indian Constitution as much as it did the minds of the makers of UDHR, 1948. In other words, the framing of the Constitution of India had started about two years before the Universal Declaration of Human Rights was adopted. However, every Article of the Universal Declaration is reflected in the Indian Constitution, which was adopted by India's Constituent Assembly on 26th November 1949, and law.

The Indian Constitution bears the impact of the Universal Declaration of Human Rights and the Supreme Court of India has recognized this. While referring to the Fundamental Rights contained in Part III of the Constitution, Sikri, Chief Justice of the Supreme Court, in Kesavanand Bharati vs. State of Kerala (AIR 1973) observed "I am unable to hold these provisions how that right are not natural or inalienable rights. As a matter of fact, India was a party to the Universal Declaration of Rights...and that Declaration describes some fundamental rights as inalienable".

The Supreme Court has also recognized the interpretative value of the Universal Declaration of Human Rights in case of Kishore Chand vs. State of H.R. 1991 ISCJ 68, 76. The Universal Declaration of Human Rights does not define the term "Human right". It refers them as "the equal and inalienable right of all members of the human family". The framers of the Indian Constitution were influenced by the concept of human rights and guaranteed most of human rights contained in the Universal Declaration. The Universal Declaration of Human Rights contained civil and political as well as economic, social and cultural rights. While civil and political rights have been incorporated in part III of Indian Constitution, economic, social and cultural rights have been incorporated in part IV of the constitution.

However, there are certain rights, which are contained in the Universal Declaration but have not been expressly mentioned in the constitution. These rights are (i) right not to be subjected to torture, or to cruel, inhuman treatment or punishment (Art. 5); (ii) Right to recognition everywhere as a person before the law (Art. 6); (iii) Right to full equality to a fair and public hearing by an independent and impartial tribunal (Art. 10); (iv) Right to be presumed innocent until found guilty according to law in a public trial [Art. 11 (i)]; (v) Right to privacy (Art. 12); (vi) Right to leave any country, including his own, and to return to his country [Art. 13(2)]; (vii) Right to nationality [Art. 15 (1)]; (viii) Right to marry and found a family [Art. 16(1)]; (ix) Right to take part in the government of his country [Art. 21(1)]. Article 32 gave the right to move the Supreme Court by 'appropriate proceedings' for the enforcement of rights guaranteed under the Constitution, which shall not be suspended except as otherwise provided for by the Constitution.

The greatest incidence of human rights violations occurred during the emergency. Many went unreported, and remedies for enforcement of rights were suspended during the period. The suspension of the Writs of habeas corpus under Article 352 which well legitimised in terms of the greater claim of national security, came up before the Supreme Court in ADM Jabalpur vs. Shivakanta Shukla (AIR 1976 SCI 207) Chief Justice Ray stated that Liberty is not an abstract or absolute freedom but a regulated freedom, and if extraordinary powers are given to the government, it is so because the emergency is extraordinary. The court had to give effect to the Presidential Order in force under Article 359. The Emergency provisions were part of the law of the Constitution for such situations.

The 44th Amendment and subsequent judicial interpretations have restored Articles 20 and 21 as being capable of enforcement, provided that they cannot be suspended under any situation. The Executive can never deprive a person of his life or liberty without the authority of law. But some habits die hard, and deaths in custody still happen, as do 'disappearances'. Important developments took place in the 1980s and 1990s in the area if the Supreme Court having the power to award monetary compensation where a citizen's constitutional rights had been violated.

It has consistently been recognised by the Supreme Court that the help of International Covenants on Human Rights, and for that matter all other International Conventions on Human Rights, which have signed and ratified by India, can be taken in interpreting constitutional provisions relating to human rights. If there is a conflict between the provisions of an international convention and provision of Indian Constitution or Indian law obviously the provision of Indian Constitution or Indian law shall prevail. But if there is no conflict between the two and the relevant provision or provisions (relating to Fundamental Rights) are of wide amplitude to encompass the provisions of the international convention can be read into the fundamental rights.

WOMEN'S RIGHTS

In the context of human rights, women's rights assume greater proportion and are also a sensitive issue. The male dominated society often ignores the rights of the women and for which reason the women remain a vulnerable section of the society. It analyses human rights in a gender perspective and focuses on the international conventions particularly meant for it. The various conventions and conferences for women's development and upliftment have been discussed in the paper. In this perspective, the paper analyses the plight of the indigenous women. Women's rights and equity have to be looked with renewed vigour and vision so as to supplement the larger goal of human rights and humanity.

The human rights of women and of the girl-child are an inalienable, part of universal human rights. The full and equal participation of women in political, civil, economic, social and cultural life, at the national, regional and international levels and the eradication of all forms of discrimination on grounds of sex are priority objectives of the international community

Recognition of the women's rights was a gradual evolution in the society. Women played a significant role in the determination of political, legal and institutional structures both in the USA and in Europe where much of the human rights debate was pursued. Civil and political rights were strived from the eighteenths century onwards in societies that were organized by men, and predominantly, for men. At that time, human rights were narrowly conceived to mean, in general, rights of the male and assertion of their dignity and common humanity against overbearing state machinery. However, at a later stage, philosophical tradition did emerge, which included J.S. Mill's *The Subjugation of Women*, Engel's *The Origin of Family, Private Property and the State* and emancipation of women and their assimilation in the society at large, but it was inadequate and hence unsuccessful. The ideas of Mill and Wollstonecraft formed the foundation of the nineteenth and early twentieth century's crusade for the recognition of women's rights as human rights, among feminists and social reformers in Europe and North America. Women's rights were further also neglected due to the indifferent attitude of the society, which undervalued their importance and to some extent ignored their existence. As society progressed, things began to change and this brought positive developments for the women.

The UN Charter was the first instrument, which recognized 'the equal rights of men and women', and the Member States adopting the aims and principles of the UN were supposed to bring an end to any discrimination on the grounds of sex. Reforms at the legislative and administrative levels were implemented to maintain the quality of both men and women. In this context, women's rights are not therefore rights which are specific, but are rather universally recognized rights held by all people by virtue of their common humanity and regardless of their sex. A particular aspect of human rights is the protection of women's fundamental rights. 'Human Rights had their origin in the natural and inalienable rights of man expressed in the seventeenth and eighteenth centuries. In the nineteenth century a few liberal reformers and radical Utopians proposed the extension of these rights to women, and thus were generated the first moves for female emancipation, which in their second wave in the mid-twentieth century became a movement for women's liberation.' In spite of a women's movement for their rights and privileges, there are innumerable instances where women are denied of their rights and privileges and suffer from varied discriminations. Gender discriminations and gender related violence is rampant and special focus is needed for it. Even though there exists a number of legal instruments for women's rights and dignity, the situation is alarming. Women, everywhere, face the harsh reality of life both in home and outside and are sometimes denied the freedom for their very existence. Entrenched structures and practices such as caste, customary laws, the family, religion, etc. continue to discriminate against women. The concept of human rights is never directly applied to situation of the category but its frequent application is seen only in unlawful imprisonment, detention, torture and custodial deaths. The implications of human rights lie in the right of human beings everywhere to a minimum standard of living and to a dignified existence free from exploitation. But are the women workforce, particularly in the rural areas, getting the free environment of a work place and the dignity of their labour? Siddiqi and Ranganathan write, "nearly thirty-five per cent of poor rural families are headed by women, two and third of rural casual labourers are women who live below the poverty line. Women constitute twenty-two per cent of India's workforce, ninety per cent are employed in the marginal and unorganized sector, which includes home-based workers, contract workers, domestic help and agricultural labour. The working conditions are exploitative, characterized by low job security, lack of unionization and welfare benefits". In spite of this hardship, their labour is not given due respect and they are considered as commodities to work. The condition of dalit women also suffers from severe constraints from the society. A dalit woman suffers doubly, that of being a 'dalit' and also of being a 'woman'. It needs to be realized that dalit women undergo double suppression—first by the males within their own community, and then under the patriarchal upper-caste domination. Due to illiteracy and low educational attainments she is not aware of her rights and the minimal requisites of a dignified existence. She is often ill-treated at her home and has to perform the domestic chores in addition to doing labour work in order to supplement to the family's income. Sexual violence may be a general problem from which women in general suffer, in the case of dalit women; it is far more intense and widespread. Because of lower social attitude towards dalit women and their economic dependence, they become victims of the high caste sexual violence, on a scale far greater than that of the non-dalit women. In spite of the protective legal acts a number of cases have been registered under the category of sexual violence towards dalit women. "Between 1981 and 1986 about 4000 dalit women became victims of rape. In 1993 and 1994 this figure rose to 798 and 992 respectively. This means annually about seven hundred dalit women fall prey to the sexual assault by high caste people". One has to understand that it is the male desire for power, for superiority that manifests itself in having a hold on woman's body; and this woman's body is used when the woman belongs to the weaker sections of society, i.e. SC/ST, and minority.

Protection of women's rights and against exploitation is now a Herculean task for the State. Effective and expeditious measures have to be taken in order to establish parity between the genders. After this has been achieved, process should be initiated to guarantee the human rights of everyone. In India, the Constitution is the Supreme law of the land and it enshrines certain Fundamental Rights in Part-Ill and has also prescribed certain principles, viz. Directive Principles of State Policy, contained in Part-IV, which the state should generally adopt while framing policies. These constitutional provisions guarantee a certain degree of rights to women. Apart from these provisions, various policies have been enacted by the legislature in order to ensure women's rights vis-a-vis human rights. Some of these legislatures are Dowry Prohibition Act, 1961, amended in 1984 and 1986; Sati Prohibition Act, 1987;

Indecent Representation of Women Act, 1986; Medical Termination of Pregnancy Act, 1971; Maternity Benefit Act, 1988; Equal Remuneration Act, 1987; etc. In order to guarantee gender equality and gender justice, the Central Social Welfare Board was established in 1953, the Department of Women and Child Welfare was set-up in 1985 under the Ministry of Human Resources Development. The National Commission for Women was set-up by virtue of an Act of the Parliament in 1990. Still there exist certain loopholes where affirmative actions are required. Empowerment of women is a major task and it needs immediate attention of all concerned for women's rights. Lack of political consensus is unnecessarily creating a hurdle in this matter. Women's reservation in Panchayati Raj Institutions (PRIs) and their participation in such institutions have proved that given the conditions, women can come forward and can reap the benefits from such protective measures. Critics also allege that women reservations in PRIs is not ensuring the proper empowerment of women as sometimes it is seen that particular women functions as a de jure authority while the de facto authority is a male number of her family. How far true this may be eroded and the scope can be more properly utilized. It is no doubt that such protective measures are essential in order to maintain gender parity in a healthy democratic society like India. Allied with this, land reform programmes and land rights issue must also be accorded so as to bring greater benefits. The land reforms programme in West Bengal has ensured greater rights to women. Some of the archaic system in our law should immediately by amended so as to ensure gender parity. For example, Section 32 of the Succession Act states that a woman's share in a piece of property can be surrendered after taking her consent in the event of her husband's death. By virtue of this clause it is seen that family members coerce woman to give up her right in the property and after this is done, she is deserted by her own family members. Consciousness regarding this has evolved now and the process of amendment of such laws has been started.

International Efforts: To talk of women's rights in the twenty-first century is a matter of grave concern and it proves somewhere there is an attitudinal fallacy to it. In spite of international concern to the issue of women's rights, it is still noted that women seldom enjoy their rights into it. They are still victims of rape, domestic violence, dowry, incest, genital mutilation, sexual harassment, prostitution and trafficking, pornography, custodial violence and armed conflicts. The United Nations has taken specific initiatives in order to bring an end to violence committed on women and to protect women's fundamental freedoms thereby guaranteeing human rights. The United Nations has always affirmed that women's rights are fundamental rights, the women should be guaranteed full participation on an equal footing in all aspects of political, civil, economic, social and cultural life and that the elimination of all forms of gender-related discrimination is one of the international community's highest priority.

Concern for the women's fundamental freedoms has not only been expressly dealt in the Universal Declaration of Human Rights or the two International Covenants on Human Rights. The International Labour Organisation (ILO) adopted (i) Convention on Equal Remuneration for Men and Women Workers for work of Equal Value 1951, (ii) Convention concerning Night Work of Women employed in Industry, 1948, and (iii) Convention concerning Maternity Protection (revised) 1952. Similarly, the UN General Assembly has adopted conventions especially concerning women. These are (i) Convention on the Political Rights of Women, 1952; (ii) Convention on the Nationality of Married Women, 1957; (iii) Convention against Discrimination in Education, 1960; prohibiting discrimination on account of sex; (iv) Convention on Consent to Marriage, Minimum Age for Marriage and Registration of Marriages, 1962; Prohibiting Child, 1989 with special emphasis on girl-child. It is apt to mention here that India, though a party to all the above UN conventions, is not a signatory to the Convention on Marriages. In 1986, the Declaration on the Right to Development was adopted by the UN General Assembly recognizing right to development as an integral part of human rights and fundamental freedom. The Declaration stressed on women's development and their active involvement in all spheres of human life.

CEDAW: The Convention on the Elimination of All Form of Discrimination against Women (CEDAW), adopted in 1979 and entered into force, is the most comprehensive instrument of human rights of the women and contains more concrete provisions aimed at the real implementation of the rights already recognized. India has ratified the Convention on 9th July 1993. The Convention guarantees prohibition of discrimination and ensures equality to women. "Discrimination against women was defined as any distinction, exclusion or restriction made on the basis of sex that has the effect or purpose of impairing or nullifying the recognition, enjoyment or exercise by women in the political, economic, social, cultural, civil or any other field. The Convention is the central and most comprehensive document in bringing half of humanity into the focus of human rights concerns. In fact, its spirit is rooted in the goals of the UN 'to reaffirm faith in fundamental human rights, in the dignity and worth of the human person, and in the equal rights of men and women".

The convention is definitely a guiding instrument for the protection of women's rights and hence is an indicator to the effect. It commits states to endeavouring to eliminate sex-role stereotyping (Art. 5); to eliminate traffic in women and the exploitation of the prostitution of women (Art. 6); to providing rights surrounding maternity such as protection from dismissal on the ground of pregnancy, the right to maternity leave, and the right to special protection for women in types of work proved harmful to them (Art. 11). For women in rural area, the convention encourages states to permit them to organize self-help groups and agricultural cooperatives in order to help them obtain access to paid employment and to have "access to agricultural credit and loans, marketing facilities, approximate technology and equal treatment in land and agrarian reforms" (Art. 14). In family law, women are to be accorded equal rights with men to enter marriage, divorce, in respects of matrimonial property, children and of personal rights (Art. 16). It may be said that the convention intends to end discrimination and not to enumerate a list of rights for women.

UNIFEM: On the occasion of the International Women's Year, in 1974, the Economic and Social Council created a voluntary fund which later became the United Nations Development Fund for Women (UNIFEM), "whose mandate is to identify and study trends and attitudes which present obstacles for women and to suggest promotional, educational and other measures designed to mitigate those problems". Since 1985, UNIFEM has been aligned with the United Nations Development Programme (UNDP) in order to expedite the process with an economic perspective. In 1976, the UN General Assembly created the International Research and Training Institute for the Advancement of Women (INSTRAW) with an object to evaluate the various programmes of women's development. The Commission on the status of women associates the INSTRAW. Under the auspices of the UN, the World Conference of the International Women's Year was held in 1975 in Mexico City and it was decided to observe the decade of 1976-85 as United Nations Decade for Women. The Conference adopted the Declaration of Mexico on Equality of Women and Their Contribution to Development and Peace. The Declaration contained provisions for the all-round development of women.

International Decade for Women: The need to define, understand and implement women's rights gained global recognition during the International Decade for Women 1976-85. In 1980, the World Conference of the United Nations, Decade for Women was held in Copenhagen. This conference dealt with three major issues, viz. 'equality, development and peace' and how to make better the living conditions of the women with a focus on their economic development. With the conclusion of the UN Decade for Women, a conference was held in Nairobi to Review and Appraise the Achievements of the United Nations Decade for Women: Equality, Development and Peace. At Nairobi Forward-looking Strategies for the Advancement of women was drawn in the conference and was based on the principle that an essential contribution to the strengthening of international peace and security would be made by the elimination of all forms of inequality between women and men and by the integration of women into the development process. It was also stressed that governments should take initiatives for the total integration of women in all aspects of civil life in their countries.

The Commission on the Status of Women has also recommended certain suggestions to remove the obstacles for the smooth facilitation of the Nairobi Forward-looking strategies: (a) awareness to the rights of women; (b) elimination of negative stereotypes role of women in books; (c) training on gender issues to teachers; (d) the ratio of women involved in economic-decision and in paid employment to be increased; (e) achieve thirty percentage of women in decision-making by 1995 and equal representation by 2000. The commission also noted that extreme poverty should be removed as it often creates hurdles in the path of women's development, access to education and health and family planning services should be given to women on priority basis. It also expressed concern to the problem of violence against women in the family, work place and in society. The increasing poverty among women has been directly linked to their unequal situation in the labour market, their treatment under social welfare systems and their status and power in the family.

Beijing World Conference on Women: In September 1995, the Fourth World Conference on Women was held in Beijing. Prior to this conference, in March 1995, the World Summit on Social Development was held in Copenhagen. This year was also the Golden Jubilee Year of the UN. The World Summit on Social Development discussed on issues of poverty, unemployment and social integration. In this summit, world leaders pledged, among other things, to achieve equality and equity between women and men, with special role of women in development and to recognize and enhance the participation and leadership roles of women in political, civil, economic, social and cultural life and in development. The Summit adopted action plan that included aims at empowering the women. The Beijing Conference, like the other conferences on women, focused on the primary areas of women, i.e. health, education, production employment, armed conflict and human rights, poverty alleviation, violence, environment and development. The Platform for Action adopted in the Beijing Conference covered a wide range of dimensions for empowerment of women. It included the following:

- Action to protect and promote the human rights of women and the girl child as an integral part of universal human rights;
- Action to eradicate the persistent and increasing burden of poverty on women;
- Action to remove the obstacles to women's full participation in public life and decision-making, at all levels-including the family;
- Action to eliminate all forms of violence against women;
- Action to ensure equal access for girl children and women to education and health services;
- Action to promote economic autonomy for women, and ensure their access to productive resources; and
- Action to encourage an equitable sharing of family responsibilities.

The United Nations was assigned with the responsibility of achieving the objectives of the Platform for Action. The then Secretary-General of the UN, Mr. Boutros Ghali assured to work on the recommendations designed by the World Conference. While concluding his address in the Beijing World Conference, he said, "Let us work together to implement the Platform for Action adopted here at Beijing. Let us tell the World—and let us tell it with pride: the empowerment of women is the empowerment of all humanity!" The Platform for Action is a sort of holistic development for women but what is required for its implementation is commitment and dedication on the part of decision-makers. According to the mission statement of the Beijing conference, the Platform for Action is a sequel to the Nairobi Forward-looking strategies and aims to accelerate it. It also reaffirms the fundamental principle laid down in the Vienna Declaration and Programme of Action, adopted by the World Conference on Human Rights that the human rights of women and of the girl-child are inalienable, integral and indivisible part of universal human rights.

Indigenous Women: Special emphasis is also required for the indigenous women. It is quite certain that indigenous women work a lot, both in their house and outside, for their and their family's well-being but it is also marked that due to inherent social problems they are often circumscribed by the problems of poverty and lack of job/economic opportunities leading to alcoholism, domestic violence, prostitution and overall ignorance to the means of their prosperity. There has been no explicit conventions or documents on the indigenous people by the UN and neither does the Universal Declaration of Human Rights or the two International Covenants on Human Rights contain any implicit reference to indigenous people with the entry into force of the convention on the Rights of Child in 1990, the notion of indigenous populations was expressly included for the first time in the text of a United Nations human rights instrument. The year 1993 was observed as the International Year of the World's Indigenous People by the United Nations. In 1994, the General Assembly decided to observe the decade of 1993-2004 as the International Decade of the World's Indigenous People and to work for them in the areas of health, education, development, environment and human rights. Prior to these developments, in 1982, the UN, to discuss about the concerns and development of the indigenous people, established a Working Group on Indigenous People. The Working Group has prepared a Draft United Nations Declaration on the rights of Indigenous Peoples. The draft declaration is now at the consideration stage by the UN. Among other things, it contains treaties between indigenous populations and states and principles and guidelines for the protection of the cultural and intellectual patrimony of indigenous populations (The International Labour Organisation's Convention No. 169 has also been adopted aiming at the protection of the rights of indigenous and tribal peoples). The indigenous people, particularly the women, should be provided with well-designed plans and opportunities for their all-round development. They must be made aware of the developments leading to dignified human existence. Indigenous women's special concerns include survival of their communities and of their cultural identity and recognition of the central role of women in the efforts to advance the interests of indigenous people everywhere. The Beijing Declaration also included concern for the development and improvement of indigenous women. Governments and the civil society were apprised of the situation of indigenous women and were requested to formulate policies and measures for the well-being of indigenous women, particularly in the sectors of human rights, education, health and economic development. It is not that indigenous women are incapable of doing anything. Many of them have done praiseworthy service for their community and have brought national pride. The Nobel Peace Awardee Rigoberta Menchu Turn, a Mayan-Indian, did commendable service for promoting human rights of indigenous people. She was exiled from her native Guatemala and lived in Mexico where she fought for the rights of Indians, on her personal experience of torture and injustice. Ms. Lois O'Donoghue, as Australian aborigine, started her fight for the rights of her people in the 1950s and is now totally involved in the aboriginal movement. Later, she became the Chairperson, of the Aboriginal and Tones Start Islander Commission, an organisation specially dealing for the advancement of aboriginals in Australia. In Columbia, Eulalia Yagari, at the age of fourteen, actively participated in the public awareness campaign on land recovery and finally succeeded in gaining more land possession grants from the government for her community. Prior to her involvement, in her village nine hundred people were living with only sixty hectares of land. She also had contributions, within her tribe, to revive their cultural traditions. Eulalia finally was able to become a member of the Provincial Assembly of Antiquia, in the north-west of Colombia and is working on social issues. These indigenous women made efforts on their own for the cases of their community and its betterment and finally achieved success in it. Instances are many where the indigenous women are deprived of their rights and face multidimensional challenges. They are deprived of their traditional land rights and do not have an independent voice in any matter, be it political, economic or cultural. A certain type of dependency attitude has been strongly imprinted in their brains. It is quite certain that as women they have been discriminated but in the case of indigenous women, there is double discrimination; that of being a woman and of being an indigenous people.

Upliftment of indigenous women has to be taken-up on a priority basis. Special plans and programmes should be developed in such a way so as to suit their environment along with providing the requisites for their improvement. They should be first made aware of the opportunities available and then a bottom-up, step-by-step approach would be suitable for them. Prior to any plans and programmes, knowledge about their interests and aptitude should be gathered so as to implement those programmes, which would be beneficial for them and will also create an interest and desire in them. In Guyana, for instance, a UNDP project helped revive the traditional skill of the woven Wapishana hammock, which were sold at US $400 instead of $15 per piece. Many indigenous women are involved in a variety of traditional craftsmanship and collection of forest produce. These have a lot of value in the international market and can fetch a fortune for them but it remains unutilized by them. Some middlemen exploit them and pocket the profits from it. Governments through its various agencies are trying to help the indigenous women by purchasing the articles and products directly from them and giving them the correct price of their labour but still many indigenous women are not aware of such facilities. The civil society has to come forward in many areas to help these indigenous women so as to properly market and sell their products.

The protection of women's rights is being strongly enforced by the United Nations and through it the Member States are appraised of the prevailing condition of women's status and means to ameliorate the degrading condition of women. It pleads for empowerment of women and giving them social equity thereby guaranteeing their dignity. Experiences from various states and nations reveal that the efforts of the international organisation is gradually creating a consciousness and awareness among the mass but it will not be wrong to say in this context, 'little done vast undone'. Although not radically ameliorative of here and now human suffering, international human rights standards and norms do empower peoples' movements and conscientious policy makers everywhere to interrogate practices of politics. The civil society is actively involving itself in women's issue and for women's cause. It is giving feedbacks to the government and associates with the latter in the implementation of women's development and welfare policies. But efforts are still not adequate in ensuring a dignified survival of women. Statistics drawn from various sources indicate a gloomy picture of women's situation in the society. Crime and violence on women are committed not only in remote rural areas of India but also in metropolis, including the national capital Delhi. Though the international instruments aiming at protection of women's rights have been enacted and are being enforced by states, violence on women has not receded. It is also marked that the international instruments do not cover the entire gambit of women's rights and liberty. Upendra Baxi writes, "the Convention on Elimination of Discrimination against Women (CEDAW), in its textual formulation, barring the solitary exception of Article 6 relating to outlawry of sex-trafficking, was concerned in original intention with discrimination, not violence, against women. Even when the CEDAW Articles 14 and 16 seek to obligate state parties to eliminate, or at least to combat, gender discriminatory practices in family relations and arrangements, they do not address these as the orders of innate and sustained violation of, and violence against, women". Contextual situations of this sort must be actively considered so as to ensure a dignified life to the women. A policy instrument intended for women's welfare and development must be free from any scope or chance for manipulation and should also cover the entire gambit for which it is intended. Any sort of gap or incoherence may lead to serious consequences resulting in a topsy-turvy situation. Gender issues and concerns are, no doubt sensitive and multi-dimensional and require thorough analysis and deliberations in order to achieve success.

To be very specific, there may be difficulty with regard to women's rights, as variations exist in different societies. Given the diversity in the forms of interpersonal relations and cultural variations which exist, say in the structure of the family, it may prove difficult to specify with sufficient precision those rights which the international community would recognize as being the rights of women. It may be presumed, after generalizations that certain patterns of women's existence may lead to certain rights which would be exclusive to women while others would be those typically claimed by women. Under the 'exclusive rights category' come child-birth and pregnancy. The CEDAW provides for right to maternity leave with pay and special protection for women during pregnancy in types of work proved to be harmful to them. The other category rights may not be due to the biological factor but "could be particularized to situations in which women would be the main beneficiaries, were such rights recognized by the state". Hence, cultural relativism should not be resorted to form an excuse for women's discriminatory treatment and attitude.

Women's rights, empowerment and equity must be looked with renewed vigour and vision. It should be an integral part of the development and welfare policies of states and international organisation.

Summing up

The civil society should also initiate awareness campaigns on women's rights and freedoms and disseminate knowledge of the various welfare measures implemented by the state and international organisation. The active involvement and association of the civil society in women's issue can accelerate the whole process as it works at the grassroots level and understands the ground reality of the situation. The local people also have faith on the civil society organisations and at times of need rely on them. The success of self-help groups of women in some parts is a proof to this. In this context it can be better for the government to take the assistance of the civil society in improving the condition of women. Promotion of women's rights supplements the human rights perspective and leads to the larger cause of humanity and in the words of Boutros Ghali, the former Secretary-General of U.N., 'human rights constitute the common language of humanity'.

7

The State

The State is the central theme of political science. It is the most powerful and most universal of all social institutions. It is an association par excellence. It is the supreme organization in society which controls and coordinates the activities of individuals and association within its territorial domain. Some kind of authority structure or government has emerged at every stage of civilization to ensure internal security, protection from external attack and ensure the observance of rules regulating social life. Aristotle says that man by nature is a political animal. The state has its roots in the natural impulses of man for regulated social life. Thomas Hobbes, John Locke, Jean Jacques Rousseau and Robert Nozick are associated with the real and actual role of the state. Political theorists such as Thomas Hobbes, John Locke, Jean Jacques Rousseau and Robert Nozick pondered issues concerning the ideal and actual roles of the state. The rise of the modern state system was closely related to changes in political thought, especially concerning the changing understanding of legitimate state power. The broad Enlightenment claims that authority should be subject to reason undermine the absolutist doctrine of divine rule and served to intensify calls to relocate sovereignty from the monarch to the people. This idea found full expression in Jacques Rousseau's theory of popular sovereignty.

In ordinary parlance, the term 'State' is used with a great deal of looseness and ambiguity. It is often confused with 'society', 'country', 'nation' and 'government'. As a concept of political science the state has a precise meaning. The rise of the "modern state" as a public power constituting the supreme political authority within a defined territory is associated with Western Europe's gradual institutional development beginning in earnest in the late 15th century, culminating in the rise of absolutism and capitalism. Cultural and national homogenization figured prominently in the rise of the modern state system. It is in this period that the term "the state" is first introduced into political discourse. Although its origins are disputed, Niccolo Machiavelli is often credited with first using the concept of the state to refer to a territorial sovereign government in *The Prince*, published in 1532. Today, the most influential definition of the modern state draws on Weber's *Politics as a Vocation*. Weber stressed the state's monopoly of the means of physical violence and legitimacy. According to Weber, without social institutions claiming a monopoly on the legitimate use of force within a given territory, anomie would quickly break out. In raising the question on why the dominated obey, Weber stresses the legitimation of such a structure of domination. He supplied the tripartite categories of "traditional", "charismatic" and "rational-legal" ideal types of legitimation of obedience.

State is the most universal and most powerful of all social institutions. It is an association of society which serves its purpose during the various phases of its historical development. State is a political association that establishes sovereign jurisdiction within defined territorial borders, and exercises authority through a set of permanent institutions. State is a set of institutions that possess the authority to make the rules that govern the people in one or more societies, having internal and external sovereignty over a definite territory. It is the central theme of political science. The contemporary concept of the state owes its origin to Machiavelli (1469-1527) who expressed this idea in early sixteenth century as the power which has authority over men. This was an important idea because it describes the nature of the state, not the end of the state which was a question of political philosophy rather than political sociology or political science. R.M. Maclver in his famous work *The Modern State*

(1926) sought to distinguish the state from other kinds of associations in that it embraces the whole of people in a specific territory and it has the special function of maintaining social order. It performs this function through its agent, the government, which speaks with the voice of law. R.M. MacIver and C.H. Page have pointed out that the state is distinguished from all other associations by its exclusive investment with the final power of coercion. Opinions differ as to the undertone of the term 'state' and as to when the concept emerged. State as a social phenomenon is an object of examination and its origin in the darkness of human history is difficult to trace. Still, political thinkers have, through the centuries, taken pains to dig out the secrets of the origin of the state. The state includes such institutions as the armed forces, civil service or state bureaucracy, courts, and police.

DEFINITIONS OF STATE

Aristotle and some thinkers after him defined state in a number of ways, some of which definitions follow:

1. **Aristotle.** "The state is a union of families and villages having for its ends a perfect and self-sufficing life". This definition by Aristotle applies only to city states. Modern states are not limited to merely villages. Modern thinkers point to four characteristics of a state—(1) Public, (2) Defined geographical areas, (3) Administration or government, (4) Sovereignty.
2. **Burgess.** "The state is a particular portion of mankind viewed as an organized unit". This definition of state lacks a delimited topography.
3. **Bluntschli.** "The state is the politically organized people of a definite territory". This definition of state does not mention sovereignty.
4. **Garner.** "The state as a concept of political science and public law is community of persons more or less numerous, permanently occupying a definite portion of territory, independently or nearly so, of external control and possessing an organized government to which the great body of inhabitants render habitual

obedience". This definition of state can be regarded as one of the best. Thus, in brief, it can be summed up, "State can be defined as an organized people living in a definite territory which has its own sovereign government".

5. **Cicero.** The commonwealth is the coming together of a considerable number of men who are united by a common agreement about law and rights and the desire to participate in mutual advantages.
6. **Bodin.** A state is an association of families and their common affairs governed by a supreme power and reason.
7. **Grotius.** The state is a perfect association of freemen united for the sake of enjoying the benefits of law and for their mutual advantage.
8. **Woodrow Wilson.** The state is the people organized for law within a definite territory.
9. **R.M. Maclver.** The state is an association which, acting through law as promulgated by a government endowed to this end with coercive power, maintains within a community territorially demarcated by the universal external conditions of social order.
10. **Laski.** By a state I mean a society of this kind which is integrated by possessing a coercive authority legally supreme over any individual or group which is part of the society. An examination of any national society will always reveal within its boundaries not only individuals but also associations of men grouped together to promote all kinds of objects, religious, economic, cultural and political, in which they are interested. Such a society is a state when the way of life to which both individuals and associations must conform is defined by a coercive authority binding upon them all.
11. **T.E. Holland.** The state is a numerous assemblage of human beings generally occupying a certain territory, amongst whom the will of the majority or of an

ascertainable class of persons is by the strength of such a majority of class, made to prevail against any of their number who opposes it.

12. **Robert Philimore.** A state is a people permanently occupying a fixed territory, bound together by common laws, habits and customs into one body politic, exercising through the medium of an organized government independent sovereignty and control over all persons and things within its boundaries capable of making war and peace and of entering into all international relations with the communities of the globe.
13. **Pennock and Smith.** We may summarize by defining the state as a political system comprising all the people in a defined territory and possessing an organization (government) with the power and authority to enforce it's will upon its members by resort, if necessary, to physical sanctions, and not subject in like manner to the power and authority of another policy.

VARIOUS NOTIONS OF STATE

State has been viewed differently by different political thinkers. The State is a historic entity. During the course of evolution of political philosophy different notions of State have emerged. A brief discussion of these notions of the State follows:

1. The Ethical Notion of the State. Plato and Aristotle regarded the State as representing the highest form of human life and looked upon it as an institution which made the virtuous life possible. They saw in the State the necessary agent for the ethical and intellectual more than the material element. The ethical notion was further developed by Rousseau, Hegel, Kant and Green. State is a necessary ethical and natural institution. It fulfills our various needs and requirements. It is an association of association and supreme association. It is an ethical institution. It embraces the whole of the human being. Aristotle said "the State has come into existence for life and exists for the sake of good life. The State is an end in itself because it is a perfect institution. The State is the highest morality. It is necessary for all-round development of man. It is within a State that man achieves moral excellence by performing his duties and enjoying his rights". Hegel endowed the State with a real personality and a will. He identified the will of an individual with the will of the State. He regarded the State as a collective person, a majestic being, the march of God on earth.

Criticism of the Ethical Notion

1. All good citizens have to conform to one single pattern laid down for him by the State. But all individuals are not alike.
2. Individuals cannot enjoy liberties in an absolute State.

2. The Legal Notion of the State. Bodin, Hobbes, Bentham and Austin interpret the State as a legal structure. It was formed for making, interpreting and enforcing law. It creates laws and norms in order to regulate human behavior. It has coercive powers in the case of violation of laws. The legal notion regards the state as a legal person having a distinctive personality and will of its own. As a legal personality State property, direct economic enterprises, may be sued in the Courts. It harmonizes activities of the various members of Society.

Criticisms of the Legal Notion

1. It does not conform to the facts of daily life.
2. It is not absolute. There are limitations on the exercise of political power by the State.

3. The Power Notion of the State. Machiavelli is the main exponent of power notion. When individuals came into contact with one another, it is but natural that conflicts and contradictions may arise in society. To resolve these conflicts and to maintain peace and harmony in society there is a need of power—a power which upholds the common good of the people. The State is the power to cope with the demands of the individuals and to resolve the contradictions in society.

Some thinkers also hold the view that it is not correct to say that the State restricts the freedom of individuals. Freedom in society is born out of the rules which every society maintains. In the absence of the rules the security of the person is endangered.

Criticism of the Power Notion

(i) Though force is an essential part of the State, yet it is not the foundation of the state.

(ii) Maclver observes, "Coercive power is only the criterion of State and not its essence".

(iii) It is the right which lends support to might and not the vice versa.

(iv) Will—not the force is the basis of the State.

4. State as a Natural Institution. The exponents of this theory say that man became civilized only in the State. The Organic theory regards State as a natural institution. The State came into existence for the sake of good life and continues to exist for the sake of good life. It is on this ground that Aristotle called man a political animal. It means that State was their right from the beginning, State is prior to man.

5. State as a Divine Institution. The Medieval thinkers considered State as a divine institution. In the medieval period the Church dominated the monarch. It was thought that God created the State and the monarch was the representative of God on earth. Thus the King was not responsible to any institution except to God only. The King was representative of God and will take care of the subjects as a father takes care of the children. He could rule according to his own will. He alone was capable of deciding well from bad. His word was considered to be the law. Any person who disobeyed him was a sinner. Kingship was hereditary i.e., after his death his son automatically became the ruler of the subjects.

6. State According to Liberal Thinkers. The Renaissance and Reformation challenged the divine theory. The French Revolution gave a rude shock to the State as a divine institution. It gave the slogan of equality, liberty and fraternity. The views of the liberals about the State can be summed up as follows:

1. State is not a divine institution but man made institution.
2. The State is only a mean not an end in itself.
3. The State is a necessary evil.
4. All laws framed by the State are opposed to man's liberty.

7. State According to Marxist Thinkers. The State is essentially a class structure. It is an organization of one class dominating over the other classes. The State took birth at a certain stage of economic development, when society was broken into classes—haves and haves-not. In history, there has been a fierce struggle between these two classes. Even today, the State is an agency for exploitation of the poor by the rich. It upholds the interests of the few at the cost of many. According to Karl Marx and Fredric Engels, the State is a man made and artificial body. It is a class organization. It represents force and oppression. They believe that a stage will come when there will be no classes and consequently the State will wither away. State is thus only a temporary organization.

Criticism of the Notion of Class Structure

The notion may be true of certain states at certain times. But it is wrong to apply it universally to all states at all times. It applies more to a diseased State than to a normal one.

8. The Totalitarian Notion of the State. The modern totalitarian notion of the State regards the whole life of an individual as coming within the jurisdiction of the State. There is no part of a man's life which he can call his own. If he lives, he lives for the State and if he dies, he dies for the State. Mussolini stated the totalitarian view in these words, "All within the State none outside the State none against the State". The motto which he placed before the people was: "to believe, to obey, to fight".

Criticism of the Totalitarian Notion of the State

Totalitarian view means regimentation of the life of the individual. It is wholesale denial of the worth and dignity of man. Individual is regarded just a log in the wheel of the State.

The Pluralists opposed the absolute sovereignty of the State and pleaded for the decentralization of political power. They regarded State like other association and asked for the division of power between them.

ELEMENTS OF THE STATE

A brief discussion and explanation of the state is necessary. The state has four essential elements. These are explained below:

- Population
- Territory
- Government
- Sovereignty (or independence)

The first two elements constitute the physical or material basis of the state while the last two form its political and spiritual basis. The state is a human institution. So population is its primary element. There is no hard and fast rule about population. The ancient Greek writers like Plato and Aristotle favored a small population. According to Plato, an ideal state should have a population of 5040. Aristotle laid down a general principle that the population of a state should be large enough to make it self-sufficient and small enough to make good. The primary requirement for the existence of the state is population. The state, being a human institution, cannot be conceived of without people. Political philosophers have long tried to lay down some standard rules as to the number of people required to form the state. Plato said that an ideal state should have 5,000 citizens. Rousseau opined that an ideal state should have a population of 10,000. He thought that a small state is proportionately stronger than a large one. Aristotle avoided this mathematical precision and said that the population of a state should not be stated here that Plato and Aristotle lived in the era of small city-states. The state cannot be formed without a definite and fixed territory. Nomads or wandering tribes who have no permanent residence don't form a state. Even specialized people like Jews did not possess a state till the formation of Israel in 1948. They were scattered all over the world. As in the case of population, no limit is fixed for the territory of a state. There is no hard and fast rule regarding the size of population or territory.

The modern states differ considerably in their size of population or territory. According to Garner, government is the agency or machinery through which common policies are determined and by which common affairs are regulated and common interest promoted. Friedrich Engels in his *Origin of the Family, Private Property, and the State* (1884) notes that the formation of the state is accompanied by a division of population according to territory. In the pre-state society when people lived as nomadic tribes, moving from one place to another in search of food, the members of the tribe are held together by the ties of kinship. With the formation of the state citizens are allowed to exercise their rights and duties wherever they settle, irrespective of genes and tribes. The organization of citizens according to locality is the common feature of all states. John Seeley holds that a fixed territory is not an essential aspect of a state. The nomadic tribes, who do not possess fixed territory, do constitute a state.

DIFFERENT VIEWS OF STATE

State has been understood in three very different ways:

- From an idealistic perspective,
- From a functional perspective, and
- From an organizational perspective.

The idealistic approach to the state is most clearly reflected in the writings of Hegel. Hegel identified three moments of social existence—the family, civil society and the state. Within the family, he argued a particular altruism operates that encourages people to set aside their own interests for the good of their children or elderly relatives. In contrast, civil society was seen as a sphere of universal egoism in which individuals place their own interests before those of others. Hegel conceived the state as an ethical community underpinned by mutual sympathy—"universal altruism". The functionalist approaches to the state focus on the role of state institutions. The central function of the state is invariably seen as the maintenance of social order, the state being defined as that set of institutions that uphold order and deliver social stability. Such an approach has been adopted by modern Marxists, who have been inclined to see the state as a mechanism through which class conflict is ameliorated to ensure the long-term survival of the capitalist system. The organizational view defines the state as the apparatus of government in its broadest sense. It distinguishes clearly between the state and civil society. The state comprises the various institutions of government: the bureaucracy, the military, the police, the court, the security system and so on. It can be identified with the entire body-politic.

THEORIES OF THE STATE

Social Contract Theory of the State

The theory of the social contract presents a typical version of origin of the state from the liberal point of view. This theory treats the state as a product of the mutual agreement of men, created with a definite purpose, to serve certain social needs. The theory of the social contract can be seen as a justification for the formation of the state. Social contract theories relied on a specific anthropological conception of man as either "good" or "evil". The social contract theory of the origin of the state implies that there was a time when men lived or would have lived without any recognized civil law, without the state. This stage or life-pattern of men is described as the 'state of nature'. The state was created through the voluntary agreement of all individuals who constitute the state.

Liberal Theory of the State

The liberal theory originated from the mechanistic concept of the state although some later thinkers, T.H. Green (1936-82) and H.J. Laski (1893-1950) joined the liberal stream without subscribing to the mechanistic concept. In short, the mechanistic theory treats the state. This implies the possibility of two life-patterns; one before the origin of the state, the other after the creation of the state. According to this theory, the state is not a natural institution, but an artificial device or instrument invented by men for their mutual benefit; it is intended to serve the interests of all individuals or all sections of society. It regards the state as the product of the will of society; hence, it is an expression of 'superior will'. The idea of the creation of the state through a contract is found in a rudimentary form in ancient thought both of the East and the West. Kautilya's *Arthashastra* makes a pointed reference to it while some sophists of ancient Greece described the state as an outcome of the contract between men. Some traces of the theory are also found in ancient Roman law. But all these references should not be taken to mean that the theory of the social contract has been prevalent from ancient times. On the contrary, this theory was systematically formulated at a particular point of European history, in order to drop a curtain on the values of the feudal system and to introduce the new values of the capitalist system.

Exponents of the Theory

Thomas Hobbes (1588-1679), John Locke (1632-1704) and Jean Jacques Rousseau (1712-78) are regarded as the main exponents of the theory of the social contract. Of these, Hobbes and Locke are from England while Rousseau belongs to France. This theory held the field in Europe in the seventeenth and eighteenth centuries. Some later thinkers, such as, Immanuel Kant (1724-1804), Herbert Spencer (1820-1903), John Rawls (1921-) and Robert Nozick (1938-) made use of this theory to elaborate their own systems of thought. Hobbes was a tutor to Charles-II of England. He sought to justify the absolute power of the sovereign in his famous work *Leviathan*. He condemned the Civil War of 1642 as he saw in it the forces of disintegration. He sought to establish the absolute sovereignty of the state as an essential condition of social solidarity. Locke, on the other hand, sought to justify the Glorious Revolution of 1688. He was an ardent advocate of constitutional monarchy. In his two treaties of Government, Locke argued that if the monarch ever behaved in a despotic manner, the people had the right to remove him from authority. Brought up in the tradition of British conservation, Locke was not the sworn enemy of monarchy, but he sought to establish it in the consent of the people. Roussesu had no such particular purpose to serve yet he was a brilliant writer whose whole ideas not only inspired poets and men of letters but induced the revolutionary upsurge that shook the French polity to its foundations in 1789. He is regarded as the source of inspiration of the great French Revolution. The social contract theory of the origin of the state implies that there was a time when men lived or would have lived without any recognized civil law, without the state. This stage or life-pattern of men is described as the 'state of nature'. The state was created through the voluntary agreement of all individuals who constitute the state. Hobbes, Locke and Rousseau have drawn different pictures of the 'state of nature', 'terms of the contract' and the character of sovereignty which came into existence as a consequence of the birth of the state. It is important to note here that the whole theory of the social contract is based on speculation. It seeks to trace the origin of the state through logic, not through historical or scientific evidence. Locke refers to historical fact to illustrate the point, but illustration is no evidence.

State of Nature

The state of nature denotes how men live or would have lived without the authority of civil law, state or political control. At this stage, there is no industry, no systematic production. Men live not only close to nature; they have to depend on the bounty of nature for their survival. Their behavior is largely governed by their inner impulses, in restrained by civil law, although a 'natural law' is supposed to have existed. Men have no recognized rights, although they enjoy some 'natural rights'. As all these conditions are determined by logic or particular lines of argument, not on the basis of any scientific evidence, they do not lead to any uniform conclusions. Different authors have, therefore, given different versions of the state of nature, etc.

Hobbes

Hobbes draws a gloomy picture of the state of nature. This is natural corollary of his concept of human nature. Hobbes postulates that man is selfish by nature; self-interest is the mainspring of human action. Men are moved to action not by intellect or reason, but by their appetites, desires and passions.

In the absence of law and justice, the state of nature is characterized by a perpetual struggle, ceaseless conflict and constant warfare. In Hobbes's own forceful words, the life of man at this stage is 'solitary, poor, nasty, brutish and short'; 'every man is enemy to every man'. In pursuance of his own pleasure, man wants power over others; but as the physical and mental powers of natural men are nearly alike, nobody is able to overpower the other. Hence, men stand in natural fear of each other. It is a state of total insecurity. In such a state there is no room for industry, 'Might is right' is the order of the day. Men are free to take what they can, and to rob whomever they can. There is no law to prevent oppression or to contain the 'law of the jungle'. It is a state of perfect anarchy. Hobbes is quite clear that he is not describing a historical fact, but only trying to demonstrate what would happen if there were no settled government for any length of time. Hobbes argues that there can be no morality or consciousness of duty or obligation in the state of nature, because these are possible only after the establishment of law and government. Natural rights are, therefore, nothing more than the natural powers of men, used to oppress others. At best, natural liberty is nothing but 'the liberty for each man to preserve his own life'. This urge for 'self-preservation' is embodied in the law of nature of natural law. This conforms to the rules of prudence and expediency. It is natural law which prompts men to abandon the state of nature and to establish law and government. It consists in the rules of self-preservation, particularly as follows: (a) Everybody should aim at securing peace; (b) Men should be willing in concert with others, to give up their natural rights; (c) Man should keep their contracts; and finally, (d) Men should show gratitude or return beneficence for beneficence. Thus, the requirements of self-preservation itself created a sense of duty in the minds of men which prompts them to form the state.

Single Contract of Hobbes

Hobbes postulates a single contract by which men abandon the state of nature and establish society and state together. Through this historical fiction he tries to convey a philosophical truth that the government does not rest on sheer force; it rests on the will of the people. The social contract, according to Hobbes, is concluded among the people themselves who emerge from the state of nature. The sovereign is not a party to the contract. According to Hobbes's logic, the sovereign did not exist before the conclusion of the contract, he comes into existence as a result of this contract, hence he cannot be a party to the contract. It is contract of each with all and of all with each, to set up a sovereign authority. But by this contract every man gave up his natural rights and powers to a common power who would 'keep them in awe' and given them security. Men entered into a social contract to set up a ruler, as if every man should say to every man; "I authorize and give up my right of governing myself to this man, or to this assembly of men, on this condition, that thou give up thy right to him, and authorize all this actions in like manner". Thus, the social contract brings a sovereign into existence who enjoys supreme and absolute authority. All men in society, apart from the sovereign himself, become his subjects. All the natural rights of men are surrendered to the sovereign once and for all. The power conferred on him cannot be withdrawn, because if men chose to revive their natural rights, they would revert into the state of nature, characterized by anarchy and total insecurity. Hobbes, therefore, does not admit people's right to revolt or revolution. On this basis, he condemned the civil war of 1642. Since, according to Hobbes, the state and society come into existence together through a single contract, repudiation of the contract would result not only in an overthrow of the government but a disintegration of society itself. That is why Hobbes treats sovereignty as absolute, individual and inalienable. He creates unlimited political obligation.

Locke

Locke draws an entirely different picture of the state of nature. In his view, it is not a state of constant warfare. On the contrary, it is a state of peace, goodwill, mutual assistance and preservation; it is a state of liberty, not a state of license. The majority of people at this stage obey the law of nature, that is, the law of inward morality. Men are by nature rational beings, impelled by their inner nature to treat humanity—whether in their own person or in that of any other persons—in every case as an end, never as a means only. But still, there are a few persons who set aside the rules of morality in pursuance of their self-interest. In the absence of any established authority in the state of nature, it becomes very difficult to deal with such offenders. If men become judges of their own cases, justice would not be secured. In this respect, the state of nature proves to be inconvenient. In order to rectify this defect, men abandon the state of nature and enter into civil or political society by means of a contract. Natural law, according to Locke, consists in the rules of morality implanted in the human conscience, natural rights consists in the 'perfect freedom and equality' of every man "not only to preserve his property, that is his life, liberty and estate, against the injuries and attempts of other men, but to be judged of, and punish the breaches of natural law" committed by other. When men enter into political society, they surrender their natural rights to be judged in case of breaches of law—this power is now vested in the community instead of in individuals; but they still retain their natural rights to 'life, liberty and property'. Locke's picture of the state of nature is, again, hypothetical, not a historical account. As W.T. Jones (Master of Political Thought, Vol. II) has elucidated: Locke means by the natural law...a rule for human behavior only, and one which is not a description of how men do behave, but a statement of how they ought to behave. Hence by his state of nature, paradoxically enough, Locke primarily means something which is not natural or historical.... By saying, for instance, that in a state of nature men are free and equal, he does not merely mean that there was a time in the past when men were, in fact free and equal: he means rather than to assert that they ought to be free and equal. Locke tries to overcome this difficulty by postulating several stages of the contract. As Jeremy Waldron has elucidated: "Contract and consent have three stages in Locke's description; first, men must agree unanimously to come together as a community and pool their natural powers so that they can act together to uphold one another's rights; second, the members of this community must agree by a majority vote to set up legislative and other institutions; third, the owners of property in a society must agree, either personally or through their representatives to whatever taxes are imposed on the peoples" (*The Blackwell Encyclopedia of Political Thought*, edited by David Miller, p. 294). This theory of several stages of the contract marks a clear departure from Hobbes's position. Hobbes postulates that society and state are formed together; they are dissolved together. On the contrary, Locke believes that society and state were created in different steps; creation of society is the primary step; setting up of the government is a secondary step. So, if the government is dissolved, society does not disintegrate. Order will be restored by setting up another government in its place.

In Locke's system of thought the nature of government resembles a 'trust'. In other words, a government, like a trust, is bound to act within the terms of its Constitution. By drawing a distinction between the process of formation of society and state, Locke places the government under the control of society. This leaves no scope for absolutism. As Waldron has significantly observed: "Absolutism of the kind Thomas Hobbes envisages is ruled out on the grounds that people hold their natural rights of life and liberty as a sort of trust from God and, therefore, cannot transfer them to the arbitrary power of another. Since government is set up to protect property and other rights, and not to undermine them, the government may not take or redistribute property without consent". While Hobbes creates absolute sovereignty, Locke evolves a constitutional government. Hobbes postulates an unconditional surrender of natural liberty to the sovereign, because in his system of thought natural liberty is the source of constant conflict and consequent anarchy. Locke postulates conditional and partial surrender of natural rights, because some natural rights are fundamental; they cannot be given up because they are the cornerstone of human freedom. According to Locke, people give up their natural right to 'judge and punish the offenders of natural law' in their own case or in the case of other persons. This right is now vested in the community, 'common power' or the government which assumes the rule of 'umpire'. But this right is surrendered on the condition that their rights to 'life, liberty and property' will be protected and kept intact. Society retains the authority to watch whether the government is exercising its powers strictly in accordance with the terms of the contract or not. This implies (a) in the first place, the government must govern with the 'consent of the people'. It is the people who are endowed with the faculty of 'reason'—conscience, sense of morality, knowledge of right and wrong. The government is created by the will of the people, but as an artificial device it cannot embody 'superior reason'; and (b) secondly, if in any case the government falters from its duty, the people have the right to overthrow that government and set up another government in its place. Thus, Locke recognizes the people's right to revolution. It is on this basis that he justifies the 'bloodless' or 'glorious' revolution of 1688, which had led to the flight of James II from England and the establishment of William and Mary on the throne.

It is significant that Locke treats 'right to property' as fundamental natural right which cannot be surrendered to the government. He proceeds on the assumption that property consists in one's 'fruit of labor'. Locke argues that when an individual mixes his labour with natural resources, this act is sufficient to establish his exclusive right on the product which does not depend on the consent of other people. Locke's theory of taxation also based on his notion of the citizen's right to property. He postulates that the governments should take only what is necessary to carry on its business. It has no power to take anything more without the owner's consent.

Natural Rights

Natural rights are the basis for the theory of government shared by most branches of liberalism including libertarianism. In this view, human beings are born with certain natural rights, and governments are established strictly for the purpose of protecting those rights. What the natural rights actually are is a matter of dispute among liberals; indeed, each branch of liberalism has its own set of rights that it considers to be natural, and these rights are sometimes mutually exclusive with the rights supported by other liberals. Natural rights (also called human rights) are universal rights that are seen as inherent in the nature of people and not contingent on human actions or beliefs. When discussed in political contexts, the notion of natural rights is developed and detailed into the notion of human rights. As a result, there is some debate between natural rights theorists, ranging from modern writers such as Tibor Machan to Enlightenment thinkers such as Locke, Kant, or Jefferson. One theory of natural rights was developed from the theory of natural law during the Enlightenment in opposition to the divine right of kings, and provided a moral justification for liberalism. The concept of a natural right can be contrasted with the concept of a legal right: A natural right is one that is claimed to exist even when it is not enforced by the government or society as a whole, while a legal right is a right specifically created by the government or society, for the benefit of its members. The question of which rights are natural and which are legal is an important one in philosophy and politics. Critics of the concept of natural rights argue that all rights are legal rights. The idea of human rights descended from that of natural rights; some recognize no difference between the two and regard both as labels for the same thing while others choose to keep the terms separate to eliminate association with some features traditionally associated with natural right.

Criticisms of Natural Right of Locke

Marx, Nietzsche or Freud, Hannah Arendt, Lacan, Althusser, Foucault, Deleuze or Derrida, etc. have criticized the theory of Natural rights. Contractualism is based on a philosophy of rights being agreed to in order to further our interests, which is a form of individualism: each individual subject is accorded individual rights, which may or may not be inalienable, and form the basis of civil rights, as in the 1789 Declaration of the Rights of Man and of the Citizen. It must be underlined, however, as Hannah Arendt did in her book on imperialism, that the 1789 Declarations, in this agreeing with the social contract theory, bases the natural rights of the human-being on the civil rights of the citizen, instead of doing the reverse as the contractualist theory pretends to do. This individualist and liberal approach has been criticized since the 19th century by thinkers such as Marx, Nietzsche or Freud, and afterward by structuralist and post-structuralist thinkers, such as Lacan, Althusser, Foucault, Deleuze or Derrida. Several of those philosophers have attempted, in a spinozist inspiration, of thinking some sort of trans individuality which would precede the division between individual subject and collective subject.

FUNCTIONS OF MODERN STATE

A. Compulsory Functions

1. *Defence against Foreign Attack.* The most urgent function of the state is defence of the country against foreign attack. It has to make adequate preparations in the form of weapons and land, sea and air forces. It has to take special notice of things which can create the danger of attack from other countries.
2. *Internal Peace and Security.* The policy of a state at home is quite as important as is its foreign policy. It is the prime duty of the state to maintain internal peace and security. An increase in communal riots, thefts, cases of dacoity and rebellion can endanger the existence of the state itself. The state maintains peace and order through police and army.
3. *Protection of the Rights of Citizens.* In every state the citizens possess certain rights like rights to life, property, freedom of thought etc. It is incumbent upon the state to protect these rights, for which it has to formulate essential laws, arrange for proper administration and organise justice.
4. *Justice.* In this way justice is a compulsory function of the state. This provides for obedience of laws in the state, maintains order and protects the rights of everyone.

B. Voluntary Functions

Besides these compulsory functions of state the following are its voluntary functions:

1. *Education.* In the modem age, all states consider it their duty to make adequate arrangement for the education of their citizens. A state of uneducated citizens can never progress. Thus the state makes arrangement for primary schools and colleges and universities so that higher education in sciences, agriculture and the humanities may become possible. Arrangements are made for adjoining research centres, libraries, zoos, store houses and art classes etc. Efforts are made to provide free primary education. Capable students are awarded scholarships by the state. But the state should avoid unnecessary interference in educational centres.
2. *Health.* Along with education, modern states try to provide for the protection of health. Provision is made for sanitation, hospitals, free medicine, vaccination and essential energizing foods for the poor. Medical colleges are opened to end the dearth of capable doctors. Government research centres and training schools for nurses are opened.
3. *Protection of the Old, Poor and Invalid.* Modern states have also begun making arrangement for the old, unemployed people who are given pension. The facility of insurance insures the security of everyone. Orphanages and homes for destitutes are created.
4. *Arrangement of Public Welfare Services.* The state organises the railways, postal and telegraphic wireless facilities, etc. It is the duty of the state to make arrangements for means of transportation such as buses, railways, aeroplanes and ships, etc.
5. *Social and Economic Improvement.* Another of the state's duties is affecting social and economic improvement. The state lays down laws against harmful customs and makes necessary arrangements for their enforcement.
6. *Encouraging Trade and Industry.* It is also the duty of the state to encourage trade and industry and to

develop it as well. Almost everywhere in the world, it is the state which controls economic system and the mint. It is the state which standardizes the scales of measurement and weighing. The country cannot benefit by international trade if it does not make the proper laws for import and export. The state should establish factories of the key industries in order to implement and initiate other industries in the country. The state should also encourage cottage industries.

7. ***Organisation of Labour.*** The state should direct its efforts to the improvement of conditions of labourers and lay down rules to obviate the probability of their exploitation. It is the responsibility of the state to make efforts towards labour welfare.
8. ***Proper Use of Natural Resources of the Country.*** A country can become powerful by land, forests, rivers, minerals and agricultural products. Maximum benefit should be extracted from them. On this subject, the state should direct the necessary precautionary measures, research and search for new mineral products and lay down laws for the utilisation of forests, mines, land, etc.
9. ***Arrangement of Recreation.*** In order to maintain the novelty and excitement in the life of the public the state should provide means for recreation. For this, film industry, dramatic societies, etc., ought to be encouraged.

Actually, the function of a modern state is not merely administration but an integral welfare and development of its subjects. Thus, its functions have been aggrandized. The turbulence of local situations does make an appreciable though slight alteration in them, while different political schools of thought have recognized different functions of the state. Thus nothing final can be said upon this subject. The only theory which can be universally acceptable is that the state should function in a manner calculated to add to public welfare but the scholars differ in their opinions about that in which lies this public welfare. It is here that the guidance of the sociologist is needed. He has to determine the supreme and ultimate objective of the individuals. The state shall collect the means to the attainment of this ideal. As an example, the supreme ideal of an individual is self-realisation or an integral development. Thus, it is for the state to utilize the means to his physical, mental and spiritual development.

STATE AND COMMUNITY

Many people come to treat the state as a community. But the state is only a political association in the community. Defining Community, G.D.H. Cole has written, "By community I mean a complex of social life, a complex including a number of human beings, living together under conditions of social relationships, bound together by a common however constantly changing stock of conventions, customs and traditions and conscious to some extent of common social objects and interests". The same scholar of political science has defined state as a means which organises particular human society, both in internal and external relation, into a corporate body. Accordingly, the state is actually the means for the welfare community. It can be scribed as a part of community. It is created for the fulfillment of certain objectives.

State is more Limited than Community

A state is more limited when compared to community. It is of course true that it does control a major part of social functions and relations but still many aspects of human life are excluded from it. Communal life is more comprehensive than the life of a citizen. In community, the individual is a member of many other associations, besides the state. The laws of the state exert their influence upon a very small part of the person's life. MacIver has truly written, "As social beings, we are more than merely citizens of a state. We enter into many relationships; we carry on many social activities, not as members of state but as social beings, as friends, or lovers, as members of families, of churches, of clubs or other groups". As a self-conscious being, the individual thinks independently of others and tempts self-development. Moral life is even wider than the political and social life. An individual acts more as a social being than as a citizen and more as a self-conscious being than as a social being. And this moral nature of his is the most comprehensive of all.

State is an Association

Actually the state is an association despite some differences which professes from the other associations. The state is here referred to an association in the sense that its establishment is motivated by particular objectives. It has some special functions. It can neither perform all functions and nor does it exercise sovereign authority over the individual. There are other associations besides the state in society which cannot be replaced by state, in the implementation of whose functions the state is neither appropriate nor capable. The state was made the sovereign in some countries like Italy or Germany, but the experiment did not prove a success. Maclver has said quite correctly, "The state can effectively supervise only the external aspects of life. Beyond all else, it cannot under any conditions be a substitute for those cultural organisations which express the variant beliefs, opinion of modern interests and ideals of the diversified groups society". Actually, the state is a political association whose objective is to maintain peace and order in the community and to raise the standard of living while creating circumstances conductive to the integral development of every citizen. There are a number of activities like religious, moral, economic, social and psychological which the state cannot perform. Even the sovereign state of Germany could not take into its hands the functions of the church.

State is a Means to the Welfare of Community

In this way, state is not itself an end. It is a means to which rights are assigned for governing over society and individual for their own benefit. When the state ceases to be of any use to the individual, its need will also end. According to Engels, the state will dissolve of itself. Many thinkers like Marx, Engels, Gandhi, Kropotkin, Tolstoy, Sri Aurobindo etc., have recognised the disutility of state in an ideal order. The theories of the origin of society also support this view that it is a means, not an end. The end is the integral development of the individual and society. The state is accorded its rights by the society and individual. It governs because that is what it is meant for. It is created for the proper utilization of natural resources, maintaining peace and order, defence of the country from external aggression, protection of health arrangement for means of transport and communication and other activities of a similar nature. It does not annihilate other associations but organises and encourages them. Even in sovereign states like the U.S.S.R., the state has not interfered in the activities of the family. The state in Germany never triumphed over the Church. F.L. Schuman has written, "in the church and church alone, the Nazi dictatorship has found an insuperable obstacle to its absolutistic pretentions". Actually, a good State is one which makes its objective the benefit of community and works for its attachment. It is useless in the event it fails to achieve the communal benefit and is changed by revolutionaries. In the words of Maclver, "It is best conceived of as an agency of the community with very broad and important functions, but nevertheless limited". From the moral viewpoint the state is a means to the integral development of society and the individual.

STATE AND SOCIETY

In political science, the term is used to mean the totality of human relationships, generally in contrast to the State, i.e., the apparatus of rule or government within a territory: the state is a summation of privileges and dominating positions which are brought into being by extra-economic power. Society is the totality of concepts of all purely natural relations and institutions between man and man. The term state is sometimes used synonymously with society. A distinction between state and society is desirable, not only for scientific precision but also for saving individual from absolutist, authoritarian, and totalitarian rule. The state is usually described as society politically organized. Society is an association of human beings which fulfills all their needs of life from cradle to grave. The state fulfills their particular need of political organization—it subjects them to binding laws and decisions to provide for order and security, and common services. When a society is governed by a common set of rules, regulations and a supreme decision-making authority, only then does it qualify for being a state. Society binds men into multifarious relationships that are usually determined by necessity, custom, courtesy, morality, mutual understanding, agreement or even contract. Political relations are mainly determined by command and obedience. Society may coincide with the state, especially when society takes the form of a nation. The state is formed out of society. Society is a primary association. Society which chooses the pattern of its political grouping. States may be created, altered or dissolved, but society goes on forever. Man can live without a state, but not without society. That is why man is described as a social animal by nature. The state depends on society for its existence, not vice versa.

STATE AND GOVERNMENT

The word 'government' is derived from the Greek which means 'to steer' or 'to control'. Typically, 'the government' refers to the executive function of the state. Government is a body that has the authority to make and the power to enforce rules and laws within a civil, corporate, religious, academic, or other organization or group. R.M. Maclver in his book (*The Web of Government*) has said that every social organization must have a focus of administration, an agency by which its policies are given specific character and translated into action. The idealistic theory does not make a distinction between state and government. It creates an image of the perfect state. (State is the march of God on Earth.) The liberal democratic theory is more rational in this respect. It treats the state as a product of the will of society an instrument of conflict resolution and of securing the common interest. In its broadest sense, 'to govern' means to administer or supervise, whether over a state, a set group of people, or a collection of assets. In many countries (particularly those having parliamentary systems), the government refers to the executive branch of government or a specifically named executive, such as the Blair government (compare to the administration as in the Bush administration in U.S. usage). In countries using the Westminster system, the party in government will also usually control the legislature.

8

Civil Society

The concept of civil society in the process of nation-making is now engaging the attention of policy makers, teachers and research scholars all over the world. As the name indicates, civil society refers to that part, or kind of society which is civil in nature. When members of a society possess civic virtues we may ordinarily call it civil society. Civicness among the inhabitants makes the society civil. A sense of group living, group engagements and interactions among individuals for their common interests constitute the major features of civil society. It is the sphere in which a community enjoys independence and acquires the strength to organize itself to achieve common good. To Calhoun, civil society is "the capacity of political community to organize itself independent of the specific direction of state power". Here the emphasis is on the political culture, or character of the society. Men in cooperation and co-ordination provide the base for the growth of civil society. It is that form of society where the "real will" of individuals play the decisive role. According to Axel Hadenius and Fredrick Uggla, civil society manifests itself, when people combine themselves to pursue their common objectives. Mutual trust, inter-relatedness, concern for "other-selves", voluntarily organizing and sharing norms are the chief ingredients of civil society.

Civil society is purely an analytical concept. The institutions of civil society are, therefore associational and representative, in character. Civil society stands outside the arena of political system, free from state authorities. The state may be considered as the product of civil society. For instance, Gramsci the Italian theorist has conceived the state as the "political constitution of civil society". But the essence of civil society lies in its autonomy from the state. The relationship between civil society and the state is of mutual nature. The functioning of civil organisations and associations depends upon their recognisation by the state. The state, for its part, also needs civil society in order to attain its goal. According to Robert Putnam "...joint efforts on the part of civil society and the state may offer the most efficient way of carrying out political reforms". At the same time, the state has the ability to strengthen civil society. According to Tocqueville, governmental bodies with a firm footing in the local community make an ideal breeding ground for democratic civil endeavours. The state cannot be abstracted from civil society and vice versa. Since the political actors basically belong to the civil society subsystem, they know the demands and the requirements of the people. But by the influence of power and money, they became fluid to the other causes. The sane society produces both the political actors and the civil society. It is only that the failure of one subsystem as an effect on the other thus relating to a particular effect.

Civil society is a modern phenomenon. Membership of civil Society is open to all and not based on inheritance. The concept of this society embraces an entire range of assumptions, values and institutions, namely, socio-political rights, democratic institutions, free associations etc.; which are essential pre-conditions of democracy. Civil society is conceptualized as space where human beings can pursue self-defined ends in an associational area of common projects. Human emancipation or promotion of human welfare constitutes the case of civil society's functioning, civil society trains men in the values of collective action. It is here, where individuals enter on their own into social relationship with each other. In turn, the civil association paves the way for political associations. The state, being the highest form of political associations, cannot be oppositional to the civil society. The term civil society has come to enjoy much intellectual currency. Precisely, we can therefore say that civil society combines in itself the social capital civic engagements and voluntary associations which aim at common benefits. The concept social capital refers to three features of social life—interpersonal trust; networks, and shared norms—that enable people to act together more effectively to pursue shared objectives. The central premise of social capital refers to the collective value of all "Social Networks" and the inclinations that arise these networks to do things for each other. To Putnam, social capital in short, refers to social connections and the attendant norms and trust. There is strong correlation between social trusts and civic engagements. Putnam, on the other hand, has conceived civic engagements, as people's connections with the life of their communities. We consider civic engagements as individual's activities aiming towards welfare of "other self", and not for his own self. In short, it is individual's concern for others. Voluntarily organizing for public good is the essence of social capital.

It is viewed that in India civil society is represented by these social groupings voluntarily formed, representing the interests of their associations. At the same time, the Indian social activists conceive society as a combination of protest movements posing challenges to arbitrary actions of the state. According to Monor, civil society has been conceptualized as a popular sphere against the centralizing tendencies of Indian state, which cultivates the soil for democracy. In short, civil society has been conceived as a non-state domain of challenge and protest. Civil society has to perform mainly two types of activities in a country. The first is the complementary role with that of government in ensuring that the policies and programmes of the government are carried out properly and that yield result that are expected. Secondly, they should take up the problems of the citizens with the administration and get it solved. It is rightly said that civil society works for empowering the people, for their increased participation in the process of administration, for enforcing accountability and transparency and for efficient production of goods and services. The devices used for this purpose should be within the framework of liberal democracy.

Agencies of Civil Society

1. Policy institution
2. Community-based organisations
3. Non-governmental organisations
4. Gender group
5. Environmental groups
6. Professional associations
7. Social and sports clubs, etc.

THEORIES OF CIVIL SOCIETY

Gramsci's Theory of Civil Society

Gramsci's theory of hegemony is tied to his conception of the capitalist state. Gramsci focused on the structure of domination in the culture of the capitalist society. Gramsci justified rules through force plus consent. According to Gramsci, the institutions of civil society—family, school, and church familiarize the citizens with the rules of behaviour and teach them to show natural respect to the authority of the ruling class. These structures lend legitimacy to the rule of the bourgeois class so that even injustice involved in this rule would carry the impression of justice. That is why these are called structure of legitimation. They enable the bourgeoisie society to function in such a manner that the ruling classes seem to be ruling with the consent of the people. When the power is apparently exercised with the consent of its subject, it is called hegemony. Gramsci divides state between 'political society', which is the arena of political institutions and legal constitutional control. Gramsci defines 'civil society', which is commonly seen as the 'private' or 'non-state' sphere, including the economy. Gramsci claims that under modern capitalism, the bourgeoisie can maintain its economic control by allowing certain demands made by trade unions and mass political parties within civil society to be met by the political sphere. The bourgeoisie engages in 'passive revolution' by going beyond its immediate economic interests and allowing the forms of its hegemony to change.

According to Gramsci, the bourgeoisie society consists of:

- Base (capitalist mode of production)
- Superstructure (Legal and political structure, religion, morals, etc.
- Structure of Domination (civil society, political society)
- Civil society consists the structure of domination and political society consists of structure of coercion. Gramsci points out that the structure of legitimation within the bourgeois society usually prevents any challenge to its authority. Bourgeois society largely depends on the efficiency of these structures for its stability. It is only when civil society fails to prevent dissent that political society is required to make use of its structures of coercion, including police, courts and prisons.

Hegel's Theory of Civil Society

Georg Wilhelm Friedrich Hegel, a German philosopher, made this distinction in his Elements of the Philosophy of Right. In this work, civil society (Hegel used the term "buergerliche Gesellschaft" though it is now referred to as Zivilgesellschaft in German to emphasize a more inclusive community) was a stage on the dialectical relationship between Hegel's perceived opposites, the macro-community of the state and the micro-community of the family. Hegel broke with this tradition by identifying civil society as pre-state society. Influenced by British writers Adam Smith and Adam Ferguson, Hegel accepted that prior to the state there was some natural order to social life within the sphere of mutual dependence known as the economy. Hegel used the term civil society to refer to this sphere of life, between the family and state, which brought individuals into relationships of cooperation with others on the basis of their own inclinations to work and live. For Hegel the state stood above civil society, ensuring that the negative aspects of its organization, such as pauperization, were eradicated.

Marx's Theory of Civil Society

In defining Civil Society, Marx has identified the study of bourgeois society. It became a description for all non-state aspects of society. Karl Marx brought the end of the first life of the idea of civil society, replacing it with the more politically charged term 'bourgeois society'. He was sure that civil society as Hegel defined it was where the real action was, but argued that civil society was so strongly shaped by class antagonism that it was more accurately described bourgeois. For the next century and a half, political philosophers and sociologists, both liberal and socialist, emphasized economic relations as the principle factor shaping society in general. It is no coincidence that the term civil society re-entered the vocabulary of political science through the struggles against those states that had repudiated its existence.

Marxism's denunciation of civil society as ideological mystification of the real social relations of exploitation was in a large measure responsible for the denial of any autonomous role for either law or society against the state in communist societies. The fact that Marx identified civil society as the place where the real action of history occurred did not prevent the state in communist societies from dominating civil society in the name of civil society's freedom. Soviet societies, characterized by what Feher, Heller and Markus called a 'dictatorship over needs' (1984), had denied society any autonomy from the party-state in the formation of opinions, needs, and so forth. Pushing back the state and establishing democracy became the project of social movements such as Poland's solidarity.

Almond, Sidney and Tocqueville's Theory of Civil Society

The relation between civil society and democracy has their root in early liberal writings like those of Tocqueville. They were developed in significant ways by 20th century theorists like Gabriel Almond and Sidney Verba, who identified the role of civil society in a democratic order as vital. The political scientists said that political element of many civil society organizations facilitates better awareness and a more informed citizenry. They can make better voting choices, participate in politics, and hold government more accountable as a result.

Robert Putnam's Theory of Civil Society

Putnam has questioned how democratic civil society actually is. The civil society actors have now obtained a remarkable amount of political power without anyone directly electing or appointing them. Robert Putnam has acknowledged that non-political organizations in civil society are vital for democracy. Putnam has put more emphasis on social capital to hold society together. Trust and shared values may be transferred into the political sphere to keep the society transparent. These core values facilitate an understanding of the interconnectedness of society. In 1995 he published *Bowling Alone: America's Declining Social Capital* in the Journal of Democracy. Some critics argued that Putnam was ignoring new organizations and forms of social capital; others argued that many of the included organizations were responsible for the suppression of civil rights movements and the reinforcement of anti-egalitarian social norms. Over the last decade and a half, the United States had seen an increase in bowlers but a decrease in bowling leagues. In 2000, he published *Bowling Alone: The Collapse and Revival of American Community*, a book-length expansion of the original argument, adding new evidence and answering many of his critics. Though he measured the decline of social capital with data of many varieties, his most striking point was that much traditional civic, social and fraternal organization— typified by bowling leagues—had undergone a massive decline in membership while the number of people bowling increased drastically.

Putnam makes a distinction between two kinds of social capital: bonding capital and bridging capital. Bonding occurs when you are socializing with people who are like you: same age, same race, same religion, and so on. But in order to create peaceful societies in a diverse multi-ethnic country, one needs to have a second kind of social capital: bridging. Bridging is what you do when you make friends with people who are not like you, like supporters from another football team. Putnam argues that those two kinds of social capital, bonding and bridging, do strengthen each other. Consequently, with the decline of the bonding capital mentioned above inevitably comes the decline of the bridging capital leading to greater ethnic tensions. In recent years, Professor Putnam has been engaged in a comprehensive study of the relationship between trust within communities and their ethnic diversity. His conclusion is based on Robert David Putnam (born 1941 in Rochester, New York) a political scientist and professor at Harvard University. Putnam developed the influential two-level game theory that assumes international agreements will only be successfully brokered if they also result in domestic benefits. His most famous (and controversial) work, *Bowling Alone*, argues that the United States has undergone an unprecedented collapse in civic, social, associational, and political life (social capital) since the 1960s, with serious negative consequences. Over 40 cases within the United States is that, other things being equal, more diversity in a community can mean less trust both between and within ethnic groups.

Major Works of Putnam

- *The Beliefs of Politicians: Ideology, Conflict, and Democracy in Britain and Italy* (1973).
- *The Comparative Study of Political Elites* (1976).
- *Bureaucrats and Politicians in Western Democracies* (with Joel D. Aberbach and Bert A. Rockman, 1981).
- *Hanging Together: Cooperation and Conflict in the Seven-Power Summits* (with Nicholas Bayne, 1984, revised 1987).
- *Making Democracy Work: Civic Traditions in Modern Italy* (with Robert Leonardi and Raffaella Nannetti, 1993).
- *Bowling Alone: The Collapse and Revival of American Community* (2000).

- *Democracies in Flux: The Evolution of Social Capital in Contemporary Society* (Edited by Robert D. Putnam), Oxford University Press, (2002).
- *Better Together: Restoring the American Community* (with Lewis M. Feldstein, 2003).

Michael Sandel (1953) Theory of Civil Society

Sandel is a contemporary political philosopher. Sandel subscribes to the theory of communitarianism (although he is uncomfortable with the label), and in this vein he is perhaps best known for his critique of John Rawls' *A Theory of Justice.* Rawls' argument depends on the assumption of the veil of ignorance, which allows us to become "unencumbered selves".

Fukuyama Theory of Civil Society

Fukuyama is best known as the author of *The End of History and the Last Man.* He said that the progression of human history as a struggle between ideologies is largely at an end, with the world settling on liberal democracy after the end of the Cold War and when the Berlin wall fell in 1989. In defining the concept of civil society, Fukuyama justified that human nature is governed by a desire for recognition. To him, civil society means the satisfaction of the need for recognition and it can provide the end point of history. Civil society explores where social norms come from and talks about how the current disruption, due to the shift from the manufacturing age to the information age.

Jiirgen Habermas Theory of Civil Society

Habermas is a German philosopher and sociologist in the tradition of critical theory and American pragmatism. His work focuses on the foundations of social theory and epistemology; the analysis of advanced capitalist industrial society and of democracy; the rule of law in a critical social-evolutionary context; and contemporary—especially German—politics. Habermas concept of civil society refers to the study of reason and emancipation of man. This theory of civil society advances the goals of human emancipation, while maintaining an inclusive Universalist moral framework. Habermas puts more emphasis on more humane, just, and egalitarian society through the realization of the human potential for reason, in part through discourse ethics.

Locke's Theory of Civil Society (Political or Civil Society)

John Locke (1632-1704) wrote his Second Treatise of Government early in the 1680s and published it in 1690. In it Locke proposed a social contract theory of government and argued against the idea of "divine right", which held that rulers had a legitimate claim on their office because they were God's emissaries on earth. Locke believed that government derived from an agreement between men to give up life in the state of nature in favour of life in a political or civil society. They set up political society in order to guarantee their natural rights: life, liberty, and estate (or property). Locke's emphasis on a social contract that protected natural rights shaped the views of the American revolutionaries. No man in civil society can be exempted from the laws of it. For if any man may do what he thinks fit and there be no appeal on earth for redress or security against any harm he shall do, I ask whether he be not perfectly still in the state of nature, and so can be no part or member of that civil society, unless any one will say the state of nature and civil society are one and the same thing, which he has never yet found any one so great a patron of anarchy as to affirm. For Locke, individuals are compelled to consent to community by natural law. Lockean natural law, still anchored in theism, regulates both individual conscience and society. Thus the concept of civil society is one born out of a peculiar blend of reason and revelation.

Seligman's Theory of Civil Society

In Seligman's view, then, the concept of civil society is a product of secularization. It is the attempt to provide a moral self-representation of society about a transcendent, or at least a theistic, reference that is more than peripheral. Seligman, a Weberian-oriented sociologist, simply assumes a straight-line secularization theory and focuses on the internal problem of the "civil society tradition", namely, once society is held to derive from the choice of individual moral agents, sociality per se is secondary, epiphenomenal. Autonomy and solidarity as ideals are mutually exclusive.

Seligman explores this problem in a most insightful way. He asks why individuals should trust in or sacrifice for their society. In what ways do we reconcile our private interests with the demands of social existence? Many of the distinctive problems of modern societies, he tells us, e.g. the expansion of welfare state entitlements versus traditional free market liberalism, reflect this fundamental tension between a desire for a common good and the profound individualism of our culture.

John Keane's Theory of Civil Society

John Keane has contributed significantly to the study of civil society. His latest book, *Global Civil Society* aims to clarify the concept of a global civil society and to contribute his own perspective on what is positive in the developments he outlines. Global civil society can only refer to non-state society, because there is no global state. He called it as 'a new cosmology', begins by outlining the emerging interest in studying a new socio-political environment: the global. From this emerging political landscape Keane discerns a set of relationships, institutions and processes that he names global civil society. He writes that global civil society properly refers to a dynamic non-governmental system of interconnected socio-economic institutions that straddle the whole earth, and that have complex effects that are felt in its four corners. These non-governmental institutions and actors tend to pluralize power and to problematize violence.

Reviving the idea of civil society in nation states reflected renewed interest in citizens' role in making society democratic, just and peaceful. Similarly, the developing literature on global civil society reflects the emergence both of efforts towards justice and democracy among people and peoples, and of social scientific interest in understanding the sources and nature of these efforts. To this end, Keane attempts to flesh out what kinds of relationships constitute global civil society—who makes the rules, which norms dominate, and what sorts of institutions and processes are operating. Keane takes on three tasks: 'defining the relationship between formal power and people; sorting out what institutions make up global civil society; and defining the values that characterize and give a coherence to its participants'.

Michael Edwards' Theory of Civil Society

Michael Edwards' slim volume Civil Society is less scholarly and pretentious yet more satisfying than Keane's. It is both about civil society and for civil society; Edwards surveys with economy some main approaches to civil society and concludes with Lenin's question 'What is to be done?' His main argument is that social equality underpins a healthy 'associational ecosystem'. He surveys various justifications of civil society, which he classifies as focusing on associational life, the public sphere, and the good society, usefully drawing out the main currents in the renewed American focus on civil society. The benefits of associational life, notably extolled by Robert Putnam, are often linked with the production of 'social capital'; trust, reciprocity, and civic mindedness. Edwards points out that although social capital usefully highlights the resources that community groups rely on, associations by themselves can accomplish relatively little.

Gramsci, Hegemony and Civil Society

Antonio Gramsci, an Italian (1891-1937), was a leading Marxist thinker. Like Althusser, he rejected economism, insisting on the independence of ideology from economic determinism. Gramsci also rejected crude materialism, offering a humanist version of Marxism which focused on human subjectivity. Gramsci used the term hegemony to denote the predominance of one social class over others (e.g. bourgeois hegemony). This represents not only political and economic control, but also the ability of the dominant class to project its own way of seeing the world so that those who are subordinated by it accept it as 'common sense' and 'natural' Commentators stress that this involves willing and active consent. Common sense, suggests Geoffrey Newell-Smith, is 'the way a subordinate class lives its subordination'.

However, unlike Althusser, Gramsci emphasizes struggle. He noted that "common sense is not something rigid and immobile, but is continually transforming itself". As Fiske puts it, "Consent must be constantly won and rewon, for people's material social experience constantly reminds them of the disadvantages of subordination and thus poses a threat to the dominant class.... Hegemony...posits a constant contradiction between ideology and the social experience of the subordinate that makes this interface into an inevitable site of ideological struggle". References to the mass media in terms of an ideological 'site of struggle' are recurrent in the commentaries of those influenced by this perspective. Gramsci's stance involved a rejection of economism since it saw a struggle for ideological hegemony as a primary factor in radical change.

Criticisms of Althusser's Theory

The rise of neo-Marxism in social science represented in part a reaction against 'functionalist' models of society. Functionalists seek to explain social institutions in terms of their cohesive functions within an inter-connected, socio-cultural system. Functionalism did not account for social conflict, whereas Marxism offered useful insights into class conflict. At the time of the European ascendancy of neo-Marxism in media theory (primarily in the 1970s and early 1980s), the main non-Marxist tradition was that of liberal pluralism (which had been the dominant perspective in the United States since the 1940s). As Gurevitch *et al.* put it:

Pluralists see society as a complex of competing groups and interests, none of them predominant all of the time. Media organizations are seen as bounded organizational systems, enjoying an important degree of autonomy from the state, political parties and institutionalized pressure groups. Control of the media is said to be in the hands of an autonomous managerial elite who allows a considerable degree of flexibility to media professionals. A basic symmetry is seen to exist between media institutions and their audiences, since in McQuail's words the 'relationship is generally entered into voluntarily and on apparently equal terms'...and audiences are seen as capable of manipulating the media in an infinite variety of ways according to their prior needs and dispositions, and as having access to what Halloran calls 'the plural values of society' enabling them to 'conform, accommodate, challenge or reject'.

In contrast, they continue: Marxists view capitalist society as being one of class domination; the media are seen as part of an ideological arena in which various class views are fought out, although within the context of the dominance of certain classes; ultimate control is increasingly concentrated in monopoly capital; media professionals, while enjoying the illusion of autonomy, are socialized into and internalize the norms of the dominant culture; the media taken as a whole, relay interpretive frameworks consonant with the interests of the dominant classes, and media audiences, while sometimes negotiating and contesting these frameworks, lack ready access to alternative meaning systems that would enable them to reject the definitions offered by the media in favour of consistently oppositional definitions.

Base and Superstructure

Economism (also called 'vulgar Marxism') is a key feature of 'classical Marxism' (orthodox or fundamentalist Marxism). In economism, the economic base of society is seen as determining everything else in the superstructure, including social, political and intellectual consciousness. Theories positing economic relations as the basic cause of social phenomena are also called materialist theories, and Marx's version is also known as 'historical materialism'. Economism is related to technological determinism. Marx is often interpreted as a technological determinist on the basis of such isolated quotations as: 'The windmill gives you society with the feudal lord: the steam-mill, society with the industrial capitalist'.

Mass media research in this fundamentalist tradition interprets the 'culture industries' in terms of their economic determination. According to this view, 'the contents of the media and the meanings carried by their messages are primarily determined by the economic base of the organizations in which they are produced'. Consequently, 'commercial media organizations must cater to the needs of advertisers and produce audience-maximizing products (hence the heavy doses of sex-and-violence content) while those media institutions whose revenues are controlled by the dominant political institutions or by the state gravitate towards a middle ground, or towards the heartland of the prevailing consensus'. Marxists of the 'political economy' variety (such as Graham Murdock) still see ideology as subordinate to the economic base. The base/superstructure model as applied to the mass media is associated with a concern with the ownership and control of the media.

Critics regard economism as reductionist, failing to account for diversity. Althusserian Marxists propose 'the relative autonomy of the superstructure with respect to the base and the reciprocal action of the superstructure on the base'. According to this view ideological practices such as the mass media are relatively autonomous from economic determination. The notion of 'relative autonomy' has been subject to criticism. Under the influence of Althusser, Stuart Hall and other 'culturalist' Marxists reject the base/superstructure formulation, argüing that there is a dialectic between what Marx termed 'social being 'and 'social consciousness's. The Frankfurt School of 'critical theory' was regarded by orthodox Marxists as 'revisionist' partly because it criticized economism and crude materialism, and partly because of its eclecticism. In media theory, it is important for offering the first Marxist attempt to theorize about the media. However, it provided no real way forward for the study of the mass media. The most notable theorists connected with the Frankfurt School were Theodor Adorno, Herbert Marcuse and Max Horkheimer—all committed Marxists—who were associated with the Institute for Social Research, which was founded in Frankfurt in 1923 but shifted in 1933 to New York. The Frankfurt School was influenced by predominantly conservative notions of 'mass society', though it gave this perspective a leftist slant. The so-called 'father of the New Left', Herbert Marcuse, in *One-Dimensional Man* (1972), presented the media very pessimistically as an irresistible force:

The means of communication the irresistible output of the entertainment and information industry carry with them prescribed attitudes and habits, certain intellectual and emotional reactions which bind the consumers...to the producers and, through the latter to the whole social system. The products indoctrinate and manipulate; they promote a false consciousness which is immune against its falsehood. Thus emerges a pattern of one-dimensional thought and behaviour. For Marcuse, the mass media defined the terms in which we may think about the world. The Frankfurt School in general was profoundly pessimistic about the mass media. As Janet Woollacott puts it, their work 'gives to the mass media and the culture industry a role of ideological dominance which destroys both bourgeois individualism and the revolutionary potential of the working class'. Theodor Adorno and Max Horkheimer coined the phrase 'the culture industry', referring to the collective operations of the media. The Frankfurt School's focus on ideology helped to undermine economism, but it was criticized by other Marxists for elitism and for Hegelian idealism.

Althusser

Louis Althusser (b. 1918) was a French Marxist philosopher who saw Marxism as a science. His work is in the structuralist tradition. One feature of Althusserian Marxism is a rejection of Marx's Hegelian essentialism. Essentialism is a reduction of things to a single principle or essence. Althusser rejected two kinds of Marxist essentialism: economism (economic determinism) and humanism (in which social developments were seen as expressive of a pre-given human nature). So Althusserian Marxism is anti-economist and anti-humanist. In rejecting economism he saw ideology as itself a determining force shaping consciousness, embodied in the material signifying practices of 'ideological state apparatuses', and enjoying 'relative autonomy'. Althusser's work represents a move away from a preoccupation with economic determination. Ideology, for Althusser 'represents the imaginary relationship of individuals to their real conditions of existence' (cited in Stevenson 1995: 37). Ideology transforms human beings into subjects, leading them to see themselves as self-determining agents when they are in fact shaped by ideological processes.

Tony Bennett notes that since he represents all ideological forms as contributing to the reproduction of the existing system, Althusser comes 'dangerously close to functionalism', representing capitalist society as monolithic, and failing to allow for internal conflict (Bennett 1982: 53). Stuart Hall adds that in Althusser's theory it is difficult 'to discern how anything but the "dominant ideology" could ever be reproduced in discourse' (Hall 1982: 78). In Althusserian theory mass media texts 'interpellate the subject' whereas many current media theorists argue that the subject projects meaning onto the media texts. For the notion of a 'struggle over meaning' one must turn to Volosinov and Gramsci. Althusser's influence has been held responsible by some critics for leading some of his followers into purely formalist readings of the signifying systems of mass media forms, neglecting their modes of production and reception. However, Althusser is 'the central conduit through which developments in structuralism and semiotics have both entered into and lastingly altered Marxist approaches to the media'.

Limitations of Marxist Analysis

Critics argue that Marxism is just another ideology. Some Marxists are accused of being 'too doctrinaire'. Fundamentalist Marxism is crudely deterministic, and also reductionist in its 'materialism', allowing little scope for human agency and subjectivity. Marxism is often seen as 'grand theory', eschewing empirical research. However, research in the Marxist 'political economy' tradition in particular does employ empirical methods. And the analysis of media representations does include close studies of particular texts.

The orthodox Marxist notion of 'false consciousness' misleadingly suggests the existence of a reality 'undistorted' by mediation. The associated notion that such consciousness is irresistibly induced in mass audiences does not allow for oppositional readings. Marxist perspectives should not lead us to ignore the various ways in which audiences use the mass media. Neo-Marxist stances have in fact sought to avoid these pitfalls. The primary Marxist emphasis on class needs to be related to other divisions, such as gender and ethnicity.

Unlike many approaches to the mass media Marxism acknowledges the importance of explicit theory. Marxist 'critical theory' exposes the myth of 'value-free' social science. Marxist perspectives draw our attention to the issue of political and economic interests in the mass media and highlight social inequalities in media representations. Marxism helps to situate media texts within the larger social formation. Its focus on the nature of ideology helps us to deconstruct taken-for-granted values. Ideological analysis helps us to expose whose reality we are being offered in a media text. Whilst Althusserian Marxism helps to undermine the myth of the autonomous individual, other neo-Marxist stances see the mass media as a 'site of struggle' for ideological meaning, opening up the possibility of oppositional readings.

Marxist theory emphasizes the importance of social class in relation to both media ownership and audience interpretation of media texts: this remains an important factor in media analysis. Whilst content analysis and semiotics may shed light on media content, marxist theory highlights the material conditions of media production and reception. 'Critical political economists' study the ownership and control of the media and the influence of media ownership on media content cannot be ignored. It also remains important to consider such issues as differential access and modes of interpretation which are shaped by socio-economic groupings. Marxist media research includes the analysis of representation in the mass media (e.g., political coverage or social groups) in order to reveal underlying ideologies. We still need such analyses: however oppositional it may sometimes be, audience interpretation continues to operate in relation to such content. Because of the distribution of power in society, some versions of reality have more influence than others.

Conclusion

Natural law philosophers (such as Hobbes, Locke, Rousseau and Kant) used the term civil society as an antonym for natural society. In natural society each person had only the rights they could defend for themselves. Civil society, by contrast, equipped each person with such rights as the state defended for them. For Kant, civil society was a higher form of social life because it transformed what each had only by force into theirs by right.

In this phase of its life, civil society was synonymous with the existence of a state. A natural law approach like this defines civil society by the existence of laws that make natural rights into positive rights; rights protected by laws backed by a state. However, no one but the most hardened libertarian accepts that civil society is defined purely by the existence of basic laws. This juridical approach emphasizes the important role law plays in civil society, but ignores the equally significant role of an autonomous social space where citizens can form opinions dealing with important social questions. Renewed interest in civil society reflects a renewed interest in the role that individuals can play collectively in linking law and society together, or, in other words, making democracy work through the efforts of citizens themselves.

9

Citizenship

Citizenship is membership in a political community (originally a city or town but now usually a country) and carries with it rights to political participation; a person having such membership is a citizen. The idea of citizenship in its early form is found in the ancient Greek and Roman state system. In a modern democratic state all members of a community are regarded as its citizens. But in Ancient Greeks very few inhabitants enjoyed the status of freemen who were treated as full citizens. These citizens were equal among themselves as regards their rights. There was no discrimination between the rich and the poor among freemen. The concept was developed by Aristotle in his books *Politics*. Aristotle regarded citizenship as a privilege of the ruling class. After the decline of the Greek city-states a new definition of citizenship was evolved in the Roman Empire. Initially, few citizens were confined to the power holder. Later it was extended to the ordinary people and those vanquished in war.

Thus diverse types of people came within the ambit of citizenship. During the medieval period, political authority was eclipsed by ecclesiastical authority. Temporal citizenship was no longer considered to be important. In the 15th century and 16th century with the advent of modern thought, the idea of citizenship again occupied the Centre stage in Italian republics; Machiavelli the famous Italian thinker gave a new lease of life to this idea. In 17th century in England James Harrington (1611-77) and John Milton redefined the idea. Harrington drew a picture of an ideal system of the future which would be an empire of the laws, not of men. The exponents of Glorious Revolution (1688) of England particularly popularized the idea of citizenship.

In the 18th century this idea became very popular during the days of American Revolution. The idea of citizenship reached its zenith with the French Revolution (1789) and the consequent Declaration of Rights of Man and Citizen. This declaration echoes the views of Jean Jacques Rousseau (1712-78). Rousseau in his Social Contract (1762) wrote that citizen is a free and autonomous person. In the 19th century the ascendancy of liberalism gave rise to market relations which promoted a new notion of citizenship. Now the idea of natural rights came to be regarded as the basis of citizenship. The idea of natural rights in this sense was advanced by John Locke in England. Locke had argued that the right to life, liberty and property was the mainstay of natural rights. The citizen set up a state for the protection of these rights.

DEFINITIONS OF CITIZENSHIP

Aristotle said that one who has the power to take part in the deliberative is a citizen of that state. Laski defines Citizenship as the contribution of one's "Instructed Judgment" to the public good. Barbalet defines citizenship is in the nature of a "Political Bond". Marshall defines citizenship as a status attached to full membership of a community, and those who possess this status, are equal with respect to the rights and duties associated with it (Citizenship and Social Class). Brogan defines that Citizenship has two aspects (1) every citizen has the right to be consulted in the conduct of political society and the duty to contribute something to the general consultation and (2) the "reverse: the citizen who has a right to be consulted, is bound by the results of that consultation". Bryan S. Turner said that citizenship in terms of three major dimensions. They are: "Civil Citizenship, Political Citizenship and Social Citizenship". Karl Marx said that the modern democratic citizenship is called "Bourgeois Citizenship". Anthony Giddens said that Citizenship and Democracy are associated with the expansion of state sovereignty. He puts forth the dialectics of control stating that the increase in sovereignty led to the increase in administrative power, which needed cooperation from the other sections of the society and hence citizenship was reciprocity between the rulers and the ruled. Giddens calls this as two-way expansion of power or dialectics of control. Green said that citizenship means positive freedom, the positive capacity of the individual to develop his personality in the social context. Bentham and Mill defines that the essence of citizenship lies in individual liberty, participation and just apportionment of property.

TYPES OF CITIZENSHIP

Naturalized Citizenship

In law, naturalization refers to an act whereby a person acquires a citizenship different from that person's citizenship at birth. Naturalization is most commonly associated with economic migrants or refugees who have immigrated to a country and resided there as aliens, and who have voluntarily and actively chosen to become citizens of that country after meeting specific requirements. However, naturalization that is at least passive and often not voluntary, can take place upon annexation or border adjustments between countries. Unless resolved by denaturalization or renunciation of citizenship, naturalization can lead to multiple citizenship. In general, basic requirements for naturalization are that the applicant hold a legal status as a full-time resident for a minimum period of time and that the applicant promise to obey and uphold that country's laws, to which an oath or pledge of allegiance is sometimes added. Some countries also require that a naturalized national must renounce any other citizenship that he currently holds, forbidding dual citizenship, but whether this renunciation actually causes loss of the person's original citizenship will again depend on the laws of the countries involved.

Multiple Citizenship

Multiple Citizenship, or multiple nationalities, is a status in which a person is concurrently regarded as a citizen under the laws of more than one state. Dual citizenship (being a citizen of two nations), or dual nationality, is by far the most common type of multiple citizenship, as nothing in international law prevents anyone from establishing citizenship in two countries. Multiple citizenships can be acquired because countries use different and not necessarily mutually exclusive criteria to bestow their citizenship. Some countries bestow citizenship automatically at birth to persons with a parent who is one of their nationals (jus sanguinis), or to persons born on their territory (jus soli), or through marriage to persons wedding their nationals. In addition, citizenship can be granted on request through naturalization.

Second-Class Citizenship

(i) Second class citizen is an informal term used to describe a person, being a member of a discriminated group, who is systematically discriminated against within a state or other political jurisdiction. The discrimination exists due to membership within the group despite the person being a citizen of that state.

(ii) While not necessarily slaves, outlaws or criminals, second-class citizens have limited legal rights, civil rights and economic opportunities, and are often subject to mistreatment or neglect at the hands of their putative superiors. Second-class citizenry is generally regarded as a violation of human rights.

Subnational Citizenship

Citizenship most usually relates to membership of the nation state, but the term can also apply at subnational level. Subnational entities may impose requirements, of residency or otherwise, which permit citizens to participate in the political life of that entity, or to enjoy benefits provided by the government of that entity. But in such cases, those eligible are also sometimes seen as "citizens" of the relevant state, province, or region. An example of this is how the fundamental basis of Swiss citizenship is citizenship of an individual commune, and thus of a canton and of the Confederation.

Honorary Citizenship

Some countries extend "honorary citizenship" to those whom they consider to be especially admirable or worthy of the distinction. By act of United States Congress and presidential assent, honorary United States citizenship has been awarded to only six individuals. Honorary Canadian citizenship requires the unanimous approval of parliament. The only three people have received honorary Canadian citizenship are Raoul Wallenberg posthumously in 1985, Nelson Mandela in 2001 and the 14th Dalai Lama, Tenzin Gyatso on June 22, 2006. In 2002, South Korea awarded honorary citizenship to Dutch football (soccer) coach Guus Hiddink who successfully and unexpectedly took the national team to the semi-finals of the 2002 FIFA World Cup. Honorary citizenship was also awarded to Hines Ward, a black Korean American football player, in 2006 for his efforts to minimize discrimination in Korea against half-Koreans. American actress Angelina Jolie received an honorary Cambodian citizenship in 2005 due to her humanitarian efforts.

RESPONSIBILITIES OF CITIZENSHIP

The duties of responsible citizenship include:

(i) Paying taxes

(ii) Serving in the country's armed forces when called upon

(iii) Obeying laws enacted by one's government

(iv) Demonstrating commitment and loyalty to the democratic political community and state

(v) Constructively criticizing the conditions of political and civic life

(vi) Participating to improve the quality of political and civic life

(vii) Respecting the rights of others

(viii) Defending one's own rights and the rights of others against those who would abuse them

(ix) Exercising one's rights.

CIVIL RIGHTS OF CITIZENSHIP

(i) Right to Property

(ii) Right to Family

(iii) Right to Work
(iv) Right to Religion
(v) Right to Education
(vi) Right to Form Association and Move about Freely
(vii) Right to Equality
(viii) Right to Life

THEORETICAL PERSPECTIVES OF CITIZENSHIP

In the contemporary political discourse, several theories have been advanced regarding the logical basis and the proper scope of citizenship. In this context, the five theories are very important and informative.

Liberal Theory of Citizenship

According to this theory civil rights constitute the foundation of citizenship. It is also described as evolutionary theory of citizenship. T.H. Marshall is regarded as the chief exponent of this theory. In his *Citizenship and Social Class* (1950) Marshall observed that citizenship prescribes equal rights and duties, liberties and constraints, powers and responsibilities for different individuals. Citing the example of Modern England, Marshall has shown that the idea of citizenship begins with the provision of civil rights, and proceeds further by giving rise to political and social rights respectively.

Libertarian Theory of Citizenship

This theory regards citizenship as a product of free choice and contract among individuals. It considers "market society" as a suitable model of civic life. Robert Nozick is the life exponent of this theory. In his *Anarchy State and Utopia* (1974) Nozick has observed that individuals resort to private activity, market exchange and voluntary association in order to realize their values, beliefs and preferences. Nozick likens the state to a large enterprise, and citizens as its customers or clients. Men hire protective institutions for the protection of their rights to property.

Communitarian Theory of Citizenship

As against the libertarian theory, the communitarian or "republican theory of citizenship" insists on a strong bond of affinity between individual and the state. The exponents of this theory include—Hannah Arendt (The Human Condition, 1958). Michael Walzer {Spheres of Justice, 1983) and Benjamin Barber (Strong Democracy, 1984). The main tenet of this theory is that a citizen should identify himself with the community of which he is a member, and take active part in its political life.

Marxist Theory of Citizenship

This theory treats the rights associated with citizenship as the product of class conflict. Anthony Giddens is the chief exponent of this theory. In his two important works *A Contemporary Critique of Historical Materialism* (1981) and *Profiles and Critiques of Social Theory* (1982), Giddens has contradicted Marshall's view in order to bring forth his own viewpoint. Marshall treats the development of citizenship as if it were something that unfolded in phases according to some inner logic within the modern world. Giddens finds that an oversimplification of the role of the state and politics, as if the whole process was supported and buttressed by the beneficent hand of the state. Giddens argues that the underprivileged have achieved their citizenship in substantial degree only through struggle; they succeeded to tilt the balance of power in their favor only during the times of war.

Pluralist Theory of Citizenship

Pluralist theory of citizenship treats the development of citizenship as a complex and multidimensional process. The theory is now in the process of formation. Davi Held in his *Political Theory and the Modern State*, 1989 has observed that from the ancient world to the present-day, citizenship has meant a reciprocal relationship between individual and community. Pluralist theory insists that on inquiring into all types of discrimination against people, whether on grounds of gender, race, religion, property, education, occupation or age. In contemporary world so many social movements have been launched against different types of social discrimination. These include feminist movement, black movement, religious movement, workers movement, children rights movement, Dalit movements, adivasi movements, and ecological movement among others. Pluralist theory recommends that the problem of citizenship should be analyzed in the context of all these movements.

In recent years, the debate over citizenship rights has expanded to recognize a variety of groups for the basic rights of women and ethnic minorities. New social movement is one of the trends over the debate of citizenship at the time of globalization. This is called cosmopolitan citizenship. Rights can be well documented as an identity of a citizen of a global community with the rise of nation-state, citizenship education is meant to foster a personal and perpetual relationship of allegiance between king and his subjects. The concept of citizenship includes not only civil and political dimensions but also a social component. The pursuit of equal membership in the new political set coloured the concept of citizenship. In a federal state, there should generally be "dual citizenship" or double citizenship for two sets of governments— the federal, central government on the one hand and governments for different units of the federation like state or provincial governments on the other. This dual citizenship is very clear in the USA. In Switzerland, a citizen is primarily a citizen of a canton and his cantonal citizenship automatically leads to acquisition of citizenship of Swiss Federal Republic. Though India is a federation, there is single citizenship in the country. This is done with the purpose of highlighting national integration and as an antidote to separatist tendencies. Successful working of democracy requires alert, intelligent and public spirited citizens. A good citizen must possess common sense and knowledge to understand the problems of social life and far-sightedness and acumen to solve them.

Aristotle's Theory of Citizenship

Aristotle states that "the politician and lawgiver is wholly occupied with the city-state, and the constitution is a certain way of organizing those who inhabit the city-state". His general theory of constitutions is set forth in *Politics III*. He begins with a definition of the citizen (polites), since the city-state is by nature a collective entity, a multitude of citizens. Citizens are distinguished from other inhabitants, such as resident aliens and slaves; and even children and seniors are not unqualified citizens (nor are most ordinary workers). After further analysis he defines the citizen as a person who has the right (exousia) to participate in deliberative or judicial office (1275b, 18-21). In Athens, for example, citizens had the right to attend the assembly, the council, and other bodies, or to sit on juries. The Athenian system differed from a modern representative democracy in that the citizens were more directly involved in governing. Although full citizenship tended to be restricted in the Greek city-states (with women, slaves, foreigners and some others excluded), the citizens were more deeply enfranchised than in modern representative democracies because they were more directly involved in governing. This is reflected in Aristotle's definition of the citizen (without qualification). Further, he defines the city-state (in the unqualified sense) as a multitude of such citizens which is adequate for a self-sufficient life (1275b, 20-21). It is largely coterminous with nationality, although it is possible to have a nationality without being a citizen (i.e., be legally subject to a state and entitled to its protection without having rights of political participation in it); it is also possible to have political rights without being a national of a state. Citizenship often also implies working towards the betterment of one's community through participation, volunteer work, and efforts to improve life for all citizens.

Roman Theory of Citizenship

The citizenship in ancient Greece and Rome, as well as in cities that practised citizenship in the Middle Ages, was very exclusive and inequality of status was widely accepted. Those who were citizens had a much higher status than those who could not obtain the status of a citizen, such as women, slaves or 'barbarians'. Women were considered not to be rationally capable of political participation for example (although some, most prominently Plato, disagreed). There were also other methods used to determine whether someone could be a citizen or not, at certain times this had to do with wealth (the amount of taxes one paid), political participation, heritage (both parents had to be born in the polis).

FIVE MODES OF ACQUIRING CITIZENSHIP

(i) By Birth: Born on the soil of India whose one or both parent is Indian citizen.

(ii) By Registration: Certain categories who can acquire Indian citizenship by registration, before the prescribed authority.

(iii) People of Indian origin.

(iv) Citizens of a country mentioned in the first schedule.

(v) Woman married to Indian citizen.

(vi) Minor children of Indian citizen.

(vii) By Descent: A person from outside India on or after January 16, 1950 shall be a citizen of India if his father is a citizen of India at the time of the person's birth.

(viii) By Naturalization: A foreigner can acquire citizenship on application for naturalization to government of India. A person acquiring citizenship by naturalization has to take an oath of allegiance by the Constitution of India.

(ix) By Incorporation of Territory: If any new territory becomes a part of India, the Government of India specifies the persons of that territory who shall be citizens of India.

TERMINATION

The three modes of losing citizenship are as follows:

(i) **Renunciation:** An Indian citizen may voluntarily renounce his Indian citizenship.

(ii) **Termination:** Termination of Indian citizenship automatically takes place if a person voluntarily acquires citizenship of some other country.

(iii) **Deprivation:** This is a compulsory termination of the citizenship obtained by Registration or Naturalization on charges of using fraudulent means to acquire the citizenship.

The Indian Constitution, though federal, provides for a single citizenship, namely, the citizenship of India.

Many countries have a law named Citizenship Act, to regulating the Citizenship.

There are following laws of that type (amongst others):

(i) The Bhutanese Citizenship Act 1985

(ii) The Bhutanese Citizenship Act 1958, repealed by the 1985 Act

(iii) The Canadian Citizenship Act 1946

(iv) The Ceylon Citizenship Act

(v) The Citizenship Act (Slovakia)

(vi) The Black Homeland Citizenship Act (South Africa)

(vii) The British Nationality and Citizenship Act 1948

(viii) In the United States:

- (a) The Child Citizenship Act of 2000
- (b) The Citizenship Reform Act of 2005

(ix) The Indian Citizenship Act of 1924.

CITIZENSHIP IN INDIA

Citizenship of India can be acquired by:

1. Birth
2. Descent
3. Registration
4. Naturalization
5. Incorporation of territory
6. Termination
7. Renunciation
8. Acquisition of another country
9. Deprivation

Citizenship by Birth

Every person born in India on or after the 26th January, 1950, is a citizen of India by birth except if at the time of his birth:

(a) his father possesses such immunity from suits and legal process as is accorded to an envoy of a foreign sovereign power accredited to the President of India and is not a citizen of India; or

(b) his father is an enemy alien and the birth occurs in a place than under occupation by the enemy.

From 1st July, 1987 i.e. the date of enforcement of the Citizenship (amendment) Act, 1986, (except as provided at 9a & 9b) above, every person born in India on or after 26th January, 1950 but before the commencement of the act and on or after such commencement and either of whose parents a citizen in India at the time of his birth, shall be citizen of India by birth:

Citizenship by Descent

A person born outside India-

(a) On or after 26th January, 1950, but before the commencement of the Citizenship (Amendment) act, 1992, shall be a citizen of India by descent if his father is a citizen of India at the time of his birth; or

(b) On or after such commencement, shall be a citizen of India by descent if either of his parents is a citizen of India at the time of his birth:

Provided further if either of the parents of such a person referred to in clause (b) was a citizen of India by descent only, that person is not to be a citizen of India by virtue of this section unless:

(a) his birth is registered at an Indian Consulate within one year of its occurrence or the commencement of the Citizenship (amendment) act, 1992, whichever is later, or, with the permission of the Central Government, after the expiry of the said period; or

(b) either of his parents is at the time of his birth, in service under a Government of India.

Citizenship by Registration

Subject to certain conditions and restrictions, the Central Government, in the Ministry of home Affairs, may, on application made in this behalf, register as a citizen of India any person who is not already such citizen and belongs to any of the following categories:

(a) Persons of Indian origin who are ordinarily resident in India and have been so resident for five years immediately before making an application for registration. Prior to the coming into force of the Citizenship (Amendment) Act, 1986 i.e. 1st July 1987, this period was six months.

(b) Persons of Indian origin who are ordinarily resident in any country or place outside undivided India;

(c) Persons who are or have been married to citizens of India and are ordinarily resident in India and have been so resident for five years immediately before making an application for registration. Prior to the Citizenship (amendment) act, 1986 the clause read "women who are or have been married to citizens of India"

(d) Minor children of persons who are citizens of India; and

(e) Persons of full age and capacity who are citizens of a country specified in the first Schedule of the citizenship Act, 1955 (appendix 14.I)

Citizenship by Naturalization

Where an application is made in the prescribed manner by any person of full age and capacity who is not a citizen of a country specified in the First Schedule 14.I for the grant of a certificate of a naturalization to him, the Central Government may, if satisfied that the applicant is qualified for naturalization under the provisions of the Third Schedule, grant to him a certificate of naturalization.

Provided that, if in the opinion of the Central Government, the applicant is a person who has rendered distinguished services to the cause of science, philosophy, art, literature, world peace or human progress generally, it may waive all or any of the conditions specified in the Third Schedule of Citizenship act, 1955.

The person to whom a certificate of naturalization is granted shall, on taking a oath of allegiance in the form specified in the Second Schedule, be a citizen of India by naturalization as from the date on which that certificate is granted.

Citizenship by Incorporation of Territory

If any territory becomes a part of India, the Central Government, may by orders notified in the Official Gazette, specify the persons who shall be citizens of India by reasons of their connection with that territory, and those persons shall be citizens of India as from the date to be specified in the order.

Termination

Citizenship is terminated either by renunciation or acquisition of citizenship of another country.

Renunciation of Citizenship

If any citizen of India of full age and capacity, who is also a citizen or national of another country, makes in the prescribed manner a declaration renouncing his Indian citizenship; the declaration shall be registered by the prescribed authority, and upon such registration, that person shall cease to be a citizen of India. Provided that if any such declaration is made during any war in which India may be engaged, registration thereof shall be withheld until the Central government otherwise directs.

Where a person ceases to be a citizen of India, every minor child of that person shall thereupon cease to be a citizen of India, provided that any such child may, within one year after attaining full age, make a declaration that he wishes to resume Indian citizenship and shall thereupon again become a citizen of India.

For the purpose of this section. Any woman who is, or has been, married shall be deemed to be of full age.

Acquisition of Citizenship of another Country

Any citizen of India who by naturalization, registration or otherwise voluntarily acquires, or has at any time between the 26th January 1950 and the commencement of this Act voluntarily acquired, the citizenship of another country, cease to be a citizen of India. However, this does not apply to a citizen of India, during any war in which India may be engaged, voluntarily acquires the citizenship of another country, until the Central Government otherwise directs.

If any question arises as to whether, when or how any person has acquired the citizenship of another country, it shall be determined by such authority, in such manner, and having regard to such rules of evidence, as may be prescribed in this behalf.

Deprivation

The Central government under section 10 of the Indian citizenship Act, 1955 deprives any citizen of Indian Citizenship if it is satisfied that-

(a) the registration or certificate of naturalization was obtained by means of fraud, false representation or concealment of any material fact; or

(b) that citizen has shown himself by act or speech to be disloyal or disaffected towards the Constitution of India as by law established; or

(c) that citizen has, during the war in which India may be engaged, unlawfully traded or communicated with an enemy or been engaged in or associated with, any business that was to his knowledge carried on in such manner as to assist any enemy in that war; or

(d) that citizen has, within five years after registration or naturalization, been sentenced in any country to imprisonment for a term of not less than two years; or

(e) That citizen has been ordinarily resident out of India for a continues period of seven years, and during that period, has neither been at any time a student of any educational institution in a country outside India or in the service of a Government of India or of an International organization of which India is a member, nor registered annually in the prescribed manner at an Indian consulate, his intention to retain his citizenship of India.

(f) The Central Government shall not deprive a person of citizenship unless it is satisfied that it is not conducive to the public good that person should continue to be a citizen of India.

CITIZENSHIP AMENDMENT ACT, 2003

The act has amended the Indian Citizenship Act, 1955 and provides for acquiring overseas citizenship of India to peoples of Indian origin (PIOs) in sixteen countries who have acquired citizenship in those countries. These countries include USA, UK, Canada, Australia, New Zealand, the Netherlands, France, Portugal and Italy. The Act defines overseas citizen of India as a person of Indian origin, being a citizen of a country specified in the act or was a citizen of India immediately before becoming citizen of a country specified in act and is registered as overseas citizen of India by union government.

Overseas Indian Citizens

(i) Entitled to carry Indian passport

(ii) No need for visa to enter India

(iii) His property rights and all his investments in India will enjoy the same legal protection which a citizen of India enjoys

(iv) He may be given special provisions regarding admissions in educational institutions in India

(v) No right to vote

(vi) No right to hold constitutional offices.

Jus Soli and Jus Sanguinis

Citizenship, which is explained above, is the political rights of an individual within a society. Thus, you can have a citizenship from one country and be a national of another country. One example might be as follows: A Cuban-American might be considered a national of Cuba due to his being born there, but he could also become an American citizen through naturalization. Nationality most often derives from place of birth (i.e. jus soli) and, in some cases, ethnicity (i.e. jus sanguinis). Citizenship derives from a legal relationship with a state. Nationality can be lost, as in denaturalization, and gained, as in naturalization.

10
Sovereignty

Sovereignty is the most important constituent element of a Modern State. It is this element which distinguishes the state from all other associations. We cannot think of any state without Sovereignty. It is the supreme power over citizens and associations. The concept of Sovereignty has been called the very basis of Modern Political Science. It is this concept which distinguishes state from other institutions and places a state over and above every other institution or association. But it has given rise to a lot of controversy and confusion. It is a term about which there exists confusion and contradiction of thought. In fact, the concept has been changing with the transformation of social, economic and intellectual forces. Sovereignty denotes the supreme power of the state. This rests with the person or persons and exercises the power and is called Sovereign. It is the essential element of a state. Any state which is internally and externally free is called a Sovereign state. Sovereignty is absolute, exclusive, universal, permanent, unalienable and indivisible.

Two Views on Nature of Sovereignty

Sovereignty is an essential element of state. It is an attribute that makes state the pre-eminent association of society. As C.L. Oyseau says, "Were the state deprived of it, it would no longer be a state and whoever had it would have the state in as much as he would have the sovereign authority (supreme power). For sovereignty is the form which causes the state to exist; indeed, the state and sovereignty in the concrete are synonymous. Sovereignty is the summit of authority, by means of which the state is created and maintained".[1] It manifests itself in the form of a law binding on all concerned individuals and their groups.

NATURE OF SOVEREIGNTY

1. *The Traditional view.* It holds that the state is an absolute and morally supreme organisation endowed with a coercive power for assuring the realisation of the ideal of peace and security. This is the very *raison deter* of a political organisation. Hence, the state can legitimately claim total allegiance of man to its authority issuing in the forms of law. It may punish those who violate its commands being its 'will' in the concrete form. The traditional view is called 'monism', because it regards sovereignty as absolute, unlimited and indivisible.

2. *Pluralist view.* Opposed to monism the 'pluralists' seek to justify the limited and divisible nature of sovereignty. They attack the doctrine of an absolute state. They contend that there "are other essential associations on parity with the state. Man's social nature, as they maintain, finds expression in numerous groupings, pursuing various ends — religious, social, economic, professional, and political; no one of the groups is superior, morally or practically, to the others".[2]

Thus sovereignty is an essential attribute of state. It is the only element that distinguishes state from any other association like a family or a school, or from a whole set of associations and relations like a society or a nation. According to Prof. C.H. Mcllwain, sovereignty "is the central formula under which we may try to rationalise the complicated facts of our modern political life".[3] It finds its place in the supremacy of the will and power of the state. As Garner points out "in every fully independent state there is some person, assembly or group (e.g., the electorate) who or which has the supreme power of formulating in terms of law, and of executing the collective will; that is, the final power to command and enforce obedience to its authority. Other associations have collective wills, and may formulate opinions, but it is the peculiar characteristic of the state that its will alone dominates and over-rides in the event of conflict all other wills, whether of persons or of associations. To it all other wills are potentially subject. The will of the state, once declared, represents the last word regarding the matter upon which it has made a decision".[4]

THE MEANING OF SOVEREIGNTY

The sixteenth-century French political thinker, Jean Bodin (1530- 96) was the father of the modern theory of sovereignty. Published in Paris in 1576 his *De la Republique* contained the first systematic presentation of his theory. Sovereignty, defined Bodin, is "the supreme power of the state over citizens and subjects, unrestrained by law".[5] Thus sovereignty was identified with royal absolutism. The power of the sovereign monarch was absolute and unlimited, unrestrained by any human authority. It was equipped to resist the Universalist claims of the papacy and the Empire. The earlier writers— Bodin, Hobbes, Locke, Rousseau and modern political scientists—Jellinek, Duguit, Kelsen, and Laski interpreted sovereignty in varying terms. During the modern period, it has frequently changed its content, its laws, and even its functions.[6] It has given rise to the concept of "popular sovereignty." It has been regarded as a major stumbling block to hopes and plans for supranational organisation and cooperation. "Few political conceptions," observed Professor Mcllwain, "have been the subjects of so much discussion amongst us in the last hundred years".[7] "No word in political science," declared Professor Coker, "is used with a greater variety and meanings".[8] Some political scientists contend that the concept is obsolete, or even dangerous. Sovereignty is a concept of modern political theory. The Greeks had no idea of this term. We may take note of the fact that Aristotle used the term 'supreme power' of the state in different sense. During middle ages the jurists, the theologians and other writers used terms like *summa potestas* (highest power of the state) or *plenitudopotestatis* (supreme authority of the state) in a sense different from what we mean now by the term sovereignty.

DEFINITIONS OF SOVEREIGNTY

1. **Grotius.** Sovereignty is the supreme political power vested in him whose acts are not subject to any other and whose will cannot be over-ridden.

2. **Blackstone.** Sovereignty is the supreme, irresistible, absolute, uncontrolled authority in which the highest legal power of the state resides.
3. **Jellinek.** Sovereignty is that characteristic of the state by virtue of which it cannot be legally bound except by its own will or limited by any other power than itself.
4. **Pollock.** Sovereignty is that power which is neither temporary not delegated, not subject to particular rules, which it cannot alter, nor answerable to any other power on earth.
5. **Wilson.** Sovereignty is the daily operative power of framing and giving efficacy to the laws.
6. **Willoughby.** Sovereignty is the supreme will of the state.
7. **Duguit.** Sovereignty is the commanding power of the state, it is the will of the nation organised in state; it is the right to give unconditional order to all individuals in the territory of the state.
8. **Burgess.** Sovereignty is the original, absolute and unlimited power over individual subjects and associations of subjects.
9. **Laski.** The sovereignty of the state issues orders to all men and all associations within its area; it receives order from none of them. It will is subject to no legal limitations of any kind. What it proposes is right by mere announcement of intention.
10. **Jenks.** Sovereignty is an authority which, in the last resort, controls absolutely and beyond appeal the actions of every individual member of the community.
11. **Carre de Malberg.** Sovereignty is not power but rather a quality; it is the supreme characteristic of a power—supreme in the sense that this power admits no other above it and no other competes with it.
12. **Donald F. Russell.** Sovereignty is the strongest power and supreme authority within a state, which is

unlimited by law or anything else, since otherwise it would neither be strongest nor supreme.

13. **Oppenheim.** Sovereignty is supreme authority, an authority which is independent of any earthly authority.
14. **Kelsen.** In its original and only specific meaning, sovereignty means supreme authority.

DIMENSIONS OF SOVEREIGNTY

1. Internal dimensions. In the internal sphere the idea of sovereignty means that the state has highest authority within the area under its control. All people and their associations are under the control of the state. The state has the power to make and enforce a law throughout its territory. State is the final power to command and enforce obedience. State is subject to no legal limitations. As Gettell says: "Sovereignty, properly speaking, deals with the internal relations of a state to its inhabitants; it is a term of constitutional law rather than of international law. It is a legal concept and deals with positive law only. It would be conducive to clearness of thought and would avert much controversy if the term 'sovereignty' were applied only to what is usually called internal sovereignty and the term 'independence' were used for what is sometimes called external sovereignty".[9]

2. **External dimensions.** In external sphere the idea of sovereignty implies freedom of state from any alien subjection. A dependent people cannot be called a state. They live and have to act according to the will of another state. However, if in pursuance of some international treaty or agreement a state accepts limitations on its freedom of action, it does not amount to the loss or destruction of its sovereignty, it is a self-imposed limitation. For example, the association of a sovereign state with the Commonwealth of Nations or with the United Nations. In fact, the external aspect of sovereignty is an extension of its internal aspect in the international sphere. In the words of Le Fur "it is only an abbreviated expression for designating the totality of rights by which internal sovereignty manifests itself vis-a-vis foreign states".

The above mentioned two aspects of sovereignty should not be distinguished too much. Both these are two sides of the same attribute. Sovereignty has its expression in the form of a 'command' given by the state that is binding on all concerned with it. According to Giddings, "In all the dictionaries there is no other word that has more disastrously been conjured with by the metaphysical juggler.... Jurists and political theorists, losing sight of concrete fact, gave their minds to abstractions. And sovereignty became for political science a thing that never was on sea or land".[10] It issues forth in the form of the law of the state. Thus, from the legal standpoint, "the state is a total order and the only total order precisely because the state and the law are identified".[11]

ESSENTIAL CHARACTERISTICS OF SOVEREIGNTY

1. Universality. The power of the state is all-comprehensive. It covers all people and their associations living under the area of its control. It is co-extensive in its operation with the jurisdiction of the state. It comprehends within its scope all powers and things within its territory, except the embassies, consulates and legations where the law of the foreign country is applied. Even that takes place according to the will of the state. The state accepts some principles of international law for manifesting its commitment to the behaviour of the civilised nations of the world. It shows the quality of exclusiveness. It implies the quality by virtue of which there "can be one but supreme power in the state, legally entitled to the obedience of the inhabitants. To hold otherwise would be to deny the principle of the unity of the state and to admit the possibility of an imperium in *imperio* (state within a state)".[12]

2. Absoluteness. The authority of the state is supreme as well as absolute. It knows no limits on the formulation, expression and realisation of its will. The state may make and enforce any law and it is binding on all concerned. There can be no other authority to revoke or rescind the law of the state. However, a state may deny to itself some area of action by the logic of self-imposed limitations as specified in its constitution or in the text of some international treaty or convention. Sir

Henry Maine refers to social customs and traditions as important limiting factors on the power of the sovereign. Laski says that in purely juristic terms this implies that, in practice, legally unlimited power "turns out to be power exercised under condition fairly well-known to each generation".[13]

3. Permanence. Sovereignty is the permanent quality of the state. The holder of sovereignty may die, but the power of the state survives. It is passed on to his successor. A state may lose its sovereignty only when it is conquered by some other state and converted into a colony or a dependency. In the national anthem of English people 'God save the King', the word 'king' signifies both the head of the state and the immortal authority as supreme power of the state. The phrase, 'King is dead, long live the King', implies that "sovereignty does not cease with the death or temporary dispossession of a particular bearer on the reorganisation of the state, but shifts immediately to a new bearer, as the Centre of gravity shifts from one part of a physical body to another when it undergoes external change."[14]

4. Inalienability. Sovereignty cannot be alienated. It is the very essence of the personality of the state. When a sovereign dies, his office is given to his successor. It is change in the government and not an abdication or surrender of sovereignty. However, a state may cede away a part of its territory to another state by some voluntary or involuntary agreement. This is not the surrender of its whole sovereignty. Lieber points out that sovereignty can no more be alienated than a tree can alienate its right to sprout, or a man can transfer his life or personality to another without self-destruction.[15] Thus, by the quality of inalienability is meant that attribute of the state by virtue of which it cannot cede away any of its essential elements without self-destruction".[16]

5. Indivisibility. Then, the sovereign power of the state is indivisible. The will the state cannot be divided into many wills. Maintaining this view Hobbes, Rousseau, Hegel and Austin are called monists. As Calhoun says that "sovereignty is a whole thing, to divide it is to destroy it. It is the supreme power in a state, and we might just as well speak of half a square, or half a triangle, as of half a sovereignty".[17] A federal system is not based on the division of sovereignty. In it the powers of the government are divided between a central (national or federal) government on the one hand and provincial (regional or constituent) governments on the other. Thus, a federal system stands on the principle of the distribution of governmental powers and not that of sovereignty of the state. As Gettell says: "What is divided in a federal system is not sovereignty which resides as a unit in the state as a whole, but the exercise of its various powers, which are distributed in accordance with a constitutional system among various governmental organs".[18] To sum up, sovereignty is the exclusive, all-comprehensive or universal, inalienable, permanent and indivisible power of the state.

KINDS OF SOVEREIGNTY

1. Nominal and real sovereignty. These may be distinguished as follows: A nominal or titular sovereign is one whose authority is in name only; a real sovereign is one who actually uses his powers. The English monarch is the best example of a titular sovereign who reigns but does not govern. The real exercise of powers is vested in the ministers under the Prime Minister, who are collectively responsible to the Parliament. Hence, it is said that 'king can do no wrong'. The President of India also belongs to this category. But the Presidents of the United States and France belong to the category of a real sovereign. They exercise the power of the state according to their best judgment. They may be held accountable for any wrong entailing from an act of their commission or omission.

2. Legal and political sovereignty. A legal sovereign has the highest power of making and enforcing a law. A law made by him is binding on all concerned people and parties. It may be changed or repealed by the same authority. The British Parliament may make any law as per its best judgments. It is omnipotent in that it "can adjudge an infant of full age; it may attain a man of treason after death; it may legitimise an illegitimate child, or, if it sees fit, make a man judge in his own case".[19] But, the voters can make and unmake a parliament. The members of the parliament cannot make a law that is not acceptable to the voters. If it happens, the voters may rise in revolt and thereby change their parliament. Thus political sovereignty lies behind legal sovereignty. According to Gilchrist, "political sovereignty is the sum-total of influences in a state which lie behind the law."[20] However, the idea of political sovereignty is a fiction and a matter of confusion and controversy. While the will of the legislators may be manifest through their resolution in the form of a law, the will of the electorate cannot be so ascertainable. So Gettell remarks that "any attempt to find a political sovereign at the back of a legal sovereign destroys the value of the entire concept and reduces sovereignty to a mere catalogue of influences".[21]

3. De jure and de facto sovereignty. A de jure (legal) sovereign is one who occupies his office according to the well-established laws and practices of his state. By virtue of these he has the authority to issue commands and secure their obedience by the persons concerned. His occupation of the office and exercise of all power rests on the authority of the law of the land. But a de facto (factual) sovereign occupies the highest office of the state in an illegal or unconstitutional manner and makes use of force his will. As Bryce says: "The persons or body of persons who can make his or their will prevail whether with the law or against the law, he (or they) is (or are) the de facto ruler (or rulers), the person to whom obedience is actually paid."[22] In England, Cromwell became the de facto ruler after the execution of King Charles I and dissolution of the Long Parliament in 1649. In France, Napoleon became the de facto ruler after overthrowing the Directory in 1796. In 1958, Ayub Khan became the de facto sovereign of Pakistan after wresting power from President Iskander Mirza. However, the distinction of de jure and de facto disappears when the deposed sovereign gets back his power. For example, in 1945 the Emperor Haile Selaisse of Ethiopia who had taken asylum in England in 1936, returned to his country and once again became the Emperor after the defeat of Italy. The distinction also disappears when the de facto ruler legitimises his authority by changing the constitutional law of the land as was done by President Daoud in Afghanistan and by Khomeini in Iran after overthrowing the system of monarchy in their respective countries. Garner well says: "On account of the manifest advantages which flow from the exercise of power resting on strict legal right rather than upon physical force, the new sovereign sometimes has his de facto claim converted into a legal right by election or ratification".[23]

4. Popular sovereignty. Implying the highest power of the people it constitutes the foundation of a democratic order. In ancient times the Romans believed that the authority of the commonwealth was derived from the corporate power of the people. Later, in medieval period it was reiterated by the precursors of the conciliar movement like William of Ockam and Marsiglio of Padua. Rousseau of France idealised the theory of social contract by holding that the authority of the state was based on the 'general will' of the people. Thomas Jefferson harped on the theme of the highest authority of the people. Today, this idea has become an integral part of democratic theory, though in actual practice it assumes the shape of political sovereignty. As Garner says, "Unorganised public opinion, however powerful, is not sovereignty unless it is clothed in legal form, no more so than the informal or unofficial resolutions of the members of a legislative body in law. The sovereignty of the people, therefore, can mean nothing more than the power of the majority of the electorate, in a country where a system of approximate universal suffrage prevails, acting through legally established channels, to express their will and to make it prevail".[24]

AUSTIN'S INTERPRETATION OF SOVEREIGNTY

The best exposition of the idea of sovereignty is informed in its legal or juristic form. The will of the state has its best manifestation in the law of the state that has a binding character. Hence, the study of sovereignty from a strictly legal point of view, as given by Hobbes and Bentham, is important. However, the best exposition of this term is furnished by an English jurist John Austin (1790-1859). In his work *The Province of Jurisprudence Determined* (1832) Austin defined this term in these words: "If a determinate human superior, not in the habit of obedience to a like superior, receives habitual obedience from the bulk of a given society, that determinate human superior is the sovereign in that society and that society (including the superior) is a society political and independent". Stating Austin's view Henry Sidgwick wrote, "Positive law of any state is a general command to do or abstain from certain acts which is issued directly or indirectly by the sovereign of the state to a person or persons subject to his authority; the sovereign being that determinate person, or body of persons combined in a certain manner that the bulk of the members of the state habitually obey, provided that he or it does not habitually obey anyone else. It is implied in the conception of sovereign that the community, that has a sovereign, is independent in the sense that its government does not habitually obey a foreign power, and orderly in the sense that the bulk of the community habitually obeys the laws".

"From this definition together with the assumption that facts exist corresponding to the definition, two important consequences are inferred:

(a) The power of the sovereign cannot be legally limited —for, obviously, the sovereign cannot be coerced to act in a certain way by any command of his own;

(b) Sovereignty cannot, strictly speaking, be legally divided between two or more persons, or bodies of persons acting separately, because any such persons or bodies of persons must have ex hypothesis powers legally limited in certain directions—these are certain things which each of them is by law prevented from doing; but if so, they are in habitual obedience to the authority that laid down the law, and it is this latter that is the real sovereign. For example, in a federal state, such as the USA, sovereignty, strictly speaking, does not belong to the Central Government nor to the separate governments of the federated states, but to the body, whatever it may be, that is recognised as having authority to alter the conditions of federation".[25]

Nature of Sovereignty

(1) ***Supreme and absolute power.*** In every independent political community or state, there is a supreme and

absolute power in the hands of some person or persons (institution) whose will is the law of the state and, as such, is binding on all concerned persons and their associations.

(2) ***The sovereign is a determinate person.*** The highest authority of the state is vested in the hands of some person or persons who may be identified and who may exercise it as per their best judgment. They may formulate, express and realise their will. Thus, sovereignty can lie only in the legal form. Political sovereignty (supreme power of the electorate), or popular sovereignty (supreme power of the electorate) is a fiction. The vast electorate or the vast multitude of people cannot be identified with the sovereign of a state. They cannot formulate and express their resolve in the form of a law. Not natural or divine law but human laws may be the proper subject of study.

(3) ***Indivisibility.*** The sovereignty is indivisible, because sovereign does not obey any other authority. The will of the sovereign is supreme over all persons and their associations living in the state. He is under nobody's control or subjection. The laws emanating from the authority of the state are like commands that must be obeyed so as to avoid the agony of suitable punishment.

(4) ***Habitual obedience.*** The sovereign receives habitual obedience from the bulk of a given community. This obedience must be a matter of habit and not merely of an occasional ritual. It must be regular, undisturbed and continuous. However, society as a whole may not render such obedience. In every society there may be a small section of the dissenters. It is enough that obedience comes from the bulk of the major part of the community.

(5) ***Command is the essence of law.*** Whatever the sovereign wills is law. Failure to do so invites punishment. While the law of the state has a mandatory character, a usage and a custom are

volitional. While obedience to law is not a matter of volition, the people may or may not observe their customs.

Juristic Sovereignty

The argument of Austin has a juristic complexion. It expressed sovereignty in a juristic form. The sovereign power of a state manifests itself in the form of a law that is a command to be obeyed by the persons and groups concerned. As Austin says: "Every positive law, or every law, simply and strictly so called, is set by a sovereign person or a sovereign body of persons to a member or members of the independent political society wherein that person or body of persons is sovereign or supreme". He further says: "To that determinate superior the other members of the society are dependent. The position of its other members towards that determinate superior is a state of subjection or a state of dependence. The mutual relation which subsists between that superior and them may be styled the relation of sovereign and subject, or the relation of sovereignty and subjectivity". In short, the law is the regulator of the behaviour of the people and sovereign is the maker and enforcer of this law. There can be no political society without a sovereign power which "is the Centre of gravity in a mass of matter".[26]

Austin's interpretation of sovereignty assimilates all the five characteristics of sovereignty—absoluteness, all-comprehensiveness, inalienability, indivisibility, and permanence. It is regarded as the best exposition of the idea of sovereignty in juristic terms.

Limitations of Austin's View

1. ***No real sovereign.*** So far there has been no sovereign in the world that may be truly identified with the model of the Austinian sovereign. Sir Henry Maine contends that even the great Tartars of China and the Mughals of India could not be taken as the concrete examples of the Austinian sovereign, because even the most power-drunk rulers of the world bowed their heads before the might of some natural or supernatural agency. The power of the sovereign has certain limits. These

may be in the form of some religious or social customs having their sustenance in the deep-rooted convictions of the people. Only a despot with a 'disturbed brain' may be the sole conceivable example of Austin's sovereign. There exists a vast mass of moral influences that perpetually shapes, limits, or forbids the actual direction of the forces by its sovereign.[27] Figgis makes a convincing observation: "But the truth is that this state in the sense of an absolute super-entity has never existed, and that it cannot exist. In theory it represents a despot ruling over slaves; in practice, even a despot is limited by the fact that slaves are after all, human; deny their personality as you like, then comes a point at which it asserts itself, and they will kill either the despot or themselves.... Attempts are made to get out of this difficulty by saying that the sovereign power, though theoretically illimitable, is limited in practice very materially; psychologically by its own nature, and externally by the fact that there are certain things which no government can do without resistance".[28]

2. *Negligence of the power of usages and customs.* The Austinian view of sovereignty ignores the importance of social usages and customs that have a binding character. People obey their established practices in the same way they obey the laws of the state. Hence, Machiavelli cautioned the ruler against playing with the customs of the people. It is also said that the law is nothing but a custom translated into the form of a written command of the state. A wise sovereign would never commit the mistake of playing with the customs of the people and imposing upon them a law that is opposed to the well-established practices and sentiments of the people. Custom is the outcome of ages. Even an autocrat, like Peter the Great, is expected to be the guardian and servant of the customs of the people. As R.M. MacIver says all customary laws are in their origin spontaneous, not created by any deliberate will to organise, not created by the will of the state. "The state has little power to make custom and perhaps less to destroy it".[29] Again: "For custom, when attacked, attacks law in turn, attacks not only the particular law which opposes it, but, what is more vital, the spirit of law-abidingness".[30] A French

sociologist Leon Duguit goes so far as to say that it is not the state which creates laws, but it is laws which create the state. According to him, laws are merely 'the expression of social necessity'. Austin says that law is a 'command' of the sovereign and a command is a 'signification of desire' that is distinguished from other significations of desire by this peculiarity that the party to whom it is directed is liable to evil from the other, in case he does not comply with the desire. "But all laws of the state do not fit comfortably into the 'command pattern' of Austin. Many administrative orders do not fall into the category of a 'command' because of their quality of 'incomplete obligation'. One may ask what about judicial decision given by a court invalidating a law made by the legislature of the country. For instance, the American Supreme Court being the final interpreter of the constitution can make the Congress and the President mean whatever it chooses. But it is not very convincing to treat a body whose primary function is to elucidate, interpret and apply known and established rules of law, as if it were the sovereign will, on whose pleasure their existence depended".[31]

3. ***No single absolute sovereignty***. Austin's argument that the sovereign obeys none and receives habitual obedience from the bulk of a given society is disputed. In every political community there is a division of functions, though not of will. No government can be conducted effectively without such division. There is not one sovereign but three sovereigns like the executive, the legislature and the judiciary. These three ultimate authorities are independent of each other. The executive sovereign alone continues without intermission, whilst the legislature may be dissolved temporarily and the supreme judiciary is not always in session.[32] Sidgwick says that "in a modern constitutional state, political power that is not merely exercised at the discretion of a political superior—and that must, therefore, be regarded as supreme or ultimate—is usually distributed in a rather complex way among different bodies and individuals; though it is also important to bear in mind that from the many forms of government in any state we can only conjecture very incompletely the actual distribution of the power of producing political effects".[33]

4. ***Covers only legal sovereignty.*** The interpretation of Austin covers the case of legal sovereignty alone. It rejects the cases of political and popular sovereignty. According to Austin, sovereignty cannot be vested in the people as a whole or even in the body of the voters, because both have an indeterminate character. The vast body of the voters or of the people of a country cannot have a will of their own which may be translated into the law of the land. Such a view is not acceptable today. The scholars of political theory laud democratic system as one based on the 'will of the people'. It is reflected in the saying 'voice of the people is the voice of God'. Even the autocratic legislators have had to bow their heads before the voters of their country. Even the so-called sovereign British Parliament cannot make a law that is taken as 'uncivilised' or 'barbarian' by the voters (people) of the country. However, the people in general may not recognise their real force that is visible to them in the times of a popular uprising. As John Chipman Gray insisted, "the real rulers of a society are undiscoverable".[34] So Laski says that it "is impossible to make the legal theory of sovereignty valid for political philosophy.... A realistic analysis would probably content itself with saying that the will of the state is, for practical purposes, the will which determines the boundaries within which other wills must live. The will of the state, in fact, is the will of government as that will is accepted by the citizens over whom it rules".[35]

5. ***Not applicable to federal system.*** In a federal system the powers are divided between the central and provincial governments and each is taken as autonomous in the sphere allotted to it. It looks like the division of sovereignty. The provincial governments have the status of coordinate governments vis-a-vis central government. Neither the central nor the provincial governments have an authority that may be termed absolute, exclusive and indivisible—essential qualities of sovereignty as given earlier. There may be Centre-state controversies and confrontations in which victory may rest

with either side. Either the interpretation of Austin applies to a country with a unitary system, or it should be revised so as to be also applicable to a federal system. Austinian theory cannot be reconciled with a federal polity in which neither the central nor the regional governments can be termed 'sovereign'. Therefore, Laski says: "It has been pointed out that the discovery of sovereignty in a federal state is, practically, an impossible adventure".[36]

6. ***Pluralist.*** The pluralists desire to pluralise the concept of sovereignty. A very large number of social thinkers like Duguit, Durkheim, Figgis, Lindsay, Barker and Laski contend that the sovereign state has no right to discard the real significance of numerous social groups and associations that have a 'personality' of their own and also play a quite important part in satisfying needs of the people. If some portion of sovereignty is shared by these social groups and associations of the people it will be in the interest of individual liberty. As Laski says: "Men are members of the state; but they are members also of innumerable other associations which not only exercise power over their adherents, but seek also to influence the conduct of government itself.... But not less important as a limitation upon its power to determine it is the control exercised over their own sphere of activity by different associations".[37]

7. ***Need of control on state's power.*** Attack of the internationalists. Like Hobbes and Rousseau, Austin denies the existence of any authority outside and above the state. The state knows no authority above it. It is the master of its own will. Every state has the right to produce weapons of mass destruction, or to settle its disputes by means of force, or to do anything in violation of the principles of international law and international morality. However, the disasters of the two World Wars show that Austin's view of the sovereignty must be discarded. The power of the state must be regulated, even controlled, by some international authority so as to save mankind from the scourge of another great war that would bring untold sufferings. The whole idea of sovereignty should be restated in the light of the canons of internationalism. As Laski forcefully argues: "In such an aspect the notion of an

independent sovereign state is, on the international side, fatal to the well-being of humanity. The way in which a state should live its life in relation to other states is clearly not a matter in which that state is entitled to be the sole judge.... International government is, therefore, axiomatic in any plan for international well-being. But international government implies that organised subordination of states to an authority in which each may have a voice, but in which also, that voice is never the self-determined source of decision".[38] To sum up, Austinian interpretation of sovereignty is purely juristic. To quote Garner, "as a conception of strict legal nature, Austin's theory is, on the whole, clear and logical, and much of the criticism directed against it has been founded on misapprehension and misconception".[39]

VARYING IMPLICATIONS OF SOVEREIGNTY

Prof. Mcllwain observes that "few political conceptions have been the subject of so much discussion amongst us in the last hundred years".[40] Prof. F.W. Coker holds: "No word in political science is used with a greater variety of meanings".[41] The origin and history of the concept of sovereignty and closely linked with the nature, the origin, and the history of the state. In the last two hundred years, particularly in advanced countries, the growth of the idea of sovereignty has overshadowed all other associations and sometimes gone far towards absorbing all the functions of society. The students of pluralism and internationalism have sharply reacted to it. They have desired to make the concept of sovereignty compatible with democracy and international cooperation. Thus, the real meaning of sovereignty now ranges from its absolute to its limited character.

1. The case of absolute sovereignty. Sovereignty is the highest and unlimited power of the state. All social associations are under the complete and unassailable control of the state. The distinction between the society and the state has been obliterated. Hegel advocates that the predestined end of political evolution is that the nation should be absorbed into the state. The irresistible growth in the field of state activity is justified by reference to sovereignty. It was interpreted as justifying the use of political power or symbolising the actual possession of it. As F.H. Hinsley puts it "Even in federal countries what was once not true of earlier times has become true in the past hundred years; the federal form of state is always a unitary state in the process of formation or dissolution".[42]

2. The case of 'limited sovereignty'. The sovereign power of the state cannot be absolute. It should be restricted by anything like a religion or by its position as a 'satellite state'. Religion has an overriding authority over state matters in a theocratic system. Alternatively a sovereign state may become a member of some superpower's military alliance. In such a situation the sovereignty of the satellite state is truncated and the superpower has the political right to control its foreign and domestic policies and it may go to the extent of intervening in its internal affairs as the USSR did in Hungary in 1957, in Czechoslovakia in 1968, and in Poland in 1984. As Hinsley remarks, somewhat different circumstances "conspire with the doctrines of Marxism-Leninism to account for the fact that Soviet Russian state still seeks to uphold through the Brezhnev doctrine—the notion that the Communist states of eastern Europe are semi-sovereign protected states".[43]

3. The growth of internationalism. In international relations where sophisticated and less sophisticated states coexist, the concept of sovereignty might appear to have been confounded. Following the First World War the states perceived that these efforts required them to relinquish their sovereignty in at least that crucial area of relations between states which involves the decision to resort to war. As Hinsley says, "The evidence which undermines the analogy between the international system and primitive body politic is a positive evidence that the international system is a political system sue generis. And it is to be found in the fact that the states are not only moving towards the centralisation of the functions involved in applying international law which should be incompatible with their sovereignty but are advancing however slowly, in a different direction—one in which they are exercising their sovereignty to bring about an agreed redefinition of their rights and duties within the international system".[44]

4. Demarcation of internal and external sovereignty. Some scholars of international law and international relations hold that the internal and external aspects of sovereignty should be demarcated. The concept of absoluteness and indivisibility of sovereignty should be confined to internal aspect. Quincy Wright suggests that the power of self-judgment in international controversies, the power to prepare and use armed force in international relations, and the power to impose arbitrary barriers to international trade are the three aspects of national sovereignty that are in most need of limitations.[45] Act 14 of the Draft Declaration of the Rights and Duties of States prepared by the International Law Commission of the United Nations says: "Every state has the duty to conduct its relation with other states in accordance with international law and with the principle that the sovereignty of each state is subject to the supremacy of international law". Palmer and Perkins contend: "Sovereignty, in its literal sense, means supreme authority, yet it must be limited under present conditions. It is absolute and indivisible, yet it must be qualified and divided. It is incompatible with international law, yet it must be reconciled with international law".[46]

5. Divided and joint sovereignty. The traditional view of sovereignty does not accord with the growing idea of internationalism. According to new developments in the discipline of international law, the case of 'divided sovereignty' or 'joint sovereignty' has been taken into admission in the name of international cooperation.[47] Clyde Eagleton states: "Sovereignty cannot be an absolute term. It is as just foolish to say that sovereignty must be surrendered or eliminated as to say that sovereignty must be absolute and unrestrained.... The problem is not one of asking whether we should throw off a thing called sovereignty; it is rather one of asking with regard to what matters would we gain by having an international control, and in which matters would we gain more by reserving control to ourselves".[48] Today, the civilised states have put self-imposed restraints on their behaviour to play their part in the field of international peace and cooperation. When the Security Council passes a resolution of cease-fire states involved in a war stop.

To conclude, the traditional concept of sovereignty is outdated. The new idea of making sovereignty of the state compatible with the disciplines of international law and international relations is growing. To quote Carr, the concept of sovereignty "is likely to become in the future even more blurred and indistinct than it is at present".[49]

NOTES

1. *Cited in Bertrand de Jouvenel*, Sovereignty, p. 180.
2. F.W. Coker, *Recent Political Thought*, p. 497.
3. C.H. Mcllwain, *Constitutionalism and the Changing World*, p. 47.
4. Garner, *Political Science and Government*, p. 156.
5. *Ibid.*, p. 157.
6. Quincy Wright, *A Study of War* (Chicago: University of Chicago Press, 1942), II, pp. 898-99.
7. *Mcllwain*, p. 47.
8. Francis Coker, "Sovereignty," *Encyclopaedia of the Social Sciences* (New York: TheMacmillan Company, 1937), XIV, p. 268.
9. Gettell, *Political Science*, p. 123.
10. Giddings, *The Responsible State.*
11. Benn and Peters, *Social Principles and Democratic State*, p. 63.
12. Garner, *op. cit.*, p. 170.
13. Laski, *A Grammar of Politics*, p. 52.
14. Garner, *op. cit.*, p. 170.
15. Leiber, *Political Ethics*, Vol. I, p. 219.
16. Garner, *op. cit.*, p. 171.
17. Calhoun, *Works*, Vol. I, p. 146.
18. Gettell, *op. cit.*, p. 125.
19. A.V. Dicey, *An Introduction to the Study of the Law of Constitution*, p. 66.
20. Gilchrist, *Principles of Political Science*, p. 94.
21. Gettell, *op. cit.*, p. 98.
22. James Bryce, *Studies in History and Jurisprudence*, Vol. II, pp. 513-16.

23. *Op. cit.*, p. 168.
24. *Ibid.*, p. 165.
25. Sidgwick, *Elements of Politics*, pp. 651-52. It may be seen in the statement of Stephen Leacock, "The moment one passes from the dry certainty of the Austinian conception of legality, all is confusion," Elements of Political Science, p. 61.
26. Sir Henry Maine, *The Early History of Institutions*, p. 339.
27. *Ibid.* p. 359.
28. Figgis, J.N., *Churches in the Modern State*, pp. 86-87.
29. R.M. Maclver, *The Modern State*, p. 160.
30. *Ibid.*, p. 161.
31. Benn and Peters, *op. cit.*, pp. 75-77.
32. A.R. *Lord, Principles of Politics*, p. 89.
33. Sidgwick, *op. cit.*, p. 638.
34. See Laski, *op. cit.*, p. 55.
35. *Ibid.*, pp. 55-56.
36. *Ibid.*, p. 53.
37. *Ibid.*, p. 59.
38. *Ibid.*, p. 65.
39. Garner, *op. cit.*, p. 181.
40. Mcllwain, *op. cit.*, p. 47.
41. Coker, "Sovereignty" in E.A.R. Seligman (ed.), *Encyclopaedia of the Social Sciences*, Macmillan, New York, 1968, Vol. XIV, p. 268.
42. F.H. Hinsley, *Sovereignty*, London: Cambridge University Press, 1985, II Ed., p. 219.
43. Hinsley, *op. cit.*, p. 224.
44. *Ibid.*, p. 229.
45. Wright, "Fundamental Problems of International Organisation" in International Conciliation (April 1941), pp. 469-72.
46. Palmer and Perkins, *International Relations*, p. 29.
47. H.E. Cohen, *Recent Theories of Sovereignty*, p. 85.
48. Eagleton, *The Forces That Shape Our Future*, p. 176.
49. Carr, *The Twenty Years Crisis*, 1919-39, p. 230.

11

Public Obligation

MEANING OF POLITICAL OBLIGATION

Connotations of Obligation

The term 'obligation' originates from a Latin word 'obligate' implying something that binds men to an engagement or performing what is enjoined. The term obligation has its various connotations in different realms:

1. **In the realm of ethics.** In ethics obligation informs a man to fulfill or discharge a duty enjoined on him and acceptable to him by his rational understanding.
2. **In the field of jurisprudence.** Here, obligation requires a man to obey law by which he is tied to some 'performance'. Law regulates the social life of men. Hence, the principle of legal obligation takes the form of a bond between private persons tied to one another for the performance of some act as desired by the enforcement of law.
3. **In the world of politics.** In politics, obligation takes the form of a bond between man as a citizen and the authority under which he lives "to perform an act, or a number of acts, for the governing authority".[1] In the words of Benn and Peters, it implies that as man is a political animal, he is bound to live under some authority and, as such, it becomes his obligation to obey its commands. Hence, when the authorising rule is law, and the association a state, we call it "political obligation".[2]

Thus, political obligation is acceptance of the 'commands' of men-in-authority roles. The idea is integrally connected with the pattern of man's life in an organised whole. There can be no life if there is no order. And since order implies obedience, there can be no order if there is no acceptance of it. A people cannot live well without accepting the commands of the persons in charge of maintaining peace and order in the society. Thus, the principle of political obligation is based on the maxim of common prudence. As Benn and Peters observe: "Of course, there are plenty of good reasons for accepting authority in general (though they may not always apply in particular). We are often in a situation where it is more important to accept an umpire's judgement than to insist on our own.... An army will usually do better even with bad generals than with no generals at all. We accept authority, because most social enterprises would be hopelessly without it".[3]

Political obligation rests upon issues relating to the nature of authority that involves within its fold the whole world of existing rights, laws and political organisation generally. It covers the opposite situation in which people have a legitimate claim for the disobedience of authority. As Laski points out, "it is the enterprise that counts; the authority is conditional on the way it promotes or preserves it".[4] The people not only obey the laws of the state or the 'commands of the sovereign', they also scrutinise those orders in terms of the satisfaction they seek from life. Therefore, from time to time, they reject them on the ground that they are a denial of those satisfactions. To quote Laski, "Obedience, that is to say, is the normal habit of mankind; but marginal cases continually recur in which the decisions to disobey is painfully taken and passionately defended".[5]

ESSENTIAL CHARACTERISTICS OF POLITICAL OBLIGATION

1. Honest public service. As government is a difficult art, it is the duty of every conscientious person to be seriously interested in the management of public affairs. Those placed in high offices should direct their thought and action to the general good. Not merely of an intellectual character; political obligations involve obligations of an honest public service.

2. Political legitimacy and effectiveness. Political effectiveness implies actual performance in the light of the extent which the political system provides for the performance of the basic functions of government as the people and powerful groups in society perceive them. Political legitimacy refers to the capacity of the system to engender and maintain the belief that the existing social, economic and political institutions are most appropriate for society.

3. Critical attitude. The idea of political obligation not only informs people to obey the authority of those in power, it also desires them to be critical about the way authority is exercised. The people should scrutinise the actions of their rulers. They should resent any invasion on their liberties. Thus, political obligation involves resistance to authority.

Summing up the whole idea of political obligation, Benn and Peters write: "There are good grounds for accepting authority in general, but there may be good grounds for rejecting it in particular cases; if authority derives from a constitution, there would generally be good grounds for rejecting any exercise of it which is unconstitutional. Again, if its legitimacy depends on the way it is used, an invasion of a sphere where political authority is inappropriate might be a ground for disobedience or, in extreme cases, for resistance".[6]

THEORIES OF POLITICAL OBLIGATION

1. The Divine Theory. It finds its place in religious doctrines. In it the source of obedience to the commands of men-in-authority roles is traced in matters of faith. The necessity of the Divine Will stands above and apart from the citizens and the governing authority. The ordinance is "I am obliged to obey the governing authority, because I am obliged to obey God and because any governing authority is essentially an emanation and delegation of divine authority".[7] Thus, the authority of the ruler "stems not only from inheritance according to custom, or from popular acclamation, these are regarded as the consequences rather than the grounds of authority. The true source is divine and his authority is, therefore, independent both of human choice and custom".[8]

The divine theory sacrifices the nature of authority. It commands persons to obey authority as if it is an emanation of God. It led to the emergence of the dogma of divine rights of kings found in various religions like Hinduism and Christianity. It leaves no room for right to resist political authority. As it is the 'march of God on earth', the state can do no wrong.

Criticism

With the growth of new knowledge of secularism in modern times this theory has lost its significance. The new realisation is that "if men are disposed to doubt, they want reasons related to their situation, rather than dogmatic assertions that everything is as it ought to be. Any approach to political obligation that left no room for discussion in the light of the particular situation, might confirm the faith of the faithful; it could not convince the doubter".[9]

2. The Prescriptive Theory. According to this theory political authority and reverence to it are based on the principle of established 'customary rights' ripens into an association wherein lies the source of its legitimacy. As Jean Bodin says as the authority of the patriarch (head of the family) is based on the fact of historical prescription, so the authority of the king (head of the state) finds its source in the fact of long possession. An established practice has a significance of its own because it embodies the 'wisdom of the ages'. The people obey their rulers, because obedience is a well-established convention. According to Edmund Burke, all settled political institutions have a prescriptive character. He condemned the logic of the French revolutionaries that political institutions could be demolished and built anew as desired by the people. He argued that people revere their traditions in which the wisdom of the past is hidden. Such traditions have a very long record of evolution. They can be changed gradually over a very long period of time. Thus, political obligation is a result of very long traditions which the people observe as if having a 'divine' character. Thus, according to this theory, "all authority is legitimate, if it is sanctioned by custom; no further question need be asked".[10]

Limitations

(i) The source of political obligation lies not only in paying reverence to the well-established practices of the realm but also in doing away with them. People desire change and if there is frustration of their hopes, they take to the path of revolution. The advocates of this theory stick to the fact of reverence to the past and feel allergic to the idea of a revolution.

(ii) People observe their traditions so long as they have their utility. They resort to break them down when their usefulness is no longer existent. Therefore, political prescriptions may change with time.

3. The Idealistic Theory. It finds the source of political obligation in the 'moral nature' of man. It does not sanction the right to resistance. The state is a natural association. It is a moral organism. It alone can give 'good life' to its members. It is like 'a partnership in virtue'. It is a *koinonia* having its highest aim in ennobling human personality. Therefore, man should obey, rather worship, its authority. As the state represents the real will of its members, there can be no conflict between the will of the individual and the will of the state. Rousseau says that it is impossible for a sovereign to maim or harm its people. Justifying the case of a god-state Hegel says: "Nothing short of the state is the actualisation of freedom". Treitschke says, that "man should fall down and worship the state". Joad concludes: "It, therefore, follows that the actions of the State in so far as they proceed from General Will, must always be irreproachably right in the sense that they represent what is best in individual wills... The state can never act unrepresentatively".[11]

Difficulties

1. This theory is too abstract. It places very ordinary things in a highly philosophical, even metaphysical, form that cannot be understood by a man of average comprehension.
2. To teach the people to adulate political authority like deaf and dumb creatures, is to open the way for

totalitarianism. All great idealists except Green subscribe to blind obedience to the authority of the state. Referring to the ideas of Hegel, in this connection L.T. Hobhouse says: "When we are taught to think of the world which we know as a good world, to think of its injustices, wrongs, and miseries as necessary elements in a perfect ideal, then, if we accept these arguments, our power of revolt is atrophied, our reason is hypnotised, our effects to improve life and remedy wrong fade away into a passive acquiescence in things as they are; or, still worse, into a slavish adulation of the Absolute in whose hands we are mere pawns".[12]

4. Social Contract Theory. It is the theory of consent of the individuals. It dwells on the factor of consent of the people as revealed in a hypothetical social contract on which the entire structure of political obligation rests. As the people are the makers of the state, they are also its mutators. God has no place in the making of the state. In the seventeenth century England, Hobbes and Locke stressed that political authority is derived from a social contract. The people are collectively bound to obey it so long as the government works for the general good and keeps itself within limits laid down by the compact. As Locke says: "No one can be subjected to the political power of another, without his own consent".[13]

Value of Contract Theory

The system of a democratic government stands on the premise of the contract theory. This theory alone attaches importance to the 'will of the people'. The people institute a sovereign authority for the sake of their own preservation. If the sovereign puts their life in danger, they may revolt to make another contract. Locke sanctions people's right to revolt in case the government abuses the trust of the people. Thus, this theory has its distinctive merit.

Demerits of Social Contract Theory

(i) It makes state a conventional association.

(ii) It informs people to rise in revolt whenever they feel dissatisfied with the functioning of their government.

(iii) It creates fertile grounds for the occurrence of revolts. C.E. Vaughan remarks that Locke formulated not a theory of government but a theory of rebellion.[14]

5. The Marxian Theory. It denounces state as an instrument of exploitation and oppression by one class over another. People are not obligated to obey a state that is a discredited organisation. They should destroy it by revolutionary means and create a 'new state' in the form of the 'dictatorship of the proletariat' or a state of the workers and peasants. Such a state alone must be obeyed. Its aim is first to establish a classless society. It will wither away to pave way for the emergence of a stateless condition of life or a golden era in which all public affairs would be managed by the free and voluntary associations of the people and 'glorious human values' prevail. In Marxism, the theme of political obligation is converted into the theme of social obligation. Marx "envisaged the fully socialised man as one who would see no distinction between private and public interest and whose activity would be attuned to the latter".[15]

Limitations

(i) This theory on the subject of political obligation has three aspects—no obligation to a 'bourgeois state', all obligation to a 'socialist state', and eventual conversion of political obligation into social obligation in the final stage of socialism (communism). A bourgeois state is not a thoroughly discredited institution. It cannot be identified with an instrument of exploitation and oppression by one class over another. A socialist state, as conceived by the Marxists, may not be the genuine state in which people must render full obedience to its authority.

(ii) Revolution is a sacred affair in a capitalist state, but it becomes profaned when a socialist order is established.

(iii) In this theory the very theme of political obligation disappears in the final stage of social development.

> The ambivalent attitude of the Marxists "reduces the question of political obligation to a question of political expediency, and ignores the independent individual whose experience alone counts in the determination of his obedience to the laws of the state".[16]

6. Theory of Harold Laski. Discussing various theories of political obligation, one may appreciate one that stands the test of experience. One should look into the case of political obligation from a pragmatic point of view that desires "to contend for truth as tested by reality and its fruits".[17] Such a view is the approach of Laski who says that men "obey the state not merely for the sake of order, but also on account of what they deem that order to make possible. They are, in fact, judging the state from the angle of satisfactions, they think it should provide. Their judgements, no doubt, vary with time and place, expectations of what is legitimate are always born of experiences; and the demands of one society at one period will differ from those of another society at another period. But the implication is the clear one that the exercise of political authority in a society is never unconstitutional".[18]

THEORIES OF GROUNDS OF RESISTANCE

1. Thomas Hobbes. He tells us that though the state is based on a social contract whereby people surrender their all rights in favour of a leviathan without taking any commitment from him, they are bound to obey every law of the state to keep the horrible 'state of nature' away. They have a right to break the contract if the sovereign commands the people "to kill or wound themselves, or not to resist those who assault them or to abstain from the use of food, air, medicine, or any other thing, without which they cannot live".[19]

2. John Locke. The state is a creation of social contract. Society, state and government are distinguishable. The society has a pre-political character. The state is a creation of the first or open contract. It continues to exist even when the government is dissolved or changed. But the government is a creation of the second or tacit contract. It implies that the king or the government is bound by the terms of the 'contract'. The people may revolt or 'make an appeal to the heavens' if they find their king acting against the terms of the contract. They may resist the abuse of political power. They may change their ruler acting like a despot. They may have a new one of their trust in his place.[20] Explaining the meaning of the situation identifiable with the abuse of the trust of the people by the king, Laski says, "The substitution of arbitrary will for law, the corruption of Parliament by packing it with the prince's instruments betrayed to a foreign prince, prevention of the due assemblage of Parliament all these are perversions of the trust imposed and operate to effect the dissolution of the contract. The state of nature supervenes and a new contract may be made with one more fitted to observe it".

3. T.H. Green. He was an idealist like Rousseau and Hegel, but he was a liberal too. He followed the English liberal tradition. He recognised people's right to resist political authority in the event of 'cruel necessity'. He justified revolt against the abuse of political authority if it is sanctioned by the force of public conscience as being in the interest of the people as a whole.[21]

4. Harold Laski. He connects the subject of political obligation with the factor of 'moral adequacy'. According to him, people must obey the authority of the state, if it meets their satisfaction. They may disobey it, if they find that the commands of the state lack the force of utility and moral adequacy. Thus, right to resistance should be substituted by the 'duty to disobey'. It is a claim to a right which a citizen cannot surrender without denying himself the full meaning of his citizenship. It is an obligation arising out of the acceptance of and loyalty to the idea of the common good. There are circumstances in which resistance to the state becomes an obligation if claims to rights are to be given validity. However, no general rule of either time or situation can be laid down as a guide to such an action.[22]

5. M.K. Gandhi. His view is based on the premise of practical idealism. Authority is legitimate when it is based on truth and non-violence. If it is violent or untrue, the people have a right to resist it by means of ahimsa and satyagraha. The purity of means is essential for the achievement of a legitimate end.

As different answers may be furnished by different persons faced with such a situation or a series of such situations, Margaret MacDonald feels that "necessary and sufficient grounds for political obligation are not to be found".[23]

NOTES

1. Barker, *Principles of Social and Political Theory*, p. 184.
2. Benn and Peters, *Social Principles and the Development State*, p. 298.
3. *Ibid.*, p. 329.
4. Laski, *The State in Theory and Practice*, p. 17.
5. *Ibid.*
6. Benn and Peters, *op. cit.*, p. 329.
7. Barker, *op. cit.*, p. 184.
8. Benn and Peters, *op. cit.*, p. 301.
9. *Ibid.*, p. 303.
10. *Ibid.*, p. 307.
11. C.E.M. Joad, *Modern Political Theory*, p. 13.
12. E.T. Hobhouse, *Metaphysical Theory of State*, p. 19.
13. Locke, *Second Treaties of Civil Government*, Sec. 95.
14. C.E. Vaughan, *Studies in the History of Political Philosophy*, Vol. II.
15. Michael Evans, *Karl Marx*, p. 162.
16. Ray and Bhattacharya, *Political Theory*, p. 150.
17. C.E. Merriam, *History of Political Theories*, p. 15.
18. Laski, *op. cit.*, p. 17.
19. Hobbes, *Leviathan*, Ch. 14.
20. Laski, *Political Thought in England* (Locke to Bentham), p. 37.
21. T.H. Green, *Lectures on the Principles of Political Obligation*, p. 115.
22. Laski, *A Grammar of Politics*, p. 96.
23. Cited in Benn and Peters, *op. cit.*, p. 331.

12

Political Culture

Political culture is the traditional orientation of the citizens of a nation toward politics, affecting their perceptions of political legitimacy and the traditions of political practice. It was brought into political science to promote the American political system. The concept was used by Gabriel Almond in late 50s, and outlined in The Civic Culture, which was opposed by two European political scientists, Gerhard Lehmbruch and Arend Lijphart. It is a concept that characterise the specific preferences regarding politics in different political communities. The political culture of a political community can be characterized by the proportion of adherents of each way of life (its regime), and by the predominant alliance of two ways of life. The study of the concept of political culture constitutes an analysis of the sociological aspect of the theme of political development.

DEFINITIONS OF POLITICAL CULTURE

1. **A.R. Ball.** Political culture is composed of the set of "the attitudes, beliefs and values of society that relates to the political system and to the political issues".[1]
2. **Almond and Powell.** It is defined as "the pattern of individual attitudes and orientations towards politics among the members of a political system".[2] The members of a civil society share a common human nature like emotional drives, intellectual capacities and moral perspectives. The common human nature

expresses itself in the form of certain values, beliefs and emotional attitudes which are transmitted from one generation to another, though with greater or lesser modification. These constitute the general culture of the society.

3. **Beer and Ulam.** "Certain aspects of the general culture of the society are especially concerned with how government ought to be conducted and what it shall try to do. This sector of culture we call political culture".[3]

4. **Lucian Pye.** Political culture refers to "the set of attitudes, beliefs and sentiments that give order and meaning to a political process and that provides the underlying assumptions and rules that govern behaviour in the political system".[4]

5. **Dennis Kavangh.** Political culture may be defined as "the short-hand expression to denote the emotional and attitudinal environment within which the political system operates".[5]

THREE COMPONENTS OF POLITICAL CULTURE[6]

1. **Cognitive Orientations.** These imply knowledge, accurate or otherwise of the political system,

2. **Affective Orientations.** These imply feelings of attachment, involvement, rejection and the like about political objects, and

3. **Evaluative Orientations.** These imply judgements and opinions about the political objects and events.

A political culture hinges on the fact of people's attitudes and beliefs towards the political system, whether homogeneous or heterogeneous. It is a product of several inter-related factors —historical, geographical and socio-economic. It is not static. It is dynamic. It responds to the needs generated within the political system or imported or imposed from outside. A pragmatic orientation, in this direction, is known by the name of the secularisation of political culture.

Determinants of Political Culture

1. **History.** In the making of the political culture of a country the traditions of a country play their own part. For this one may go into the facts of history. For example, the British people are conservative. They follow their traditions and believe in slow and gradual change. The older values are gradually synchronised with modern attitudes undisturbed by violent internal strife or domination by foreign power. But in France, people have a radical temperament. They changed their Constitutions many times since the revolution of 1789. As the behaviour of the masters has its own impact on the culture of the slaves, one may gather many facts to show that the dependent people of India learnt from their British masters the ways of parliamentary democracy. The people of Algeria and Vietnam learnt the ways of violent revolution from their French masters.
2. **Geography.** In the determination of the political culture of a people, the geographical make-up of a country also plays a part. The insular character of the British Isles protected the country from foreign invasions and also from the massive influx of foreign races that could have created the problem of ethnic differences. On the other hand, the vast frontiers of a country like India opened ways for the foreigners to invade and even stay here with the result that Indians developed the values of independent egalitarianism in the midst of sharp ethnic and cultural differences.
3. **Socio-Economic Development.** A predominantly urban industrialised society is a more complex society, putting a premium on rapid communications. Educational standards are higher, groups proliferate, and participation in the decision-making process is by necessity wider. As the rural societies are not geared to change and innovation, states with a predominantly peasant population are more conservative. The developments in the fields of

science and technology have their impact on the growth of agriculture and industry. They also have their impact on the process of transportation and communications, migrations and immigrations, imports and exports, revolutions and warfares. On account of the immense economic and technological development of a country like the United States, the labour class has become so much 'embourgeoisified' that the Marxian law of inevitable revolution has lost its relevance there. An economically and also technologically advanced state may establish its hold over a weak country and relinquish it after imposing a new political culture there through the process of its secularisation. As Almond and Powell say, "The process of the secularisation of political culture means increasing political awareness of the people enabling them to have growing information about their political system and their role as a political actor in it. It is through the secularisation of political culture that these rigid, ascribed and diffuse customs of social interaction come to be over-ridden by a set of codified, specifically political and universalistic rules".[7] The Americans put Japan under their occupation for a period of about two years after the Second World War and left it after the imposition of the MacArthur Constitution establishing parliamentary democracy there in 1947.

POLITICAL STABILITY AND CHANGE

1. **Role of political culture.** A study of the western and developed or eastern and developing political systems of the world leaves the impression that political culture plays a very important role in the political stability and change. If political culture "is the pattern of knowledge, evaluation and communications relating to political authority",[8] it informs us to treat political orientations of the people towards authority as a very important determinant or an explanatory variable in accounting for the

stability, effectiveness and representativeness of a democratic political system.[9] The builders of a state should remember that the political system should be in consonance with the pattern of their political culture, otherwise it would not work. John Stuart Mill said that democracy cannot be successful in a country where the people are barbarians, though enlightened and capable rulers of a country may seek to impose a new culture by coercive or persuasive means. Turkey under Kemal Ataturk is an example of the former, India under Nehru of the latter.

2. **Dichotomy of tradition and modernity**. The people, in general, are tradition-ridden, but they also desire change. The practicable way is to effect slow and incremental change in the attitudes and orientations of the people. Very revolutionary changes lead to political instability. However, the rulers use very harsh and despotic methods to achieve their aims as happens in a country under Fascism or Communism. In such countries a danger of counter-revolution persists until the men of old generation are thoroughly liquidated and a new generation with a culture foisted on it takes its place. However, experience shows that leaders who strive for a gradual change get ample success in their endeavours. Thus, the very stability and integration of the political culture depend on promoting orderly changes and achieving a political consensus depends on the politician's ability to strike a balance between the old and the new.[10]
3. **The congruence of the political system with the political culture**. In the case of advanced democratic countries of the West this has become an established fact, however, in such countries there are problems the kind of which we find in the rebellious attitudes of the negroes in the United States, or of the 'blacks' in the South Africa, or of the French people in some provinces of Canada. But such problems are very few.

In the developing and undeveloped countries of the Third World such problems are numerous. According to Kavangh four reasons may be assigned for this:[11]

(i) If change of culture is to be effected speedily, it will have to be directed by the state, usually by means of secondary and formal agencies.

(ii) The scope of politics is large in such states; society becomes identified with the state, good man or good citizen is a good party man.

(iii) Given the recent discontinuities in the history of many new states, the creation of new attitudes is important in weakening the pre-revolutionary or pre-independence outlooks. New orientations are necessary to support new institutions ad new forms of activity.

(iv) The internalisation of regime-approved norms and values is important in strengthening the regime's legitimacy and in encouraging voluntary compliance with its commands.

CONCLUSION

Thus, political culture acts as an impediment to political change if the rulers desire to introduce some innovations. The remedy is to adopt the method of slow and incremental change. A political system would not get the quality of stability if its institutions clash with the norms of political culture. It is the reason of the failure of Western representative system in many Muslim countries of the Middle East. But the possibilities of this kind do not occur in advanced countries of the world where the problems of political instability have been solved by making the political culture congruent to it. The cause of failure of democracy in many countries of the Third World, should be related to the wide gap between the democratic rules of the conduct of government and the authoritarianism found in the military, the bureaucracy, the political parties and the family. As Apter says, "High congruity in the political culture equals great stability in the political system".[12]

Thus, the whole idea of political culture involves the vita, attitudes, sentiments, convictions and commitments of the people in respect of political values like rights, liberty, equality, justice, rule of law, freedom of the press, independence of judiciary and the life. What the people, in general, feel and do about them reveals their political culture. As it plays an important part in the success or failure of political system, contemporary political scientists have sought to include it in the discipline of new political theory. Referring to the case of liberal-democratic countries, it is asserted that the "independence is prized, men say they would rather be known for their capacity to get along in a discussion; they value leaders who give the impression of independence".[13] To conclude with Kavangh, "Values and attitudes are undoubtedly relevant to an explanation of the performance of political systems, but eventually we have to go back and explain how the political culture came to be formed and expressed the way that it is".

NOTES

1. A.R. Ball, *Modern Politics and Government*, p. 56.
2. Almond and Powell, *Comparative Politics*, p. 50.
3. Beer and Ulam, *Patterns of Government*, p. 32.
4. Lucian Pye, *op. cit.*, p. 104.
5. Dennis Kavangh, *Political Culture*, p. 10.
6. S. Almond and Powell, *op. cit.*, p. 50.
7. Almond and Powell, *op. cit.*, p. 60.
8. Peter Nettel, *Political Mobilisation*, p. 57.
9. E.A. Nordlinger, *The Working Class Tories*, p. 49.
10. Kavangh, *op. cit.*, p. 39.
11. *Ibid.*, p. 40.
12. David E. Apter, *Introduction to Political Analysis*, p. 250.
13. Robert E. Lane, *Political Ideology*, pp. 19-20.

13

Concept of Property

Man seeks to acquire property. He needs property for his development. The concept of property is crucial to modern political theory. It is the basis of modern state and society. Nothing has played such a vital role in the development of state, civilization and culture. Many of the laws relating to property are much fuller, precise and more exacting than even laws relating to life and liberty. In the 20th century, the right to property became very controversial. The Marxists are against the institution of property. The Anarchists condemn private property. For them property is theft and the root cause of all prevailing evils and crimes in the society. It divides the society into two warring factions—haves and have-nots. The haves or capitalists exploit the have-nots—the workers. Liberals advocate the right to private property. According to them it emancipates man from the care of morrow the ghost of starvation and the dread of want. It enables him to lead a comfortable life and seek intellecteral attainments.

MEANING OF PROPERTY

The word property is derived from the Latin word 'Proprites' which means 'one's own'. Thus whatever one owns is his property. Ownership and, control of material goods is property. Property is the control by man over things or on appropriation of material objects recognised by society.

DEFINITIONS OF PROPERTY

1. **Asirvatham.** Property may be defined as the control by man over things or an appropriation of material

objects recognised by society. "It does not mean mere possession which confers only a delegated right". It calls for exclusive and permanent control over things.

2. **Sidgwick.** The property is "the complete right of exclusive use including the right to destroy and the right to alienate but not necessarily the right of bequest". Property is needed to satisfy physical wants and requirements of human beings.

CHARACTERISTICS OF PROPERTY

1. **Complete control.** Property is those material goods over which we have complete control. Complete control means the right to destroy and the right to alienate also.
2. **Social sanction.** Like all other rights, right to property also requires social sanction or recognition. A right is meaningless if it does not have behind it the sanction of society.
3. **Natural right.** John Locke believes that property is a natural right but others consider it a legal right. It exists within the state.
4. **Creation of society.** Socialists believe that property is the creation of society so the right to property is relative and not absolute. This means that the property should be used for the good of the society as a whole.

EVOLUTION OF THE CONCEPT OF PROPERTY

The origin of property lies in the instinct of acquisition in human beings. In the primitive society communal property was the universal order. There was no private property. Everything was held in common by the society. But Hobhouse thinks that in the early society there was private property also. It included his weapons which he used in hunting and protecting himself from wild beasts and animals. Property in the form of domestic animals also came into existence when the animals came to be domesticated for milk, wool and ludes etc. Property in the form of land, factories, house came into existence with the evolution of society through various stages hunting, pastoral, agricultural, handicrafts, etc. Aristotle the father of political science considered slaves as a part of property. He supported the institution of private property on the ground that is natural and necessary. During Middle Ages Christianity advocated trusteeship of property.

PRIVATE PROPERTY

Property is usually equated with private property. It is the right of an individual to exclude others from some use or benefit of something. The issue of private property has made property a contentious moral issue. It was attacked by Plato as incompatible with the good life for the ruling class. It was defended by Aristotle as essential for the full use of human faculties and as making more efficient use of resources. Machiavelli was the first political thinker to say that property is the source of power. According to him, "Men forget more easily the death of their fathers than the loss of patrimony". Hence, Machiavelli warns the rulers not interfering with the property of the people.

Legal Theory of Property

Hobbes advocated the legal theory of property. Property is possible in the state. Locke considered property as a natural right. Individualists and utilitarian justified private property. But in the 19th century the institution of private property came under severe criticism. Proudhan called property a theft. Anarchists and communists opposed the institution of private property because it was responsible for all kinds of moral, physical and social immorality. Ownership of means of production should be in the hands of society. It should be used for the interests of society as a whole. The protagonists of various schools of thought disagree about the utility, role, place and functions of private property in society.

Liberal Theory of Property

Theory of property is an integral part of the philosophy of liberalism. As an economic, social and political doctrine liberalism arose in defence of capitalism, the capitalist market society and the interests of the capitalist class after the decline of feudalism. The right to property was needed to operate the capitalist market economy. Liberalism defended the right to property. Prof. Laski, Adam Smith, Herbert Spencer, Jeremy Bentham, J.S. Mill, T.H. Green and other liberal theorists advocated the right to private property and the private ownership of the means of production. They defended capitalism and private property. They advocated freedom for trade and industry. They opinioned that trade and industry flourished well under free competition. The free movement of capital and trade and adjustment of prices on the basis of demand and supply would lead to the best economic adjustment in the economy. It stimulates production, keep wages and prices at their normal level, prevent excessive rates of interest, increase national wealth and promote individual and social welfare. They demanded free trade, freedom of occupation, unrestricted competition and along with it inviolable property rights.

Property as Reward

The liberal theory is based on the assumption that property is the reward for one's labour. A man is fully entitled to own what his labour and ability have produced. A man should have a right to ownership and private property. In the private market economy the forces of demand and supply automatically bring about the best equilibrium between production, prices and consumption. The right to property is inherent and natural. However, inequality in society is not because men were unequal by birth. Instead the liberals found a rational explanation of inequality in man's ability and capacity. In a free capitalist society a man working hard and having requisite ability can accumulate any amount of property as the reward of his labour and ability. It is in the interest of the society to respect the right to property and ownership. The liberal theory of property pleads for an exclusive and absolute right of the individual to property.

CONCEPT OF PROPERTY AND VIEWS OF JOHN LOCKE

At the hands of John Locke (1632-1704) the liberal theory of property received a great fillip. He began with the contention that the earth and its fruits were given by nature to mankind in common. Every person has a property in his own person. Labour creates property rights. The labour of the body and hands creates property rights.

Locke uses the term property in two senses

(a) a narrow sense of goods and possessions

(b) an extended one to cover life, liberty and estate.

Locke justifies the natural right to private property. Labour is the personal property of man. Whatever the man appropriates from the common property bestowed by nature becomes his private property. But the right to this property is not absolute and unconditional. It is subject to their remaining a sufficiency of fruits available for others which they too may appropriate. To waste is to offend against the common law of nature. No man has a right to take more than he can himself consume. No one has a right to waste property and one must leave enough for others. Money solved the problem of waste. It enabled man to store up wealth in a non-perishable form. It made possible a great increase in production and commerce. The state did not create property. It was created to protect it. One of its main purposes is the defence of established system of property rights. Without the express consent of the people, the Government has no right to abridge or abrogate the right to property. Property is not only a natural right but a legal right as well.

The Main Points of the Liberal Theory

1. ***Private property*** is the real property. Earlier no difference was made between private and public property.
2. ***Private property*** is the reward of labour. Labour and ability are the personal and private property of man which is the result of his labour and therefore should be accepted as right.
3. ***Control of the state on economic system.*** The socialist liberal theory asserts that right to property should be used for public good. If right to property is

to be utilized for public good then it is necessary that the economic system is controlled by the state.

4. ***Theory of compensation.*** Modern liberals accepted the institution of private property but they want that excessive property must be surrendered for public service. Property should not be confiscated by the state. If it is taken by force in public interest, he should be paid compensation.

Defence of Right to Property

1. ***Economic ground.*** In the absence of the institution of private property production will suffer. Free competition is essential for the economic development of the society.
2. ***Psychological ground.*** The institution of private property is essential for an incentive to work. A man puts more labour because he gets better reward.
3. ***Ethical ground.*** Private property is the reward of labour and ability which he puts to earn more and more.
4. ***Logical ground.*** It is logical to give freedom to enterprises for better production.
5. ***Historical ground.*** History shows that private property was held by the individuals from the time memorial. Civilisation has developed due to institution of private property.

Though the liberals are in favour of institution of private property they want some restrictions on the right of private property in the interest of general welfare of the society as a whole. They are not in favour of abolishing right to property. They are confident that evils of private property can be checked through proper legislation.

THEORIES OF JUSTIFICATION OF PRIVATE PROPERTY

Ownership and control of material goods is property. It is the control of man over things or an appropriation of some material object recognised by society. Right to property requires social recognition. It is nothing if it does not have the sanction of society behind it. John Locke believed that property is a natural right but others consider it legal right. It exists within the state. Socialists believe that property is the creation of society so the right to property is relative and never absolute. This means that the property should be used for the good of the society as a whole. Following are various themes about justification of private property:

1. **Natural Theory.** According to this theory the right to property is a natural right. It is prior to society and state. Natural theory is of two kinds. In the beginning, things belonged to none. Everything in nature was held in common. But after some time one who enclosed piece of land became its owner. Thus the institution of property came into existence.
2. **Labour Theory.** It was supported by John Locke. He asserts that man has a natural right to that with which he has mixed the labour of his body and mind. He says, "The labour of his body and the work of his hands are his property whatsoever; thus, he removes out of the state that nature hath provided and left it in, he hath mixed his labour with and joined it something that is his own and thereby makes it his property".
3. **Legal Theory.** Hobbes and Bentham are the great supporters of this view. They maintain that there can be no right in the state of nature because rights are created and maintained by the state. According to this theory, the civil law is able to furnish not only the legal but the ethical basis for the institution of private property. "Property and law" writes Bentham, "are born-together". Before laws were made there was no property. Take away law and property ceases. "Rousseau adopts the general view that it is only in an institution made secure by the protection of the political authority that the foundation of property is to be found in law".
4. **Idealistic Theory.** The Idealists support private property on the basis of personality. In the words of

Kant, "Property is necessary for the realisation of one's will". It is necessary for the fulfillment of personality. According to T.H. Green appropriation of property is an expression of will. It is an effort of the individual to give reality to a conception of his own good which is at the same time a common good. Property does not rest on contract or on supreme force. It is an instrument of self-expression and satisfaction.

Arguments for Private Property

1. ***Fundamental Right.*** Individualists and liberals consider the right to property as the most fundamental right. According to Locke, political authority was established to support the right to property. Classical Economists like Adam Smith and Ricardo also supported the institution of private property. Liberal thinkers like J.S. Mill and T.H. Green support the institution of private property though they do not consider it as absolute. They put some limitations on it in the interest of the society.
2. ***Psychological and Physical Satisfactions.*** The possession of private property gives man a sense of security. It emancipates him from the ghost of starvation and the dread of want. Those who are without any property lead a very miserable life. They are always in the grip of uncertainties. In the modern industrial society they are no better than the slaves. Property enables a man to provide for the future and affords a sound basis for family independence.
3. ***Social Status.*** Property gives a man a status in society which ultimately leads to happiness and contentment. Machiavelli rightly remarks, "Men forget more easily the death of their fathers than the loss of patrimony."
4. ***Peace and Stability.*** A man of property is said to be a man of deliberation and prudence. As such he is not likely to be swept off his feet by every new fanged doctrine leading to violent change. This leads to

political stability in the country. Peace and stability are the primary requirements for progress and prosperity.

5. ***Development of Personality.*** Property helps the individual in the development of his personality. A man of property can develop his talents and faculties of mind to the maximum extent. It promotes a sense of independence. It emancipates him from the yoke of involuntary work and the drudgery of undesired activity.
6. ***Creative Life.*** In the development of civilisation and culture property is an end. A man of property can devote his means to the fostering of art, culture, science, literature and technology. Thus it enables him to have creative life.
7. ***Incentive to Work.*** Private property provides an incentive to work. It is the reward of one's own labour. When one knows that he will get the reward of his efforts, he works sincerely and to the best of his capabilities and efficiency.
8. ***Support by History.*** Historical experience justifies the institution of private property. The states which have recognised the right to private property have progressed more and at much faster rate than the states which did not recognise this right.

Arguments against the Private Property

1. **Division of Society.** The institution of private property has divided the society into two classes—haves and have-nots. The gap between the rich and poor is ever widening. Hence Laski says, "It remains historically obvious that a community divided into rich and poor when the latter are numerous, built upon the foundations of sands".
2. **Anti-Democratic.** There can be no democracy in an economically unequal society. In capitalist societies, rich people have monopolies over the means of communication and transportation. They have full

control over the three wings of government. All the laws of the country favour the rich class.

3. **Moral and Physical Evils.** Private property is responsible for all kinds of moral and physical evils. It brings economic dependence for the poor. It brings superfluous luxury for the rich and laborious toil for the poor. It is responsible for spiritual and social immobility.
4. **Offence against Justice.** Kropotkin condemns the institution of private property as an offence against justice. It allowed a few persons to enjoy what was created by the efforts of many. Human progress was the outcome of collective efforts and not individual efforts and consequently there was no justification for private property.
5. **Exploitation.** Property is a tool in exploitation of the poor. It is an instrument which is used to dominate and enslave the weaker classes of people. Millions of people remain ill fed, ill clothed and ill housed. The growth of children is checked.
6. **Economic and Political Evils.** Property leads to over production, large scale production, use of machinery, division of labour, technology, etc. It leads to imperialism and colonisation. Thus, property is at the root of war and destruction.
7. **Other Rewards of Labour.** Private gain need not be the only incentive to labour. Lord Haldane remarks that the desire to distinguish himself in the service of the state is as potent motive with the brain workers as the desire to amass a fortune. Plato claimed that the satisfaction derived from performing a congenial task or rendering public service was a great reward in itself.

The institution of private property has got its own merits and demerits. The individual should be given the right to property but it should be controlled and regulated by the state in the interest of the society as a whole. A striking balance must be maintained between the private property and social service.

MARXIST THEORY OF PROPERTY

For Marxists, property is important for its productive value and not as the means of personal gratification. They view property in the totality of the economic system and social relationship of man in this system. The form of property has always been changing with the change in the mode of production and the relations it establishes in the society. In the primitive society there was no such thing as private ownership.

Origin of Ownership of Property

With the decline of primitive society, domesticating of animals instead of killing them became prevalent. Emergence of handicrafts changed the material conditions of society. People started owning tools, implements and domestic animals and land and slaves. This gave rise to the concept of private property. Once it came into existence, it continued unabated though its form changed with the march of civilisation. The capitalist private property is the capital. It is the means of production of wealth in an economic system. It comes into being by the transformation of the system of self-earned property into capitalist private property. A close associate of Karl Marx Engels discussed about the origin of private property in his famous book, *The origin of the Family, Private Property and the State.* In primitive society there was no private property. It was the stage of primitive communism when forms of production were a few and they were possessed by society as a whole. No man exploited another. Men used to wander from one place to another in search of food. They depended on nature for their livelihood through hunting, fishing and fruit and root gathering. Whatever they got, they distributed among them.

New forms of production were discovered as the civilisation advanced. People started domesticating animals instead of killing them. Agriculture developed gradually. This brought a revolutionary change in the life of society. The stronger compelled the weak to work on their land. The society was divided into haves and have-nots. There were two types of people, one the diligent, intelligent and frugal elite, and the other lazy, rascal, spending their substance. The former sort of people accumulated wealth and the latter had nothing to sell except their own skin.

Theory of Surplus Value

Surplus value is the difference between the value of a commodity produced by labour and the wages received by the labourer. According to Marx, as the value of a thing is due to labour alone the whole of the surplus value of the thing should be paid to the labourer. However, this is not done in actual practice. The capitalists give only a little to the labourer and pocket the rest of it. It is robbery on the part of the capitalists to keep anything to themselves. This theory of surplus value of Marx showed how the employers steal the value created by the labourers.

Evils of Capitalism

Marx attacked private property and capitalism from various angles:

1. **Social Evils.** He condemns capitalism because it exalted the fortunate few at the expense of the oppressed many and cheated millions of people of the just fruits of their labour.
2. **Moral Evils.** From the ethical point of view capitalism is exploitative, oppressive and dehumanizing. It is unfair and results in inequality of wealth and income in society. It deprives the poor of the major part of their rightful earnings. The appropriation of surplus value is nothing else but a highway robbery.
3. **Aesthetic Evils.** On aesthetic ground also capitalism is undesirable and harmful. Production under capitalism is hostile to art. It is responsible for ugliness and vulgarity. It fills the land with factories which give out smoke, stench and filth endangering health of the people. It raises mansions for the rich and hovels for the poor. All creative activities depend upon the whims of the capitalists. Hence capitalism is dirty and

vulgar. It is the sinister way of life under which men who value beauty, good manners and noble thoughts cannot hope to create or even live.

4. **Economic Evils.** On economic grounds capitalism has failed to realise the material well-being of the masses. It has proved wasteful of material and natural resources. The resources of the country are not put to the best use of the economy. The majority of people have to go without bare necessities of life. Resources are used to produce articles and luxury goods for the privileged few. The goods produced on mass scale do not satisfy the wants of the common man. On account of over production and under production (Trade cycles) there are wide fluctuations in prices. The situation created under capitalism is something like—"water everywhere but not a drop to drink".
5. **Psychological Evils.** On psychological grounds capitalism injures the spirit of man. The workers are worse off psychologically than materially. On account of wide economic disparities there is constant breast burning. Machines were built by men. The goods produced by them were meant to serve his needs and he was not to become a slave of the machine.
6. **Political Evils.** Capitalism is all the more undesirable on political grounds. It distributes power and freedom unequally. It reduces democracy to mockery. It leads to imperialism, colonialism and global destructive wars. Marx condemned capitalism as defective from all angles—economic, political, ethical, psychological, etc.

In 'Communist Manifesto', the theory of communism was summed up in the abolition of private property. Private property is responsible for class war. It is a tool of exploitation in the hands of bourgeois. It keeps proletariats at the stage of permanent misery. Marx and Engels advocate for the abolition of private property and for this they have advanced moral, economic, social, political reasons.

Methods to Abolish Institution of Private Property

Abolition of the institution of private property alone can restore human values. Marxist secures human freedom and evolves a national system of production and distribution to ensure satisfaction of social needs. Marx gives revolutionary methods to abolish institution of private property. The socialist revolution will take place under the leadership of organised and class workers. Dictatorship of the proletariat will be established after the revolution. Means of production will be socialised. A socialist economy will take the place of capitalist economy. A classless society will be established. There will be no need of any state. The state will wither away. The institution of private property will wither away through communist revolution. It will pave the way for a rational and humanistic reorganisation of production and distribution. However, Marx is not against personal property consisting of small consumer goods of everyday life. The personal property is a genuine fruit of an individual's labour. The socialist property transforms the exploitative character of property into a development character.

Criticism of Marxist Theory of Property

1. **Failure to Achieve its Object.** The institution of private property is still there in communist countries. The state has not withered away. The state has become still more powerful. The state instead of abolishing the institution of private property has given shelter to it.
2. **Dictatorship of the Proletariat.** Marxist theory wants dictatorship of the proletariats through socialist revolution. It does not suggest any method to decide disputes among proletariats. In the absence of state, there will be disorder and anarchy.
3. **Classless Society.** The theory visualizes a classless society. Classes can never vanish away from the society because there are inequalities among the people on the basis of ability.

4. **No Initiative.** The theory of surplus value ignores other factors of production such as capital and organisation. This kills initiative because there is no place for incentive in this theory.
5. **Miserable Life.** If institution of private property is abolished, the life will become miserable. Property gives joy and happiness to man. It gives security from incentive in this theory.

However, one cannot deny the value of Marxist theory. It is an attack on wide socio-economic disparity in modern society. But the establishment of a stateless and classless society is a distant dream.

LASKI'S THEORY OF PROPERTY

Laski's concept of property is both a critique of the existing economic order and a justification of the existing institution of property largely on the Fabian lines of argument. He did not reject the institution of property altogether. He rather gave its defence on national grounds. He modified the theory of private property under the influence of socialist ideas of the 20th century. He wanted that one should use right to property for social good.

Present System of Property

The present system of property is not conducive to healthy economic system. The number of those who own significant property is always small. Such ownership is not related to the performance of duties. The property may be inherited. The ownership of property involves the control of capital. It involves the power to direct the lives of workers. The development of industry in modern times has made the power of capital greater than in any previous age. In a society which is divided into haves and have-nots, the poor are denied the conditions which make their effective citizenship possible. The system is not conducive to a healthy economic system. The production is carried on wastefully and without plan. Wrong commodities are produced. Those produced are distributed without regard to absolute urgency. Goods are produced for the sole object of making profit and not for the well-being of the masses. Even harmful things are produced to reap dividends. Natural resources are ruined. Commodities are adulterated. Legislators are corrupted. Thus, the present property system has distorted the economic system and led to weakening of the society as a whole.

Moral Basis of Property

Laski is not against the institution of private property. Property provides a means of harmony in the shape of security. Men get a sense of security. They develop their creative impulse. The institution of private property is not bad as such but it is possessed by few capitalists who exploit others. It gives birth to the evils of capitalism. The capitalists use private property for private profit. They do not bother for the good of others. Their production is not according to the needs of society. Distribution is rarely related to social urgency. There is wasteful expenditure. They exploit the people for their personal benefits. The hereditary property is justified only for the widows and the children of the deceased. Laski is against functionless property. No property is justified unless it is the result of the performance of socially useful functions. Moral basis of property lies where it results from personal efforts.

Theory of Reward

Liberals consider property a reward of one's labour. Laski examined several theories of right to determine the true basis of right to property. Rejecting the doctrine of equal rewards, he says, "There seems no justice in an equal reward for unequal effort, not does it seem just to reward equally where needs are unequal". Rejecting the liberal theory of rights he maintains that when workers and capitalists do not have equal bargaining power, the income should be decided on the basis of contract of demand and supply. He also rejects the theory as "each contributes to the society according to his powers and is awarded according to his needs". He thinks that there is no rod which may measure the needs of the people. The theory does not seem to be practicable.

Laski's theory of property satisfies two conditions. It enables the individual to reach out towards his best self. It preserves and develops the necessary functions of the society. It reconciles the interest of the society as a whole. In it every one will meet his minimum basic needs and society will also not suffer. No one should get remuneration more than to meet the basic needs. Thus one gets rewards for the services which one renders to the society.

Principles of Sound Theory

Laski did not favour the abolition of the right to property altogether but wanted to construct a sound theory of property. This he believed could be done only on the basis of following principles:

1. Linking the right to property with the performance of functions,
2. Collective interest of the society, and
3. A more national hereditary system of property. In short, he wanted property to be linked with the service of the community.

Property and Industrial Organisation

Laski suggests that the capital must play a limited role in industrial organisation. The capitalists must not be allowed to control the industries. The industrial system of the country should not depend upon the lust of the capitalists for profits. Social elements should be given their due share in Industrial management.

Suggestions for the Industrial Organisation

1. **Industry must be made a profession.** Just as the rules of profession are made subject to the will of society by those engaged therein, so must the rules of industry be made by the working class.
2. **No control by capitalists.** There must be alteration of the character of the owner of capital. He should be paid a fixed dividend and should not be allowed to control the business in which his capital property is invested.
3. **Control by industrial workforce.** There should be an alteration of the character of control exercised in

industry. The control should pass on from the functionless owner of capital to the industrial workforce.

4. **Emphasis on social aspect.** More emphasis should be laid on the social element in the industrial equation.

The New System of Property

In the new system of property suggested by Laski, functionless property of the capitalist system will be converted into an instrument of social good. Only those who perform social functions should be allowed to have property. One will get reward for the services he will render to the society. There will be improvement in industrial system. It will eliminate capitalists. Even if private property is allowed, only shareholders will be left. There will be self-government in industry. Under the influence of socialist ideology of 20th century, Laski justified institution of private property for social good only. Property is socially useful labour. Only that property is moral which is earned by performing socially useful functions. Laski did not plead for abolition of private property but stressed the need for change of the system. Private property must not be so large in amount that its owner experiences power by reason of its sheer magnitude. On the contrary, it must never be so small that its possessor cannot be himself at his best. To conclude, in the words of Laski, "There is nothing inherently wrong in the notion of private property. There is a sense in which it may be so held as genuinely express personality and to contribute to its enrichment. It must be derived from self-effort".